SRA Reading Mastery Plus

Plus

Teacher's Guide

Level K

**Siegfried Engelmann
Jean Osborn
Elaine C. Bruner
Owen Engelmann
Karen Lou Seitz Davis**

SRA

A Division of The McGraw-Hill Companies

Columbus, Ohio

www.sra4kids.com

SRA/McGraw-Hill

A Division of The McGraw-Hill Companies

Copyright © 2002 by SRA/McGraw-Hill.

Send all inquiries to:
SRA/McGraw-Hill
8787 Orion Place
Columbus, OH 43240-4027

Printed in the United States of America.

ISBN 0-07-568996-0

7 8 9 POH 06

NOTE TO THE TEACHER

Your hard work in practicing these *Reading Mastery Plus* exercises will provide you with a valuable set of skills for working with children of all abilities. You will learn how to present and how to correct so that children can master critical skills. You may be surprised to find the correction techniques you learn are often important in working with higher-performing children. If you have mastered the techniques, no child in your beginning reading classroom will fail to learn to read. By achieving this goal, you will provide a valuable service both to your community and to the children.

Table of Contents

Overview of Reading Mastery Plus, Level K

Reading Mastery Plus, Level K is a 150-lesson Direct Instruction program that provides children with both a solid background in the language concepts important to learning in school and a careful introduction to reading. The program is particularly appropriate for kindergarten children who are behind in language knowledge and skills. It is also appropriate for older children in bilingual or ESL programs. Children who complete *Reading Mastery Plus,* Level K will be ready to begin *Reading Mastery Plus,* Level 1.

Program Components

Reading Mastery Plus, Level K includes the following materials:

Teacher Materials

- **Three Teacher's Presentation Books for language instruction and two Teacher's Presentation Books for reading instruction** provide the teacher with exercises for directing the language and reading activities for each of the 150 lessons. These exercises indicate the teacher wording and the correct student responses for each activity. Exercises also provide directions for correcting mistakes and making sure that the children's responses are firm.

- **The Teacher's Guide** provides a complete explanation of the program and information about how to teach it. It provides placement-test and grouping information. Blackline Masters for two family letters are available in appendix C. The guide is divided into two parts—**language** and **reading.**

    (1) The **language section** of the guide summarizes the content of the language program and describes effective teaching techniques and specific correction procedures for key exercises. It also describes the Expanded Language Activities, the Responding to Literature Activities, and the Literature Lessons Selections.

    (2) The **reading section** contains remedies for students who need extra help, lists of reading words presented in the program, a sound pronunciation guide, and the rationale for the content of the program and the sequences of the activities.

- **The Literature Component** includes seven trade books and the Literature Guide containing instructions to the teacher.

- **The Behavioral Objectives** booklet provides specific objectives for each skill taught in the program.

- **A Skills Profile Folder** summarizes the skills taught in the program and provides a space for indicating when a child has mastered each skill. One folder is needed for each child.

- **Letter Chart**

- **The Answer Key** contains answers for the reading worksheet activities.

- **The Audiocassette Tape** provides instructions for presenting specific tasks and demonstrates how to pronounce the sounds for letters and letter combinations. The tape also presents a recording of the "Alphabet Song."

Student Materials

- **The Story-Picture Book** contains illustrations for selections the teacher presents orally.

- **Three workbooks** contain worksheets for 150 language lessons and worksheets for 100 reading lessons.

About This Teacher's Guide

This Teacher's Guide gives an overview of the *Reading Mastery Plus,* Level K program. The guide provides information about the use of each component and gives information about teaching the 150 lessons, about appropriately placing students in the program, and about responding to specific student-performance problems.

Reading Mastery Plus, **Level K** is research-based and has been completely field-tested. By carefully reading and studying this guide before teaching *Reading Mastery Plus,* Level K, you will be well prepared to guide children successfully through the program.

Program Summary:

Total number of lessons:	150
Number of language lessons:	150
Number of reading lessons: (Pre-Reading from 41–100; Reading from 101–150)	110
Number of mastery test lessons:	10

Phase	Lessons	Part	Instructional Time	Total Instructional Time
1	1–50	Language	30 minutes	30 minutes
2	51–80	Language Reading	30 minutes 7–10 minutes	40 minutes
2	81–100	Language Reading	25 minutes 15 minutes	40 minutes
3	101–150	Language Reading	10–15 minutes 25–30 minutes	40 minutes

Scope and Content

Reading Mastery Plus, **Level K** provides children with 150 language lessons and 110 reading lessons. The program is especially effective with kindergarten children who are behind in language knowledge and skill. These children may not be familiar with the language of the classroom. They tend to fail to learn to read in a timely manner and often lag well behind grade-level expectations for reading. They need the attention to instructional detail that *Reading Mastery Plus,* Level K provides. The program (1) allows children to start where they are, (2) lays a solid foundation for writing and oral-language expression, and (3) presents all the skills they need to decode well and understand what they read.

Through the language lessons children learn (1) basic information and build background knowledge, (2) statement patterns ranging from the simple to the complex, and (3) strategies for solving problems.

Reading Mastery Plus, **Level K** has three phases.

Phase 1 spans lessons 1–50. Phase 1 is a beginning language program that helps children learn the language of instruction. During phase 1, the daily instructional period is 30 minutes. The presentation material for the lessons in phase 1 is contained in Language Presentation Book A.

Phase 2 spans lessons 51–100. The major emphasis of phase 2 remains on language; however, beginning reading activities are introduced. Starting with lesson 51, two presentation books are used for each lesson—Language Presentation Book B and the **Pre-Reading** Presentation Book. The reading and language activities may be scheduled during the same period or at separate times. For lessons 51–80, the language lessons require about 30 minutes per day, and the reading lessons require about 7 to 10 minutes per day. For lessons 81–100, each language lesson requires about 25 minutes per day. The time required for a reading lesson increases to 15 minutes per day.

Phase 3 spans lessons 101–150. During this phase, reading becomes the primary focus of instruction. The reading lesson requires 25 to 30 minutes per day, and the language lesson requires 10 to 15 minutes per day. The reading lessons increase in length as children progress through the sequence, and the language lessons become shorter. Reading lessons for phase 3 are in the **Reading** Presentation Book, and the language lessons are found in Language Presentation Book C.

In phase 3, the writing program (copying letters, words, and sentences) and independent-work activities supplement the language and reading instruction to give children a rounded language-arts background. The independent work is closely related to the concepts and skills that children learn in the daily lessons.

Why Language in Level K?

Children who are not familiar with the language of the classroom are not well prepared to learn in school. If a child does not know what the teacher means by the direction "Touch the first word of the sentence," there is a discrepancy between the teacher's expectations of what the child should do and what the child is actually able to do. Some kindergarten children don't know the meaning of words like *touch, first, word,* or *sentence.* Children learn the meaning of these words in *Reading Mastery Plus,* Level K. The meaning of *word* is taught as an oral-language concept. Children learn to identify spoken words. Later in their reading instruction, children learn about written words. The word *sentence* is introduced as a "reading-related word." The words *touch* and *first* are taught as language concepts,

along with hundreds of other basic language concepts and word meanings.

For example, the *Reading Mastery Plus,* Level K program provides daily exercises to help children become familiar with words that tell about position—**over** the dog, **next** to the car, **under** the house. The program provides careful teaching of the instructional words that many kindergarten children do not know—for example, *all, some, none, first, last, top, bottom, front, back.* In addition, children learn a lot of the background knowledge important to reading comprehension. They learn facts about classification (for example, what kind of things are called vehicles, what kind of things are called containers), about their school, the calendar (months of the year; days of the week; the relationship between yesterday, today, and tomorrow), and about different places and occupations (what you see on a farm, what you see in a dentist's office, what you see in an airport).

Children also learn the basic language of logic and drawing conclusions. They engage in problem-solving applications in which they apply the language they are learning. For instance, they look at a picture that shows horses in a field and apply a "rule" for the horse that will go swimming: "If a horse has spots and a long tail, the horse will go swimming." The children identify the horse that has spots and a long tail, conclude that the horse will go swimming, and then see a picture that confirms their conclusion. The problem uses what children have learned, the meaning of the word *long,* the meaning of *spots,* and the meaning of the "if-then" statement. The language program provides many problem-solving applications that use concepts and facts that children have learned so that children develop the general expectation that they will use and apply what they are learning.

Why Reading in Level K?

The goal of the *Reading Mastery Plus,* Level K program is not to teach all the reading that would be presented in a first-grade program but rather to build a solid foundation of reading skills that permits children to start the first grade far ahead of where they would start without this program. Children first learn the names of the letters. They learn to identify both uppercase and lowercase letters, and they learn to write them. This teaching, which spans 110 lessons, provides children with information about the symbolic side of reading.

Children learn the other side of reading—the phonological, or oral, side—through a variety of tasks. Children learn to rhyme and to say words "a part at a time." They also learn the critical skill of oral blending. The teacher says a word slowly; the children say it fast.

Finally, children learn the relationship between the oral side and the symbolic side of reading. They learn sounds for various letters. *Reading Mastery Plus,* Level K presents the letter sounds carefully so that children have a solid understanding of the difference between the letter name and the letter sound.

The reading instruction culminates with the decoding of simple, regularly spelled words that children sound out and then identify in response to the direction "Say it fast." All the skills that children have learned are combined in this act of decoding.

The last step is for children to read stories composed of a single story word. As children learn more words, the format changes so that children read story sentences composed of three words.

Strategies for Teaching Beginning Reading

In *Reading Mastery Plus,* Level K children learn pre-reading foundation skills before they are introduced to reading. The pre-reading activities start at lesson 41. Children first learn the names of the letters and alphabetical order. They learn to identify and write both lowercase and uppercase letters. They practice phonological skills of blending and segmenting words. They learn about left-to-right sequencing. Finally, they listen to oral stories that involve the characters they will read about in the later levels of *Reading Mastery Plus.*

The alphabet song serves as the anchor for work with the letter names and letter identification. As children learn to recite the alphabet, they learn to identify the letters that are named. Children spend enough time identifying the letters and writing them to assure that they are automatic in their identification of letters.

As children continue to identify and write letters, they learn about left-to-right sequencing through games called symbol-action games. Here's a symbol-action game from lesson 113.

The children follow the arrow and do what the pictures show. The game is a variation of what children will do later in the program when they sound out words. When they sound out words they follow the arrow and say the sounds for each letter or letter combination.

Children also learn key phonological skills that involve sounds in words. Through a variety of "say-it-fast" exercises, children first say words "a sound at a time" and then blend the sounds together.

Before children begin sounding-out analysis of words, they learn how to identify symbols (letters) as **sounds.**

Reading lessons 101–123 introduce the skills that are needed for the first word-reading exercises. These lessons teach children how to say words fast, how to sequence events, and how to identify a few letters as sounds.

Word reading begins in lesson 124 and continues in every remaining lesson. Children sound out words before identifying them.

In all 50 Reading lessons, sounds and words appear in the special *Reading Mastery Plus* orthography, or print. The system is designed to point out the

regularities in words. This orthography has joined letters (such as **th,** long lines over long vowels (such as **ē,** which is pronounced as the ending sound in the word **mē**), and small letters that are not to be pronounced (such as the **a** in the word **ēₐt.**) This orthography is gradually faded at the beginning of *Reading Mastery Plus,* Level 2.

Reading Mastery Plus, Level K introduces children to a sounding-out analysis of words, starting with Reading lesson 124. Teaching the children to sound out words has these advantages:

1. Children learn more words from a given amount of teaching. If children are taught ten words as sight words, the children are capable of reading only ten words. If children learn the thirteen symbols introduced in *Reading Mastery Plus,* Level K as sounds, they are capable of reading over two hundred regularly-spelled words composed of those sounds.

2. The emphasis on sounds assures that children attend to the details of the words, or how the words are spelled. This information becomes very important when children are confronted with words that are similar in "shape," such as: **ram, ran,** and **fan.**

Before children begin sounding out words, they work on the **preskills.** These are the oral skills and the symbol-identification skills that are needed when children sound out a word by identifying each symbol in a word as a "sound" and saying the word fast. By lesson 124, children have learned six sounds in isolation. They practice saying words slowly and saying them fast. They also practice rhyming by starting with different beginning sounds and saying a specified word ending. Finally, they practice sequencing symbol action events so that they develop a general skill of combining the "first event" with the "next event."

Children continue to practice skills that have been taught earlier. For instance, after lesson 124, children continue to practice rhyming, symbol identification of earlier-taught sounds, and oral blending.

Note that as part of the word-reading practice, children learn words that are slightly "irregular" as well as regularly spelled words. The word **is** is irregular because it is pronounced in a way that is not predicted by the sounds of the individual letters. (The word **is** does not rhyme with **hiss,** which is what it would do if it were regular.)

Placement and Grouping

The grouping requirements are the same for both the language and the reading component of *Reading Mastery Plus,* Level K. Children should be assigned to the same instructional group for both components.

The groups should be small (no more than 10 children in each) and homogeneous in performance. Ideally the lower-performing groups should be smaller than the higher performing groups with no more than three groups per classroom. Children who fall outside the skill range of the three groups should be, if possible, placed in another classroom.

General Setup: The classroom setup should permit you to be very close to the children as you teach. The farther away you are, the more problems there will be with children following your directions, or with your ability to determine whether they are responding correctly.

Here is the most reasonable setup to teach the main part of the lesson:

- Have the lesson in the corner of the classroom (far from the doorway or other distractions).

- Sit so that you are facing the room. Children are seated in small chairs that are in a horseshoe arrangement, facing you.

- Provide each child with a lapboard.

- Sit close enough to the children that you can touch every lapboard without standing up. If the group is too large for you to do this, seat the highest performers in the group in a second row.

Test to see that all children can see the presentation book. Do this by holding your head next to the book and looking to see whether you can see the eyes of all the children. If you have to look almost sideways from the book to see a child's eyes, that child won't be able to see what is on the page.

Reading Group Set-up (lessons 101–150)

Keep all children in the reading group within touching distance. There will be times during the 50 Reading lessons when you will want to hand the presentation book to a child, or to reinforce a child. This will be easier if the children are all within arm's reach. Sit close to the children and group them close together.

Lowest performers should be directly in front of you. Highest performers should be on the ends of the group or in the second row. You will naturally look most frequently at the children seated directly in front of you.

You should teach until each child's response is firm. When the lowest children's responses are firm, the responses of the rest of the group will be firm. (**Note:** If some children always hold the group back, they should be placed in another group.)

Logistics: Children will need pencils, crayons, and books for the lesson. Establish rules for where they are to keep the materials not being used (ideally, on the floor under their chairs).

Worksheets: Throughout the program, children receive daily worksheets for language activities. From lessons 41 through the end of the program, children will also do worksheet activities for reading. From lessons 41 to 80, the worksheet activities for reading are on worksheets that also present language activities. These pre-reading activities are either at the top of the worksheet (41–50) or at the end of the worksheet. From lesson 81 to the end of the program, worksheets for language are on side 1 with reading on side 2.

Distribute opened workbooks (or worksheets) either at the beginning of the lesson or just before children are to do the worksheet activities. Children are to write their name on the worksheet and then follow the directions that you provide for the different parts. Children are not to start completing any worksheet part until you give them directions about what they are to do.

Group Performance: Children who are placed appropriately in *Reading Mastery Plus,* Level K should be able to complete all 150 lessons in one school year. To reach this goal, you should complete a lesson a day with each group. However, children should perform at a high level of mastery.

You may find that some lessons take more than one period to firm children. Children are firm when they respond correctly to all questions and directions the teacher presents. When the choice is between making sure that all responses are firm and completing the lesson, choose the first alternative. The best procedure is to **firm the children when new concepts and skills are first introduced.**

Occasional lessons may be long, but if you find that children typically take longer than the allotted time to complete lessons, either the group is not homogeneous (and the children should be regrouped), or there are problems with the way you are presenting the exercises.

The Placement Test

The placement test is to be administered individually to each child before instruction begins. All testing should be completed during the first week. The placement test, score sheet, and directions for testing and scoring appear later in this guide (pages 235–237).

In-Program Mastery Tests

Mastery tests start after Reading lesson 108. The 10 mastery tests are designed to show whether children have the skills that they will need in the upcoming reading lessons. The skills they need are the skills that were taught in the preceding lessons.

Teaching the Program

The lesson plans for both the language component and the reading component of all lessons are contained in teacher presentation books. The components for each lesson have the same lesson number. For lesson 86, you would present the language component labeled lesson 86 and the pre-reading component for lesson 86. (**Note:** The children's material (Story-Picture Book) does not have the same reading-lesson numbers as those in your teacher presentation books because the story-picture book is not introduced until lesson 81. The first reading lesson in the children's story-picture book is lesson 1, not 81.)

All the information you need to present the lesson exercises for the story-picture book and the independent-work exercises (worksheets) is specified in the teacher presentation books. By presenting the

exercises and following the directions for interacting with the children, you will provide children with the examples, the corrections, and the practice that they need to learn the content for each part of each lesson.

Before you present lessons, however, you should refer to this guide for information about the various exercises that you'll be teaching.

Rehearsing the exercises: You should rehearse the different exercises before presenting lesson 1. Read the exercises aloud. Use the signals that you'll use when you're working with the children. Practice giving the various corrections for mistakes that children may make. Your goal should be to smoothly present any exercise type that is scheduled for upcoming lessons. The first part of the program may require a fair amount of practice. Later lessons will require less preparation.

Getting into the lesson: Get into the lesson **quickly.** If the group is shy or tends to have behavior problems, begin with a simple "Simon Says" game ("Stand up. Touch your nose. Clap your hands."). Continue until all children are responding without hesitation. This establishes the tempo and mood for what the children are to do during the lesson. Then quickly present the first exercise. The same technique can be used if the children's attention lags during the presentation.

Teaching to Mastery: Use the following guidelines for teaching to mastery:

- Present each task until the children's responses are firm. Do not move to the second exercise in the lesson until the children's responses are firm on the first exercise.

- Use clear signals. All signals have the same purpose: They permit a simultaneous response from the group. All signals have the same rationale: If you get the group to respond simultaneously (with no one child leading the others), you will receive information about the performance of all the children, not just those who happen to answer first.

- Pace tasks appropriately. Pacing is one of the more difficult presentational skills. Pacing is the rate at which different parts of the exercise are presented. Not all portions of an exercise should be presented at the same rate. Different pacing is specified throughout this section of the guide. (Some exercises contain such instructions as "Pause" or "Wait.")

- Praise good performance. Make your praise specific. If the children have just completed a page of sounds with no errors, say something like, Good! You knew every sound! If they just said the sounds in **am** correctly, say, Good saying the sounds in **am.** Praise the children for following the rules. If all are responding well, say Good talking. I can hear everybody. Do not permit yelling or droning responses.

Independent activity: As a rule, don't leave any exercises unless children are able to perform on all parts without making any mistakes.

Lessons 41–45 · Planning Page

		Lesson 41	Lesson 42	Lesson 43	Lesson 44	Lesson 45
LANGUAGE		Actions pronouns	Actions pronouns	Actions pronouns	Actions pronouns	
		Part/Whole wagon	Part/Whole head	Part/Whole head, pencil, tree	Part/Whole head, tree	Part/Whole tree
		Opposites full/empty, wet/dry	Opposites wet/dry		Opposites big/small	Opposites long/not long
		Prepositions in	Prepositions in front of; in	Prepositions on, in		Prepositions over, on, in front of
			Information days of the week	Information days of the week	Information days of the week	Information days of the week
				Concept Application	Concept Application	
LANGUAGE WORKSHEETS		Matching		Matching	Matching	Matching
		Pair Relations	Pair Relations	Pair Relations	Pair Relations	Pair Relations
			Coloring orange	Coloring		Coloring
			Completion		Spatial First, Next, Last	
					Top/Bottom	Top/Bottom
Extra Materials		pencil, wastebasket; "Alphabet Song" cassette, cassette player	chalk, glass; "Alphabet Song" cassette, cassette player	"Alphabet Song" cassette, cassette player	"Alphabet Song" cassette, cassette player; blank piece of paper	"Alphabet Song" cassette, cassette player; blank piece of paper
READING		Alphabet Song a–d	Alphabet Song a–g	Alphabet Song a–g	Alphabet Song a–k	Alphabet Song a–k
READING WORKSHEETS		Letter Indentification c	Letter Indentification a f	Letter Indentification a c f	Letter Indentification a c f	Letter Indentification a c f
STORIES		Reread "Dozy, Bring a Hamburger"	Reread "Marvin the Eagle"	Reread "Sarah the Toymaker"	Reread "Oscar the Worm"	Poem Review: "My Cat, My Dog, My Frog"; "Painting"; "In a Tree"
LANGUAGE ACTIVITIES		See page vii for Expanded Language Activities 41–45.				
LITERATURE		Responding to Literature: Children listen to, discuss, and retell a story [teacher's choice]. You may need pictures.				

The first page of each lesson in this Presentation Book lists the Grade Level Expectations for the Sunshine State Standards that are met by using that lesson of the Presentation Book and the Workbook. A comprehensive listing of how Grade Level Expectations are met by using all components of *Reading Mastery Plus* Level K can be found in the *Florida Teacher's Handbook.*

Overview of Teacher Presentation Books

Planning Pages

Each five-lesson span in the three language presentation books and the reading presentation book begins with a planning page—a brief summary of the concepts and skills that are taught in the following five lessons. The planning pages summarize what is taught in the teacher-directed part of the lessons and what appears on the worksheets. The planning pages indicate whether the content is presented as part of the language lessons or the reading lessons. The planning pages also show the stories and other activities that are scheduled for the five-lesson span. (The planning page information for the Pre-Reading Presentation Book, lessons 51–100, is found on the planning pages in Language Presentation Book B.)

Here is the planning page for lessons 41–45. The yellow-boxed items are new skills, concepts, or activities. The planning page shows that in these language exercises children learn the color orange (worksheet lesson 42), learn the parts of a tree (lesson 43), learn the opposites *long* and *not long* (lesson 45), identify things that are "first," "next," and "last" in illustrated groups (worksheet lesson 44), and respond to directions that refer to the top and bottom of illustrated objects (lesson 44). In the reading exercises, children learn "The Alphabet Song" through the letter **k,** and learn to identify the letters **a, c,** and **f.**

Presentation Book Exercise Samples

Samples of Presentation Book exercises appear on page 19. The exercises indicate precisely how to present structured activities. Each exercise shows what you say, what you do, and what the children's responses should be.

What you say appears in blue type.

> You say this.

What you do appears in parentheses.

> (You do this.)

The responses of the children are in italics.

> *Children say this.*

Follow the specified wording in the exercises. You will communicate clearly with the children if you follow the exercises carefully, as written. The exercises provide careful wording that focuses clearly on important aspects of what the children are to do. Although you may initially feel uncomfortable "reading" from a script, present it as if you're saying something important to the children. You will observe that children respond well and that working from these exercises is not difficult.

The arrows in the exercises on page 19 show the six different things you'll do that are not indicated in the exercise plan.

1. **You signal, tap, touch, or point to make sure that group responses involve all the children.**

2. **You firm student responses in critical parts of the exercises by repeating steps.**

3. **You use information based on how the children respond to pace your presentation (proceeding quickly or giving the children more time to think before expecting them to respond).**

4. **You write things on the board.**

5. **You present exercises with abbreviated scripts.**

6. **You present individual turns.**

Arrow ❶: Signals for Group Responses

(Signal.), (Tap.), (Touch.), and (Point.)

Many tasks call for group responses. When children respond together with brisk unison responses, you receive good information about whether the children are performing correctly. The simplest way to direct children to respond together is to signal or tap in a predictable cadence—just like the cadence in a piece of music.

Signals are used to make it possible for children to initiate responses together at the appropriate rate. A tap or other audible signal (finger snap, clap) gives children a clear indication of when to respond and what to respond to.

For many Level K language and reading exercises, you hold up the teacher presentation book and display pictures and symbols that children respond to. You show children pictures, letters, or words in the teacher presentation book. For most of the pre-reading exercises, the children look at their worksheet or their story-picture book, not at your book.

Different primary signals are used to direct children to respond. **For many language activities that involve illustrations in the presentation book, you use a visual signal—a point-and-touch signal.** (See Sample A page 19.) You point to the object to which children are to respond. You present the specified instruction or question as you point. You signal them to respond together by touching the picture.

Sample A

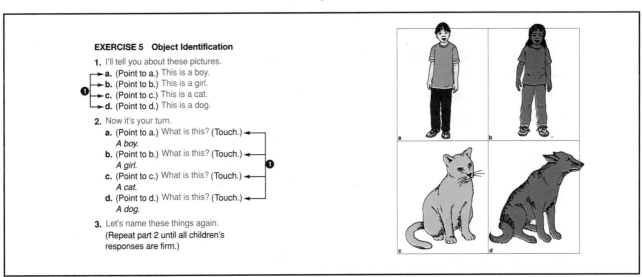

EXERCISE 5 Object Identification

1. I'll tell you about these pictures.
   - **a.** (Point to a.) This is a boy.
   - **b.** (Point to b.) This is a girl.
   - **c.** (Point to c.) This is a cat.
   - **d.** (Point to d.) This is a dog.

➊

2. Now it's your turn.
   - **a.** (Point to a.) What is this? (Touch.)
     A boy.
   - **b.** (Point to b.) What is this? (Touch.)
     A girl.
   - **c.** (Point to c.) What is this? (Touch.)
     A cat.
   - **d.** (Point to d.) What is this? (Touch.)
     A dog.

➊

3. Let's name these things again.
   (Repeat part 2 until all children's responses are firm.)

Sample B

EXERCISE 2

LETTER IDENTIFICATION

➍ a. (Write on the board:)

> o h m f j

- (Point to **o**.)
- You've learned all these letters. My turn to touch and say the names.
- (Touch each letter as you say:) **O, H, M, F, J.**

➋ b. Your turn. I'll touch each letter. You'll tell me the name.
- (Touch under **o**.) What letter? (Touch.) *O.*
- (Touch under **h**.) What letter? (Touch.) *H.*
- (Touch under **m**.) What letter? (Touch.) *M.*
- (Touch under **f**.) What letter? (Touch.) *F.*
- (Touch under **j**.) What letter? (Touch.) *J.*

c. (Repeat step b until firm.)

Worksheet 53

SIDE 2
d. (Hold up worksheet.) Find the flower. ✓
➎ • (Teacher reference:)

> a c o d b o q c a

- Some of the letters are **O.** Some are not **O.**
e. Touch the first letter in the row. ✓
   Is that letter **O**? (Signal.) *No.*
➎ f. Touch the next letter in the row. ✓
   Is that letter **O**? (Signal.) *No.*
g. (Repeat step f for **O, D, B, O, Q, C, A.**)
h. Listen. Circle all the Os. There are two **O**s. ➌
   (Observe children and give feedback.)
- Everybody, what letter did you just circle? (Signal.) *O.*

Sample C

Worksheet

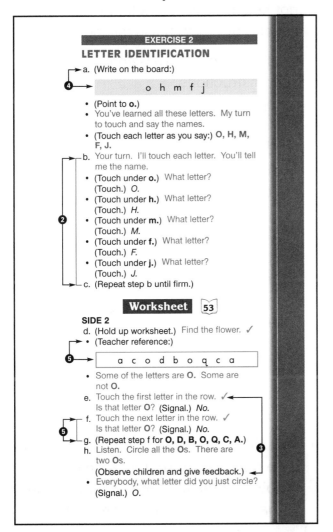

.mad.at.

STORY READING

EXERCISE 12

First reading—children sound out each word and say it fast

➊ a. Everybody, touch the ball for the first word of the story. ✓
   Sound it out. Get ready. (Tap for each sound.) *Mmmaaad.*
b. Again, finger on the ball. ✓ ➌
   Sound it out. Get ready. (Tap for each sound.) *Mmmaaad.*
   Say it fast. (Signal.) *Mad.*
   Yes, what word? (Signal.) *Mad.*
c. Touch the box for the next word. ✓
   Sound it out. Get ready. (Tap for each sound.) *Aaat.*

EXERCISE 14

➏ **Individual test**

a. Everybody, follow along with your finger as I call on different children to read one of the words.
b. Everybody, touch the ball for the first word. ✓
   (Call on a child.) First you'll sound it out and then you'll say it fast. Sound it out. Get
➊ ready. (Tap for each sound.) *Mmmaaad.*
   Say it fast. (Signal.) *Mad.* Yes, **mad.**

For some activities, you direct children to refer to specific pictures, words, or letters in their story-picture book or on their worksheet. Then you give a direction or ask a question. **For reading activities, you use an auditory signal because the children are looking at their material, not at you.** The auditory signal specified in *Reading Mastery Plus,* Level K is a tap.

Touch signals: A touch signal is used with many picture exercises. You touch a picture or a part of a picture to signal the children's response. *Touch* indicates a part of an exercise in which the touch signal is to be used. The word *touch* after a question or an instruction tells you to use the touch signal. This signal has two parts: pointing and touching. (See Sample A.)

Pointing

- Look at the picture in Sample A to demonstrate to the children that they too should be looking at it.

- Point to the picture by holding your finger about an inch from the page, just over the letter. Be careful not to cover the picture—all the children must be able to see it.

- Ask the question or give the instruction.

- Continue to hold your finger in the point position for about one more second.

Touching

- At the end of the one-second interval, quickly and decisively touch above the letter **a** in the first art cell (the boy).

- As your finger touches the page, the children should respond.

- Continue touching the picture for the duration of the children's response.

- Drop your finger when they finish responding.

Note: When pointing to or touching the pictures, be careful not to cover any important part of the picture with your arm, hand, or finger.

Watch for these common pointing problems:

- touching the picture instead of pointing to it as you ask the question or give the instruction

- not holding your point for at least one second after you finish talking

- touching the picture before you finish your instructions

- touching the picture indecisively

- covering the picture as you touch it

- not touching the picture for as long as the children are responding

Tap Signals

Three of the arrows for number 1 in Sample C specify taps for responses that have more than one part. The response expected for sounding out **mad** has three parts: **m–a–d.** You tap for each part.

Follow these rules for tapping to ensure children initiate responses at an appropriate rate:

- **Talk first. Pause a standard length of time (one second), then signal by tapping or using some other audible signal.** Don't change the timing for your signal. Children are to respond on your signal—not after it or before it. When the script directs you to tap, follow the same cadence as touch signal. After the first tap, pause a standard length of time (a second) between the remaining taps.

- Model responses that are paced reasonably. Don't permit children to produce slow, droning responses or yelling responses. These are dangerous because they rob you of the information that can be derived from appropriate group responses. When children respond in a droning way, many of them may be copying responses of others. If children are required to respond at a reasonable speaking rate, all children must initiate responses; therefore, it's relatively easy to determine which children are not responding and which are saying the wrong responses.

- Do not respond with the children unless you are trying to work with them on a difficult response. You present only what is in blue type. You do not say the answers with the children, and you should not move your lips or give other subtle clues about the answer.

Think of signals this way: If you use them correctly, they provide you with much diagnostic information. A weak response provides information about which children may need more help and suggests whether you should repeat an exercise or not. Signals are, therefore, very important early in the program.

After children have learned the routine, the signals are not as critical because the children will be able to respond on cue with no signal. That will happen, however, only if you always wait the same amount of time before signaling.

Note: More information on mastering the use of signals appears on page 195.

Arrow ❷: Firming Children's Responses

(Repeat until firm.)

When children make mistakes, you correct them. A correction may occur during any part of your presentation that calls for the children to respond; it may also occur in connection with what the children are writing. Here are the steps for corrections.

- A mistake on oral (or motor) responses is saying (or doing) the wrong thing or not responding.

- To correct: You say (or do) the correct answer, and then repeat the task the children missed.

- You correct a mistake as soon as you hear it.

For example: Touch the letter that makes the sound **sss.**

A mistake occurs if a child does not touch the letter **s**, touches the letter **s** slowly, or touches any other letter. As soon as you identify a mistake, correct it.

(Point to the letter **s.**)

This is the letter that makes the sound **sss.**

(Repeat the task:)

Everybody, touch the letter that makes the sound **sss.**

Another example: Everybody, what sound are you touching?

If children who are touching the correct letter do not say **sss,** are slow to say **sss,** say any other sound, or say the letter **name,** a mistake has occurred. As soon as you hear the mistake, correct it.

(Say the correct answer:)
That sound is **sss.**
(Repeat the task:)
What sound? (Signal.) *sss.*

Remember, wherever there's a signal, there's a place where children may make mistakes. Correct mistakes as soon as you hear them.

A special correction is needed when children make mistakes on tasks that teach a relationship. This type of correction is marked with the notation: **(Repeat steps __ through __ until firm.)** Both arrows for number 2 in Sample B indicate a section of the presentation that would be repeated (steps b and f).

When you "repeat until firm," you follow these steps.

1. **Correct the mistake.** (Tell the answer and repeat the task that was missed.)

2. **Return to the beginning of the specified steps and present the entire step.** (The part to be repeated is marked with a bracket ([) in the left margin of Pre-Reading lessons, such as sample B.)

In step b, you present one task. In step f you present two different tasks. If the

children make any mistakes, you go back to the beginning of step f and repeat the steps after you have corrected the mistakes. When you hear a mistake, you say the correct answer and repeat the questions or task. However, make sure that children's responses are firm on **both** tasks you present in each step.

Here's a summary of the steps you follow when repeating a part of the exercise until children's responses are firm.

1. **Correct the mistake.**
   Children make a mistake in step b in identifying the letter **F.** Tell the correct answer. The letter name is **F.**
   (Repeat the task:)
   (Point under **f.**) What letter? (Touch.)

2. **Repeat the step.**
   Let's see who remembers the names of those letters.
   Start at the beginning of step b and present the entire part that is in brackets.
   (Point under **O.**) What letter? (Touch.)

Repeating until the children's responses are firm is based on the information you need about the children's performance. You present the context in which the mistake occurred, and the children can show you through their responses whether the correction worked and whether their responses are firm.

The "repeat-until-firm" direction appears only in the most critical parts of exercises. It usually focuses on knowledge and skills that are very important for later work. If you're quite sure that the mistake was simply a lapse and does not mean that the children lack understanding, don't follow the repeat-until-firm directions.

Arrow ❸: Pacing Your Presentation

(Observe children and give feedback.)

You should pace your verbal presentation at a normal speaking rate—as if you were telling somebody something important. Avoid speaking too slowly.

The arrows for number 3 in sample B show two ways to pace your presentation for activities where children write or touch or find parts on their worksheet or story-picture book page. One is ✓. The other is **(Observe children and give feedback.)**

A ✓ is a note to check what the children are doing. It requires only a second or two. Monitor the responses of several "average-performing" children. If their responses are acceptable, proceed with the presentation.

The **(Observe children and give feedback.)** direction implies a more elaborate response. You monitor the responses of more children and give feedback—not only to individual children, but also to the group.

Here are the basic rules for what to do when you observe and give feedback.

- Make sure that you can see all the children's papers from where you are sitting or standing.

- As soon as children start to work, start observing. As you observe, make comments to the whole group. Focus these comments on children who are following directions and working quickly and accurately, for example, Good, a couple of children are almost finished. I haven't seen one mistake so far.

- When children put their pencils down to indicate that they are finished, you can acknowledge them by nodding your head.

- Point out any mistakes you observe. For instance, if a child circles **C,** say, You did not circle **all** the **O's** correctly.

- Make sure that you check all the independent work of lower performers and give the children feedback. Show them what they did wrong and how to fix it. Keep your explanations simple.

- When children do their independent activity, you may want to go over any parts of the lesson with the children who had trouble with the structured work.

- If there are serious problems with the lesson, repeat the difficult parts the next day, before starting the next lesson. Do not proceed to the next lesson if children are making a lot of errors.

Because *Reading Mastery Plus,* Level K is carefully designed, it is possible to help all the children learn to be self-reliant, to follow instructions, and to work quickly and accurately.

Arrow ❹: Board Work

(Write on the board:)

What you write on the board is indicated in green display boxes. In sample B, exercise 2, you write 5 letters on the board.

o h m f j

Arrow ❺: Exercise Conventions

(Teacher reference:), (Repeat for remaining letters.), (Repeat for words 2–3.), and (Repeat for . . .)

Sometimes it is difficult to keep track of where you are supposed to be reading in the teacher presentation script. It is also sometimes difficult to keep track of where the children are supposed to be touching in their story-picture books or worksheets. The arrows for number 5 in Sample B show conventions that enable you to easily track where you are and what the children are supposed to be attending to. This sample presentation script also provides a teacher reference that contains the list of all letters to be presented.

Arrow ❻: Individual Turns and Individual Tests

(Call on individual children for one of the following tasks.) and (Call on different children to . . .)

For most exercises in the early lessons, you will present individual turns immediately after presenting the exercise to the group. Make sure that group responses are firm before you present the individual turns. If you present individual turns too soon, you will find yourself repeating the same correction for different children.

Here are some things you can do to make individual turns effective:

1. Treat them as if they are very important, not merely an afterthought. Convey the message to the children that the work with the group sets the stage for the individual turns.

You can reinforce this idea by rewarding perfect performance for individual turns. (Children who do not miss individual turns receive some form of recognition.)

2. Sample the group with the individual turns. Make sure you present enough individual turns so that you see how the children are performing, but do not call on every child at the end of every exercise.

- As a rule, if there are 10 children in a group, present individual turns to 6–8 of the children. Include all the children who may be weak on the exercise.

- Do not call on children in a predictable order.

- Do not spend a great deal of time on the individual turns. They should go quite quickly.

Corrections

All children make mistakes. The mistakes children make provide you with important information about the difficulties they are having. It is important to correct mistakes immediately. Knowing how to effectively correct children's mistakes helps you help the children learn. Three kinds of correction procedures are used in the program: (1) general corrections, (2) specific corrections, and (3) statement corrections.

General Corrections: Children's responses that call for general corrections include: (1) not attending, (2) not answering, and (3) responding before or after the signal. Here are some plans for correcting these problems.

Not attending: Not attending occurs when children are not looking where they should be looking during an exercise (for example, not looking at the picture to which you are pointing). Correct not attending by looking at these children and saying, Watch my finger. Let's try it again. Then return to the beginning of the exercise. Returning to the beginning of the exercise will help the children understand your standard: Everyone has to pay attention.

Not responding: Not responding occurs when the children don't answer when you signal a response. Some children may learn not to listen the first time a question is asked and then join in later. They may become dependent on the other children's responses and may get the idea they don't have to initiate their own responses. If children are not answering, correct by saying, I have to hear everybody. Then return to the beginning of the exercise.

Responding Before or After the Signal: Remember that the purpose of a signal is to orchestrate a group response. When children do not respond on time (responding before your signal or too long after your signal), they are not attending to your signal, and you are not getting information from every child.

If you find that you are spending a lot of time correcting children who are not attending, not responding, or responding before or after the signal, your pacing of the exercise or the signal is probably too slow.

Remember that the objective of a signal is not to keep the children sitting on the edges of their seats never knowing when they will have to respond next. Rather, the pacing of signals should be predictable and occurring at a rate that permits children to think and then respond with assurance.

Specific Corrections: To correct specific response errors, follow the correction procedures below or the correction procedures that appear in some of the exercises of the presentation books. Corrections for specific response errors vary from exercise to exercise because each correction deals with the specific content of a given exercise and the types of errors that children are likely to make.

Statement Corrections: The correction for statement errors has four parts: **(1) model, (2) lead, (3) test,** and **(4) delayed test.** Here is an example of the statement correction. (Several children had trouble saying the full statement "This is a house.")

1. **The model** in step b, page 26. (Teacher: My turn. Listen. This is a house. Listen again. This is a house.) In this step you demonstrate the statement the children are to make.

2. **The lead** (Teacher: Let's say it together. You and the children: *This is a house.*) Leading gives the children the benefit of responding with you until they are confident. Some statements require a number of leads to produce firm, correct responses. Don't be afraid to continue leading until the children can

EXERCISE 6 Identity Statements

1. We're going to talk about all of these things.
   When I touch something, you tell me about it.
   a. (Point to a.) What is this? (Touch.)
   A bike.
   Say the whole thing. (Touch.) *This is a
   bike.*
   b. (Point to b.) What is this? (Touch.)
   A house.
   Say the whole thing. (Touch.) *This is a
   house.*
   c. (Point to c.) What is this? (Touch.)
   A cabinet.
   Say the whole thing. (Touch.) *This is a
   cabinet.*
   d. (Point to d.) What is this? (Touch.) *A glass.*
   Say the whole thing. (Touch.) *This is a
   glass.*
   e. (Point to e.) What is this? (Touch.) *A shirt.*
   Say the whole thing. (Touch.) *This is a
   shirt.*
   f. (Point to f.) What is this? (Touch.) *A box.*
   Say the whole thing. (Touch.) *This is a box.*

2. Let's do that again.
   (Repeat part 1 until all children's responses
   are firm.)

Individual Turns
(Repeat part 1, calling on different children for
each step.)

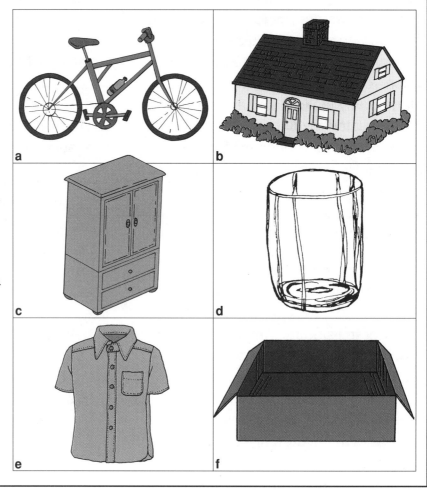

produce the statement with you. But
remember, **the lead step should be
used only when the children cannot
produce the statement.** If they can
produce the statement after the model,
skip the lead step.

3. **The test:** (Teacher: Your turn. Say the
   whole thing. Children: *This is a house.*)
   If the children say the statement
   correctly, you know the correction has
   been effective. If they still have trouble,
   you know that you must repeat the
   model and lead steps until all the
   children can pass the test step.

4. **The delayed test:** This involves going
   back to an earlier part of the exercise
   or to an earlier exercise and making
   sure the children can make the
   statement when it occurs in the context
   of the entire exercise.

   The delayed test step applies to
   specific response errors as well. After
   the children can respond to the specific
   question or instruction they had
   previously missed, you should return to
   an earlier part of the exercise and
   present the subsequent steps in
   sequence. The delayed test is very
   important. It's evidence that children
   have learned to say the statement.

Practicing Corrections: It is very important to practice making corrections. You must be able to present a correction without hesitation when the mistake occurs. By practicing the corrections, you will be well prepared for the mistakes that children commonly make.

Have other adults play the role of the children and make the specified mistake. Then present the correction. Practice it until you can do it quickly and naturally. Also practice returning to the beginning of the exercise and presenting the entire exercise. Your group is firm when they respond correctly to every step of the exercise.

Correcting Errors in Following Directions: Throughout the program, you will present directions to the children. Many of these have to do with touching words, letters, and symbols. Early in the program, children may not touch the appropriate words or symbols. For example, you say, Touch the next word, and one or two children touch the wrong word or do not respond. These mistakes can lead to serious problems if they are not corrected quickly and effectively.

Here are some guidelines:

- Make sure you observe what children are touching or reading in their story-picture book or worksheet. Children should not hold their books up, but rather keep them flat on their lapboard or desk.

- Always observe the children as you give them instructions about turning the page, touching an icon, or touching part of a picture.

- Gear your presentation to the performance of the lower performers. For example, present the instruction, Touch the picture of the dog, and quickly confirm that the lower performers are touching the picture. The confirmation should take only a second—if each child's material is visible.

- If there is a mistake, correct it quickly. For occasional lapses, quickly point to where the child should be touching. If a child seems to have more than one or two lapses a lesson, correct the mistakes by first showing the child where to touch. Then say, Fingers up. Let's do that again. Everybody, touch the picture of the dog. Good.

Use the same procedure when more than one child makes a mistake on a task. If the mistake occurred because some of the children were not able to identify the symbol or picture you referred to, show the group what it should be doing. For instance, if you say, Touch the moon, and some of the children seem lost, hold up the worksheet and point to the moon. Say, Here it is. Everybody, touch the moon. The correction should be very quick.

If you have any doubt about the ability of children to perform, provide a quick delayed test. At the end of the period, for instance, you might say, Everybody, turn back to the beginning of lesson 11 . . . Touch the picture of the moon . . . Good. Now touch the picture of the star . . . Nice job.

Letter Identification and Sound Errors:
Follow these steps to correct mistakes that children make in identifying letters or words.

1. Tell or show the correct answer. The word is man.

2. Repeat the question or instruction that the children missed.

3. Later, present a delayed test. For this test, repeat part of the exercise before repeating the item the children missed.

The delayed test lets you know if you successfully communicated the correction to the children. If mistakes do not occur very frequently, you do not need to include delayed tests. If children have trouble—particularly if you know beforehand that the children will make a mistake—use delayed tests. Make sure that the children's responses are firm before going to the next lesson.

Tracks

The Language Scope and Sequence charts and Reading Scope and Sequence chart found in Appendix A in this guide show the major skills that are taught in *Reading Mastery Plus,* Level K. Major skills are developed in tracks. Each lesson presents work from several different tracks. A particular track, such as Letter Identification, continues from lesson to lesson with new letter names introduced every few lessons. The track also provides reviews and firming of earlier-taught discriminations. The following discussion of each track for Language, Pre-Reading, and Reading presents the key exercises, points out presentation details, specifies correction and firming procedures, and provides information about the development of the track over the lesson range. When teaching the program, refer to this section of the guide to find out about presentational details and new activities.

The Language Tracks

This section presents the rationale, some teaching information, and sample exercises for each track of the Language program. The groups of tracks are displayed on the Language Scope and Sequence charts, pages 238–239.

The purpose of this overview is to give you an understanding of the concepts and skills presented in each group of tracks, to explain why they are included in the program, as well as to discuss problems children may have with specific exercises. The discussions of different tracks also present teaching techniques and corrections that are useful in solving more common problems.

This table lists when the language tracks first appear in the lessons and also gives the page numbers on which key exercises from these tracks are discussed in the teacher's guide.

Actions

Actions exercises help children learn concepts by performing actions and by describing actions illustrated in the teacher's presentation books.

The actions exercises

- provide a clear demonstration of many language concepts and word meanings;

- provide practice that the children enjoy (actions exercises are fun);

- introduce concepts that the children use in everyday activities;

Schedule of Exercises	Starting with Lesson	Page in Teacher's Guide
Actions		
Beginning Actions	1	31
Actions—Parts of the Body	4	36
Actions—Pictures	13	36
Actions—Pronouns	18	39
Tense	50	41
Tense—Pictures	54	43
Actions—Review	48	45
Descriptions of Objects		
Object Identification	1	47
Identity Statements	3	49
Common Objects	7	55
Missing Objects	18	56
Opposites	19	56
Plurals	46	60
Comparatives	126	65
Information and Background Knowledge		
Names	1	68
School Information	1	68
Days of the Week	30	69
Months of the Year	87	70
Seasons	123	72
Part/Whole	23	73
Materials	57	76
Common Information	66	79
Locations	124	82
Signs	131	84
Instructional Words and Problem-Solving Concepts		
Spatial and Temporal Relations	13	86
Prepositions	22	88
And—Actions	55	94
Same/Different	84	95
Some, All, None	87	105
Actions—Or	97	108
Before/After	95	110
If-Then Rules	120	114
Where, Who, When, What	116	117
Classification		
Classification	46	119
Rhyming		
Rhyming	55	125
Problem-Solving Strategies and Applications		
Review	28	129
Concept Applications	36	130
Absurdities	120	137
Inquiry	144	139

- provide you with immediate feedback about the children's performance (if the children don't understand the instructions for performing an action, you can identify their problem immediately);

- allow for a review of many important concepts and words that are presented in sequences of actions (not only do the children learn the concepts, but they also practice the concepts until their use becomes natural and easy);

- establish foundations for teaching more difficult language-usage conventions such as those associated with pronouns and tenses.

This guide divides the actions exercises into two types: basic actions and actions used in the development of concepts of the other tracks. The items in the first column are basic actions. The rest are actions associated with other concepts.

Basic Actions	Other Actions
Beginning Actions	Actions—Prepositions
Actions—Parts of the Body	Actions—Spatial and Temporal Relations
Actions—Pictures	Actions—Plurals
Actions—Pronouns	Actions—And
Actions—Tense	Actions—Some, All, None
Tense—Pictures	Actions—Same/Different
Review Actions	Actions—Or
	Actions—Before/After
	Actions—If-Then Rules

Beginning actions exercises focus on specific actions such as "stand up" and "touch the floor." In these first actions exercises, the children perform simple actions and label these actions. In subsequent lessons, they learn to produce the full statements that describe the actions. As children progress through the basic actions exercises, they also learn the names of parts of the body and various pronouns. They also practice the words and statements for expressing differences in tense.

Most basic actions exercises require children to perform actions. For others, children analyze pictures of people and animals performing actions. (The children describe what the people and animals are doing, what they were doing, and what they will do.) Tense actions and tense pictures give children practice in describing events that happen in present time, past time, and future time.

Review actions are exercises that provide children with opportunities to practice what they have learned. These occur on a regular basis throughout the lessons of the program.

Actions exercises are also used in the development of concepts of other tracks. Most of these tracks contain both actions and pictures exercises. For example, the teaching of prepositional concepts involves actions exercises (hold your hand in front of your nose) as well as pictures exercises (show me the man in front of the house). The introduction of the concepts *some, all, none* involves actions exercises: Hold up all of your fingers; Hold up some of your fingers; Hold up none of your fingers. Part of the teaching of *and, or,* and *if-then* involves actions (you will touch your nose *or* stand up). Discussions of actions for *same/different, before/after, prepositions,* and *if-then* appear in the various tracks. The following exercises are basic actions exercises.

EXERCISE 1 Actions—Following Directions

1. Get ready to do some actions. Watch my
   hand. Don't do anything until I signal.
   a. Everybody, stand up. (Signal. The children
      are to stand up.)
      Everybody, sit down. (Signal. The children
      are to sit down.) ● ◆
   b. (Repeat step a until all children respond to
      your signal.)

2. Let's do those actions again.
   a. Everybody, stand up. (Signal.)
      My turn. What are you doing? (Signal.)
      Standing up.
      Your turn. What are you doing?
      (Signal.) *Standing up.* ▲
   b. Everybody, sit down. (Signal.) What are
      you doing? (Signal.) *Sitting down.* ■

3. Let's do those actions again.
   (Repeat part 2 until all children can perform
   the actions and say what they are doing.)

Corrections

EXERCISE 1

● **Error**
(Children respond before you signal.)
Correction
1. You have to wait for my signal.
2. Let's try it again.
3. (Repeat step a until all children respond.)

◆ **Error**
(Children respond late.)
Correction
1. You have to do it as soon as I signal.
2. Let's try it again.
3. (Repeat step a until all children respond.)

▲ **Error**
(Children don't say *Standing up.*)
Correction
1. Standing up. Say it with me. (Signal.
   Respond with the children.) Standing up.
2. Again. (Signal. Respond with the children.)
   Standing up.
3. All by yourselves. Say it. (Signal. Do not
   respond with the children.) *Standing up.*
4. (Have the children sit down.)
5. (Repeat step a.)

■ **Error**
(Children don't say *Sitting down.*)
Correction
1. Sitting down. Say it with me. (Signal.
   Respond with the children.) Sitting down.
2. Again. (Signal. Respond with the children.)
   Sitting down.
3. All by yourselves. Say it. (Signal. Do not
   respond with the children.) *Sitting down.*
4. (Have the children stand up.)
5. (Repeat step b.)

Beginning Actions
Lessons 1–20

Lesson 1: Actions—Following Directions

In the first actions exercises, the children
respond on signal to your instructions.
The children do not make full statements
in these early exercises; rather, they learn
to follow your directions and to then label
their actions, for example, *Standing up,
Sitting down.* Exercise 1, above, is the first
exercise from lesson 1.

Teaching Techniques

• Keep your pacing brisk—say your lines
  quickly. A brisk pace will become even
  more important when the instructions
  become more complicated in later
  exercises.

• Follow each step with a hand-drop
  signal to show the children **when** to
  respond. Make your signal precise. A
  good signal is essential to the pacing of
  the exercise.

• In step a, after giving the instructions,
  pause only long enough for the
  children to stand or sit. Then
  immediately ask the question What are
  you doing? so the children realize they
  are to label the action they just
  performed.

• Do not allow the children to lead you. If
  you do not require them to respond on

signal, you will find yourself slowing the pace of the exercise, waiting for each child to perform the action before presenting the next instruction.

- Make sure the children are responding on signal before leaving this exercise on the first day it is presented.

Corrections

Follow one or more of the corrections that appear in the corrections box of exercise 1, page 32. If the children don't respond to your signal, select those children who are responding to your signal. Say, Watch them. They can do it. Repeat parts 1 and 2 with those children. Praise them for good performance. Then repeat the exercise with all the children until all respond to your signal.

EXERCISE 1   Actions—Statements

1. Get ready to do some actions. Watch my hand. Remember to wait for the signal.
   a. Everybody, stand up. (Signal. Wait.)
      Everybody, sit down. (Signal. Wait.)
      Everybody, touch your head. (Signal. Wait.)
      Put your hand down. (Signal. Wait.)
      Everybody, touch your head. (Signal. Wait.)
      Put your hand down. (Signal. Wait.)
   b. (Repeat step a until all children's responses are firm.)
   c. Everybody, stand up. (Signal. Wait.)
      What are you doing? (Signal.) *Standing up.*
      Everybody, sit down. (Signal. Wait.)
      What are you doing? (Signal.) *Sitting down.*
      Everybody, touch your head. (Signal. Wait.)
      What are you doing? (Signal.) *Touching my head.*
      Put your hand down. (Signal.)
   d. (Repeat step c until all children's responses are firm.)

2. Now let's try this.
   a. Everybody, touch your head. (Signal. Wait.)
      What are you doing? (Signal.) *Touching my head.* ●
   b. Watch me. (Touch your head. Keep touching it.) I'll say the whole thing. I am touching my head.
   c. Let's all say the whole thing. (Signal. Respond with the children.) I am touching my head.
   d. Again. (Repeat the sentence with the children until they can all say it with you.)
   e. Your turn. Say the whole thing. (Signal. Do not respond with the children.) *I am touching my head.*
   f. Again. (Signal.) *I am touching my head.*
   g. (Repeat step e until all children's responses are firm.)
      Everybody, put your hand down. (Signal.)

3. Let's go a little faster.
   a. Everybody, touch your head. (Signal. Wait.)
      What are you doing? (Signal.) *Touching my head.* ●
   b. Say the whole thing. (Signal.) *I am touching my head.*
      (Repeat step b until all children can make the statement.)
      Put your hand down. (Signal.)

4. (Repeat part 3 until all children's responses are firm.)

Individual Turns
(Repeat part 3, calling on different children for each step.)

Corrections

EXERCISE 1

● **Error**
(Children say the entire sentence when you ask, *What are you doing?*)

Correction
1. Stop. My turn. Listen. What are you doing? Touching my head.

2. Your turn. What are you doing? (Signal.) *Touching my head.*
3. Now say the whole thing. (Signal.) *I am touching my head.*
4. (Repeat steps 2 and 3 until all children can answer correctly.)
5. Put your hand down. (Signal.)
6. (Repeat part 2.)

Lesson 7: Actions—Statements

In the exercise above, the children learn to "say the whole thing"—that is, to make a statement about what they are doing. In part 1, step a, the children perform actions without responding verbally. In step c, they label their actions. In part 2, they learn to make an actions statement.

Teaching Techniques

- In part 1, page 33, make sure the children can perform all actions in step a, on signal, before you go to step c.

- Make sure the children do not respond with a complete statement in step c. (They should say *Standing up,* not *I am standing up.*)

- In part 2 lead the children through the statement as many times as necessary so that at steps e and f they can make the statement without your help.

- In part 2 make sure the children continue to do the action as they talk about it. They should keep touching their heads from the beginning of step c until the end of step f, for example. The words and statements may not have meaning unless the children are simultaneously **doing** the action they are talking about.

Corrections

- Sometimes children say the entire statement in response to What are you doing? Follow the correction specified in the corrections box.

- If a child does not follow your instructions correctly (for example, he doesn't touch his head), point to a child who has and say, Look, John is touching his head. If necessary, help the child by moving his hand to his head.

- Some children may have trouble with the response *Touching my head.* If you say, Touch your head. . . . What are you doing? and they respond *Touching your head,* they have made a mistake. To correct this error, use a model, a lead, and a test.

1. Have another child model the response: Linda's turn. Touch your head. (**Wait.**) What are you doing? *Touching my head.*

2. Lead the children:
   Let's all do it. Everybody, touch your head. (**Wait.**) What are you doing? (Signal. Respond with the children.) *Touching my head.*
   Repeat this step until all children can say *Touching my head.*

3. Test the children:
   All by yourselves. Touch your head. (**Wait.**)
   What are you doing? (Signal. **Do not** respond with the children.) *Touching my head.*

Lesson 9: Actions—Statements

This exercise establishes a pattern that is followed in many of the actions exercises throughout the program.

Teaching Techniques

- Always make sure that the children are doing the action while they are answering the question What are you doing? They must still be doing it when they "say the whole thing."

- Present each instruction quickly, emphasizing the critical word or words: Touch your **arm.**

- Make each signal crisp and clear. It is essential that these action routines be done in a brisk manner.

- If the children do not perform the action, help them. For example, take a child's hand and move it to her arm.

Corrections

If the children are hesitant to respond or are being led by some of the group, return to the beginning of the exercise. Give the instruction and then give a very precise signal. Repeat until all the children are responding on signal. This is very important as the routines become more complicated—and more fun—as the children proceed through the program.

EXERCISE 1 Actions—Statements

1. Get ready to do some actions.
   a. My turn. I can touch my arm. Watch. (Touch your arm.)
      Everybody, touch your arm. (Signal. Wait.)
      What are you doing? (Signal.) *Touching my arm.*
      Put your hand down. (Signal.)
   b. My turn. I can touch my leg. Watch. (Touch your leg.)
      Everybody, touch your leg. (Signal. Wait.)
      What are you doing? (Signal.) *Touching my leg.*
      Put your hand down. (Signal.)
   c. Your turn. Everybody, stand up. (Signal. Wait.)
      What are you doing? (Signal.) *Standing up.*
   d. Everybody, touch your ear. (Signal. Wait.)
      What are you doing? (Signal.) *Touching my ear.*
      Put your hand down. (Signal.)
   e. Everybody, touch your arm. (Signal. Wait.)
      What are you doing? (Signal.) *Touching my arm.*
      Say the whole thing. (Signal.) *I am touching my arm.*
      Put your hand down. (Signal.)
   f. Everybody, sit down. (Signal. Wait.)
      What are you doing? (Signal.) *Sitting down.*
      Say the whole thing. (Signal.) *I am sitting down.*
   g. Everybody, touch your leg. (Signal. Wait.)
      What are you doing? (Signal.) *Touching my leg.*
      Say the whole thing. (Signal.) *I am touching my leg.*
      Put your hand down. (Signal.)
   h. Everybody, touch your ear. (Signal. Wait.)
      What are you doing? (Signal.) *Touching my ear.*
      Say the whole thing. (Signal.) *I am touching my ear.*
      Put your hand down. (Signal.)

2. Let's do those actions again.
   (Repeat part 1 until all children's responses are firm.)

Individual Turns
(Repeat part 1, calling on different children for each step.)

Actions—Parts of the Body
Lessons 4–35

The children learn the names of parts of the body in many of the beginning actions exercises.

EXERCISE 1 Actions—Parts of the Body

[**Note:** If children make a mistake, demonstrate the correct action and have the children do it. Then return to step a in part 2 and repeat the exercise.]

1. It's time for some actions.
   a. I can touch my chin. Watch. (Touch your chin.)
   b. What am I doing? (Signal.) *Touching your chin.*

2. Now it's your turn.
   a. Everybody, smile. (Signal. Wait.)
      What are you doing? (Signal.) *Smiling.*
      Say the whole thing. (Signal.) *I am smiling.*
   b. Everybody, touch your chin. (Signal. Wait.)
      What are you doing? (Signal.) *Touching my chin.*
      Say the whole thing. (Signal.) *I am touching my chin.*
   c. Everybody, touch your leg. (Signal. Wait.)
      What are you doing? (Signal.) *Touching my leg.*
      Say the whole thing. (Signal.) *I am touching my leg.*
   d. Everybody, touch your head. (Signal. Wait.)
      What are you doing? (Signal.) *Touching my head.*
      Say the whole thing. (Signal.) *I am touching my head.*
   e. Everybody, touch your hand. (Signal. Wait.)
      What are you doing? (Signal.) *Touching my hand.*
      Say the whole thing. (Signal.) *I am touching my hand.*
   f. Put your hand down. (Signal.)

3. Let's do that again.
   (Repeat part 2 until all children's responses are firm.)

Lesson 20: Actions—Parts of the Body

Teaching Techniques

- You identify your chin in part 1. Make sure the children are watching you.

- Make sure the children are pointing to the right body part as they respond to your instructions.

- Move quickly through these steps. The children like these routines. Correct any mistakes and return to the beginning of the exercise.

Actions—Pictures
Lessons 13–38

For the exercises in this track the children are introduced to pictures of actions they have been performing. Children describe actions illustrated in the presentation book.

The first exercises use action words that have already been practiced in the actions exercises. In later exercises children respond to new action words and pronouns.

EXERCISE 5   Action Statements—Pictures

1. We're going to talk about some actions.
   a. (Point to the girl.) Everybody, what is this? (Touch.) *A girl.*
      Say the whole thing. (Touch.) *This is a girl.*
   b. Listen. What is this girl doing? (Touch.) *Standing.*
   c. Let's say the whole thing about what this girl is doing. (Touch. Respond with the children.) This girl is standing.
   d. Again. (Touch.) This girl is standing.
   e. All by yourselves. Say the whole thing about what this girl is doing. (Touch.) *This girl is standing.*
   f. (Repeat steps a through e until all children's responses are firm.)

2. Now we'll talk about some more actions.
   a. (Point to the dog.) Everybody, what is this? (Touch.) *A dog.*
      Say the whole thing. (Touch.) *This is a dog.*
   b. What is this dog doing? (Touch.) *Sitting.*
   c. Say the whole thing about what this dog is doing. (Touch. Do not respond with the children.) *This dog is sitting.*
   d. Again. (Touch.) *This dog is sitting.*
   e. (Repeat steps a through d until all children's responses are firm.)

3. Get ready to do some more.
   a. (Point to the cat.) Everybody, what is this? (Touch.) *A cat.*
      Say the whole thing. (Touch.) *This is a cat.*
   b. What is the cat doing? (Touch.) *Standing.*
   c. Say the whole thing about what this cat is doing. (Touch.) *This cat is standing.*
   d. Again. (Touch.) *This cat is standing.*
   e. (Repeat steps a through d until all children's responses are firm.)

4. Let's do those again.
   a. (Point to the girl.) Everybody, what is this? (Touch.) *A girl.*
   b. What is this girl doing? (Touch.) *Standing.*
   c. Say the whole thing about what this girl is doing. (Touch.) *This girl is standing.*

5. (Repeat parts 2 and 3 until all children's responses are firm.)

Individual Turns
(Repeat the exercise, calling on different children for each step.)

Lesson 13: Action Statements—Pictures

This exercise, from lesson 13, is the first exercise in the actions—pictures track. In part 1, you lead the children by responding with them as they say the whole thing about what the girl is doing. The objective is for the children to be able to respond to parts 2, 3, and 4, in sequence, without mistakes, and without your help.

Teaching Techniques

• Emphasize the words **this dog** when you say, Say the whole thing about what **this dog** is doing. This will alert the children to the difference between the action-statement form that begins with "This dog" and the identity-statement form "This is a dog."

• Because this is a picture exercise, you will use different signals than in the action routines. You will point to and touch the pictures as indicated.

• Remember to keep touching the picture as long as the children are responding. When the children say *sitting,* your finger must be on the picture while they are saying the word. When the children say, *This dog is sitting,* your finger should be on the picture while they are saying the entire statement.

- Recognize that parts 2 and 3 follow the same pattern and that part 4 is a simpler version of that pattern.

Corrections

Some children may have trouble saying the whole thing about what the dog is **doing.** They may say, *This is a dog.* Stop them as soon as you hear them say, *This is . . . .* Say, You have to tell me what **this dog** is doing. Then do a model-lead-and-test correction.

1. Model the response:
   My turn. This dog is sitting.

2. Lead the children:
   Let's say the whole thing about what **this dog** is doing. (Signal.) *This dog is sitting.*

3. Test the children:
   Your turn. Say the whole thing about what **this dog** is doing. (Signal.) *This dog is sitting.*
   Repeat parts 2 and 3 until the children can say the statement.

Lesson 19: Action Statements— Pictures

In the action statements—pictures exercise, on page 39, the children make a *not* statement about actions. (They have already learned in object identification exercises to make *not* statements in the form *This is not a . . . .*) In action exercises, the form is *This _____ is not _____.*

Teaching Techniques

- Make sure that the children can answer *yes* or *no* to all the pictures in part 1.

- Then proceed to part 2, moving quickly from one picture to the next. Recognize that each step in part 2 follows the same pattern.

Corrections

If children have trouble in steps b and c in part 2, use the model-lead-and-test correction.

1. Model: My turn. Say the whole thing about **this girl.** (Pause.) **This girl** is not eating.

2. Lead: Let's say the whole thing about **this girl.** (Signal.) **This girl** *is not eating.*

3. Test: All by yourselves. Say the whole thing about **this girl.** (Signal.) *This girl is not eating.*

4. Retest: Return to the beginning of part 2 and repeat until the children's responses are firm.

EXERCISE 6   Action Statements—Pictures

1. Look at these pictures.
   Let's see which girl is eating.
   (Point to each picture, one at a time.) Is this girl eating? (The children are to answer *yes* or *no*.)

2. We're going to talk about each picture.
   a. (Point to a.) Is this girl eating? (Touch.) *Yes.*
   Say the whole thing. (Touch.) *This girl is eating.*
   Again. (Touch.) *This girl is eating.*
   (Repeat until all children's responses are firm.)
   b. (Point to b.) Is this girl eating? (Touch.) *No.*
   Say the whole thing. (Touch.) *This girl is not eating.*
   Again. (Touch.) *This girl is not eating.*
   (Repeat until all children's responses are firm.)
   c. (Point to c.) Is this girl eating? (Touch.) *No.*
   Say the whole thing. (Touch.) *This girl is not eating.*
   Again. (Touch.) *This girl is not eating.*
   (Repeat until all children's responses are firm.)

3. (Point to b.) We're going to talk some more about this girl.
   Is this girl walking? (Touch.) *No.*
   Is this girl sitting? (Touch.) *Yes.*
   Is this girl standing? (Touch.) *No.*
   What is this girl doing? (Touch.) *Sitting.*
   Say the whole thing. (Touch.) *This girl is sitting.*

4. Let's do those again.
   (Repeat part 3 until all children's responses are firm.)

Individual Turns
(Repeat parts 1 through 3, calling on different children for each step.)

Actions—Pronouns
Lessons 18–46

Because it is less confusing for children to use pronouns in real-life situations than in book situations, all pronoun exercises are first presented as part of the daily action exercises. Before lesson 18, the children have already used the pronouns **I** and **my;** the other pronouns are formally introduced according to the following schedule:

I—you	Lesson 18	She—her	Lesson 32
You—your	Lesson 19	He—his	Lesson 33
I—my	Lesson 21	They—their	Lesson 35
We	Lesson 23	Our	Lesson 46

After lesson 46, pronouns are integrated into actions review exercises as well as into a variety of other exercises.

EXERCISE 1   Actions—Pronouns

1. Get ready to do some actions.
   a. Everybody, touch the floor. (Signal. Wait.) What are you doing? (Signal.) *Touching the floor.*
      Say the whole thing about what you are doing. (Signal.) *I am touching the floor.*
   b. Everybody, stand up. (Signal. Wait.) What are you doing? (Signal.) *Standing up.*
      Say the whole thing about what you are doing. (Signal.) *I am standing up.*
   c. Everybody, sit down. (Signal. Wait.) What are you doing? (Signal.) *Sitting down.*
      Say the whole thing about what you are doing. (Signal.) *I am sitting down.*
   d. (Repeat part 1 until all children can make the statements.)

2. We're going to talk about what I am doing.
   a. My turn. I am going to touch my ear. (Touch your ear and keep touching it.) What am **I** doing? (Signal. Respond with the children.) Touching **your** ear.
      Let's say the whole thing about what I am doing. (Signal. Respond with the children.) You are touching **your** ear.
      Again. (Signal.) You are touching **your** ear. (Repeat until all children can make the statement with you.)
   b. All by yourselves. Say the whole thing about what I am doing. (Signal. Do not respond with the children.) *You are touching your ear.*
      Again. (Signal.) *You are touching your ear.* (Repeat until all children can make the statement.)

3. Let's do some more.
   a. I'm going to touch the floor. (Touch the floor.) What am I doing? (Signal.) *Touching the floor.*
      Say the whole thing about what I am doing. (Signal.) *You are touching the floor.*
      Again. (Signal.) *You are touching the floor.* (Repeat until all children can make the statement.)
   b. I'm going to stand up. (Stand up.) What am I doing? (Signal.) *Standing up.*
      Say the whole thing about what I am doing. (Signal.) *You are standing up.*
      Again. (Signal.) *You are standing up.* (Repeat until all children can make the statement.)
   c. I'm going to sit down. (Sit down.) What am I doing? (Signal.) *Sitting down.*
      Say the whole thing about what I am doing. (Signal.) *You are sitting down.* (Repeat until all children can make the statement.)
   d. (Repeat part 3 until all children's responses are firm.)

Individual Turns
(Repeat part 3, calling on different children for each step.)

Lesson 19: Actions—Pronouns

In the exercise above from lesson 19, the children use the pronouns **I** and **you** to answer questions about what each child is doing and about what you are doing.

Teaching Techniques

- If the children have done well in previous exercises in which you ask them to say the whole thing about What are you doing? and they reply *I am* . . . , they will have little trouble with this exercise.

- Stress the words **I, your,** and **you** in part 2. (Saying **you** with the children when referring to yourself does not actually confuse the children.)

- In part 2 repeat step a only until the children can make the statement at step b without your lead.

Corrections

If children respond *We are* . . . instead of *I am* . . . , let them know their response is reasonable, but say, When I ask about **you,** you say "I." (In later exercises the children will learn to respond with **we** when you ask, What are **we** doing? and to distinguish between instructions that call for the response *I am touching the floor* and those that call for *We are touching the floor.*

Tense
Lessons 50–85

Tense changes in verbs present difficulties for many young children. Some children must learn an entire set of language conventions to describe happenings in the past, present, and future. There are several ways to express past time, present time, and future time. Children must deal with irregular past tense verbs (I ate, I sat, I ran) and must learn vocabulary for the past progressive. For the past progressive, irregular verbs are eliminated. Children must deal with

irregular verbs (I ate, I am eating, I will eat).

In the tense exercises, children not only learn the words and statements for expressing differences in tense but are also given demonstrations of the **concept** of tense. The children learn

1. present-tense actions and identity statements;

2. demonstrations of the concepts involved in changing tense—present to past, and present to future;

3. the statement patterns for describing their own actions in past, present, and future tense, using both singular and plural forms, and using the progressive for describing past tense actions;

4. to describe pictures using past, present, and future tense statements;

5. a large number of verbs, both regular and irregular, in present, past, and future tense forms.

EXERCISE 3   Actions—Tense
(Demonstration)

[**Note:** You will need a pencil and a cup.]

1. We're going to talk about a pencil and a cup.
    a. (Hold up the pencil.)
       What is this? (Signal.) *A pencil.*
       (Hold up the cup.)
       What is this? (Signal.) *A cup.*
    b. Watch. (Put the pencil in the cup
       and point to the pencil.)
       Where **is** the pencil? (Signal.) *In the cup.*
    c. Now watch. (Hold the pencil over the cup.)
       Listen. My turn. **Is** the pencil in the cup?
       No.
       Was the pencil in the cup? Yes.
    d. Listen. Your turn.
       Is the pencil in the cup? (Signal.) *No.*
       Was the pencil in the cup? (Signal.) *Yes.*
       Where **was** the pencil? (Signal.) *In the
       cup.* ●

2. Let's do it again.
    a. (Put the pencil in the cup.)
       Where **is** the pencil? (Signal.) *In the cup.*
       Say the whole thing. (Signal.) *The pencil is
       in the cup.*
    b. (Hold the pencil over the cup.)
       Listen. Where **was** the pencil? (Signal.)
       In the cup.
       Say the whole thing. (Signal.) *The pencil
       was in the cup.*

    c. Again. Say the whole thing. (Signal.)
       The pencil was in the cup.
    d. (Repeat steps a through c until all
       children's responses are firm.)

Individual Turns
(Repeat parts 1 and 2, calling on different
children for each step.)

Corrections

EXERCISE 3

● **Error**
(Children say *Over the cup.*)

   Correction
   1. The pencil **is** over the cup. I asked where
      was the pencil.
   2. Let's do it again.
      (Repeat step d.)

Lesson 50: Actions—Tense (Demonstration)

This exercise, from lesson 50,
demonstrates the difference in meaning
between present tense and past tense.
The only difference between the present
tense statement and the past tense
statement is the verbs **is** and **was.**

Teaching Techniques

- Practice the presentation before
  presenting it to the children. Stress the
  words **is** and **was** whenever they occur.

- Make sure that the children are firm
  in saying the statement at the end of
  part 2.

Corrections

In part 1, if the children don't respond
correctly to the question Was the pencil in
the cup? follow the correction in the
corrections box.

In part 2, step b, if the children say, *The pencil is in the cup* instead of *The pencil was in the cup,* correct as follows:

1. Was in the cup. Say that. Repeat until children's responses are firm.

2. The pencil was in the cup. Say it with me. The pencil was in the cup. Repeat until children's responses are firm.

3. Repeat part 2 of the exercise.

EXERCISE 4   Tense

1. Look at these pictures. They show what a cat did.
   a. (Point to a.)
   This picture shows where the cat is first. The cat is on the floor.
   Say the whole thing. (Touch.) *The cat is on the floor.*
   b. (Point to b.)
   This picture shows where the cat is next. Where is it? (Touch.) *On the couch.*
   Yes, the cat is on the couch.
   Say the whole thing. (Touch.) *The cat is on the couch.*

2. Listen.
   a. Where was the cat before it got on the couch? (Signal. Do not touch the picture.) *On the floor.*
   b. Say the whole thing about where the cat was. (Signal.) *The cat was on the floor.*

3. (Repeat parts 1 and 2 until all children's responses are firm.)

Individual Turns
(Repeat the exercise, calling on different children for each step.)

Corrections
EXERCISE 4
(Correct all mistakes immediately, then return to the beginning of the exercise.)

Tense—Pictures
Lessons 54–85

Lesson 54: Tense

The first picture presentation in the tense track appears in lesson 54. The children practice using the present and past tense of verbs in a number of contexts. In this exercise they talk about a cat, telling what the cat did **first** and **next.**

Teaching Techniques

• If the children do not give the response *On the floor* in step a, acknowledge any other correct response. (They might say *In front of the couch,* for example.) Say, Yes, the cat is in front of the couch. Is it also on the floor? **The children reply** *yes,* **and you say,** Let's say that it is on the floor. Where is the cat in this picture? The exercise will be easier to teach if you use the responses in the exercise.

- Part 2 is critical. Remember to stress the last three words of your instructions: Say the whole thing about where **the cat was.** These are the first words the children say in their response.

- In part 2 do not point to the picture of the cat on the floor. You want the children to respond on the basis of the information the words and pictures give them. Do not give away the answer by pointing to the picture.

Corrections

If the children make an error at step a in part 2, stop them and point to picture a. Then say, This is where the cat **was.** Where was the cat? Wait for the children to respond, and repeat the sequence from part 1.

If the children have trouble saying the past-tense statement, model the statement, lead them through it, and test them on it. Repeat this procedure until they can all say it. It is important that the children be able to say every statement in the tense exercises.

Lesson 116: Actions

Future tense is introduced in an actions exercise after the children have received plenty of practice in handling past- and present-tense statements. The exercise is similar to the one used to demonstrate the past tense.

EXERCISE 1   Actions

1. Here's our first action game.
   a. Everybody, we will stand up. Say the whole thing about what we will do. (Signal.) *We will stand up.*
   b. Are we standing up now? (Signal.) *No.*
   c. What are we doing now? (Signal.) *Sitting down.*
      What will we do? (Signal.) *Stand up.*
   d. Let's do it. (Signal. Stand up with the children.)
      What are we doing? (Signal.) *Standing up.*
   e. What were we doing before we were standing up? (Signal.) *Sitting down.*
      Sit down again.
   f. (Repeat steps a through e until all children's responses are firm.)

2. Here's our last action game.
   a. (Point to a girl.) She will stand up. Everybody, say that. (Signal.) *She will stand up.*
   b. What will she do? (Signal.) *Stand up.*
      Is she standing now? (Signal.) *No.*
   c. Will she stand up? (Signal.) *Yes.*
      (Child's name), do it. (The child is to stand up.)
      Everybody, what is she doing? (Signal.) *Standing up.*
   d. What was she doing before she stood up? (Signal.) *Sitting down.*
   e. (Repeat steps a through d until all children's responses are firm.)

Individual Turns
(Repeat the exercise, calling on different children for each step.)

Teaching Techniques

- Make sure that the children are saying the word **will** correctly in step a before presenting the next steps.

- Stress the word **will** in step a in part 1.

- If the children are having trouble, stress the word **were** in step e in part 1.

- Repeat part 1 until the children's responses are firm, then go to part 2.

Corrections

If children say the wrong verb in exercise 1, part 1, step a, follow the model-lead-and-test procedure to firm the children's responses.

To correct mistakes in step e, repeat that step, pausing before **were** and stressing it. Then quickly tell the children the answer: You **were** sitting down. That's what you **were** doing. Repeat step e until the children's responses are firm, and then return to the beginning of part 1.

Actions—Review Lessons 30–150

Concepts introduced in other tracks are incorporated into the daily actions exercises. These exercises provide a continual review of the concepts and of the statement patterns taught in the program.

Lesson 58: Actions

This exercise reviews the preposition **on** and the past-tense verb **was.**

Teaching Techniques

- This exercise and all the review exercises in the actions track should be done briskly. You and the children should be moving along at a good pace. Your signals should be precise and easy to follow. Pause briefly at the end of each part.

- The task should be fun for both you and the children. As you begin, challenge them to get all the way through the exercise without a mistake.

Let them know when they have done particularly well—responded correctly, clearly, and at a normal speaking rate.

- Correct any errors in a perfunctory manner, and then return to the beginning of the part in which the error occurred.

EXERCISE 2 Actions

1. It's time for an action game.
   a. Everybody, touch your elbow. (Signal. Wait.) What are you doing? (Signal.) *Touching my elbow.*
      Say the whole thing. (Signal.) *I am touching my elbow.*
   b. Everybody, touch your ankle. (Signal. Wait.) What are you doing? (Signal.) *Touching my ankle.*
      Say the whole thing. (Signal.) *I am touching my ankle.*
   c. (Repeat steps a and b until all children's responses are firm.)

2. Let's do another one.
   a. Everybody, put your hand **on** your ankle. (Signal. Wait.) Where is your hand? (Signal.) *On my ankle.*
   b. Put your hand **on** your elbow. (Signal. Wait.)
      Where is your hand now? (Signal.) *On my elbow.*
      Keep it there.
   c. Listen carefully. Where **was** your hand? (Signal.) *On my ankle.*
      Say the whole thing about **where** your hand **was.** (Signal.) *My hand was on my ankle.*
   d. Again. (Signal.) *My hand was on my ankle.* (Repeat step d until all children's responses are firm.)
      Hands down.
   e. (Repeat part 2 until all children's responses are firm.)

Descriptions of Objects

The purpose of the exercises in Descriptions of Objects is to help children learn the language concepts and sentence production required to answer the following kinds of questions:

1. What is the object's name? "A cup."

2. How do you make a statement that incorporates that name? "This is a cup."

3. What are some of the ways that you can describe the cup? "This cup is big. This cup is wet. This cup is yellow."

4. How can you compare two cups of different sizes? "This cup is big," "This cup is small," or "This cup is bigger than this cup."

5. How do you describe the presence of more than one cup? "These are cups. The cups are on the table. These cups are green."

6. What are the names of common objects in and out of the classroom?

The tracks discussed in this part of the guide all relate to the language used to describe these basic features of objects. Below is a list of these tracks and the range of lessons in which they occur:

Track	Lesson
Object Identification	1–8
Identity Statements	3–33
Common Objects	7–25
Missing Objects	18–29
Opposites	19–150
Plurals	46–74
Comparatives	126–148

The ability to respond to questions and to make statements is essential to using and understanding the language of instruction. The purpose of these tracks is to acquaint children with some of the language conventions associated with identifying objects.

The children learn

1. to give the name of an object when asked, What is this? *A dog;*

2. to produce complete statements in response to the instruction Say the whole thing. *This is a dog;*

3. to respond to the question Is this a . . . by answering either *yes* or *no;*

4. to produce *not* statements for questions that are answered *no.* Is this a ball? *No.* Say the whole thing. *This is not a ball;*

5. the names of common objects in the classroom and how to make statements about those objects. *Window, door, chalkboard, etc.*

The language skills taught in this track—object identification and statement making—are used throughout the program.

EXERCISE 4   Object Identification

1. I'll tell you about these pictures.
   a. (Point to a.) This is a tree.
   b. (Point to b.) This is a shoe.
   c. (Point to c.) This is a dog.
   d. (Point to d.) This is a cat.

2. Now it's your turn.
   a. (Point to a.) What is this? (Touch.) *A tree.*
      ● ◆ ▲ ■
   b. (Point to b.) What is this? (Touch.) *A shoe.*
   c. (Point to c.) What is this? (Touch.) *A dog.*
   d. (Point to d.) What is this? (Touch.) *A cat.*

3. Let's name these things again. When I touch something, tell me the name.
   (Repeat part 2 until all children's responses are firm.)

Individual Turns
(Repeat part 2, calling on different children for each step.)

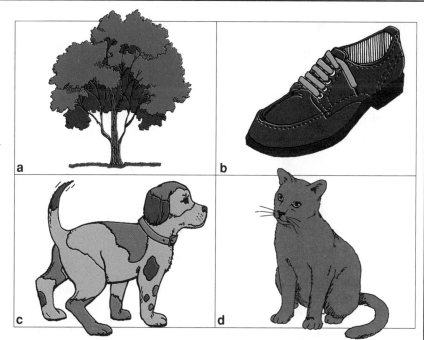

Corrections

EXERCISE 4

● **Error**
(Children give the wrong answers or no answers.)
Correction
1. (Tell children the name of the object.)
2. (Repeat part 2.)

◆ **Error**
(Children respond before you touch the picture.)
Correction
1. You have to wait until I touch it.

2. Watch. (Point to the picture.) What is this? (Touch. Respond with the children.) A tree.
3. Let's do that again. (Repeat step 2.)
4. (Repeat part 2. Do not respond with the children.)

▲ **Error**
(Children respond late.)
Correction
1. You have to tell me the name as soon as I touch it.
2. Watch. (Point to the picture.) What is this? (Touch. Respond with the children.) A tree.
3. Let's do that again. (Repeat step 2.)

4. Now do it by yourselves.
5. (Repeat part 2. Do not respond with the children.)

■ **Error**
(Children omit the word *a*.)
Correction
1. Yes, *a* tree.
2. Say it with me. (Signal. Respond with the children.) *A* tree.
3. Again. (Repeat step 2 until all children's responses are firm.)
4. (Repeat part 2. Do not respond with the children.)

Object Identification Lessons 1–8

Lesson 1: Object Identification

This exercise from lesson 1 requires the children to identify common objects by producing two-word responses. The children do not make full statements in this exercise.

Teaching Techniques

You will use the point-and-touch signal described on pages 18–20 to teach this exercise.

- Be sure to point to the letter **before** asking the question.

- Pause about one second after completing the question before touching the letter a.

- When you touch letter a, look at the tree. If you look at the children, they may look at you, not at the tree.

- As soon as the children begin to respond, quickly look at them to see who is (and who is not) responding.

- Be sure to keep touching the picture for as long as the children are responding.

When they finish a response, lift your finger and point to the next picture.

- Move rapidly from picture to picture. Ask the questions quickly and avoid long pauses between the pictures. The children will stay on task better if your pacing is relatively fast.

Corrections

On any of the pictures the children may make these errors:

1. Respond before you touch the picture.

2. Fail to respond immediately after you touch the picture.

3. Misidentify the object or fail to respond at all.

4. Omit the article.

The corrections for each of these errors appear in the corrections box. Follow the steps in the correction you are using. Remember, an error has not been corrected until **all** the children can respond correctly. Also remember to return to the beginning of part 2 after correcting any error and repeat all the questions in sequence. The children should be able to answer each of your questions correctly and on signal before you turn to the next page.

- Point to the picture as you say the whole thing, but do not touch it. You want the children to learn that your touch is the signal for them to respond.

Lesson 5: Identity Statements

EXERCISE 7 Identity Statements

1. We're going to talk about a dog. When I touch it, you tell me about it.
   a. (Point to the dog.) Everybody, what is this? (Touch.) *A dog.*
      Yes, a dog.
   b. My turn. I can say the whole thing. This is a dog. Listen again. This is a dog. Say the whole thing with me. (Touch. Respond with the children.) This is a dog.
   c. Again. (Touch. Respond with the children.) This is a dog.
      (Repeat until all children can make the statement with you.)
   d. Your turn. All by yourselves. Say the whole thing. (Touch. Do not respond with the children.) *This is a dog.*
      Again. (Touch. Do not respond with the children.) *This is a dog.*

2. (Repeat part 1 until all children can make the statement.)

3. We're going to talk about a cat. When I touch it, you tell me about it.
   a. (Point to the cat.) Everybody, what is this? (Touch.) *A cat.*
      Yes, a cat.
   b. My turn. I can say the whole thing. This is a cat. Listen again. This is a cat. Say the whole thing with me. (Touch. Respond with the children.) This is a cat.
   c. Again. (Touch. Respond with the children.) This is a cat.
      (Repeat until all children are making the statement with you.)
   d. Your turn. All by yourselves. Say the whole thing. (Touch. Do not respond with the children.) *This is a cat.*
   e. Again. (Touch. Do not respond with the children.) *This is a cat.*

4. (Repeat part 3 until all children can make the statement.)

Individual Turns
(Repeat parts 1 and 3, calling on different children for each step.)

Identity Statements
Lessons 3–33

In these exercises the children identify a pictured object with a two-word response and then make the whole identification statement about the object.

Lesson 5: Identity Statements

Teaching Techniques

In part 1, step b of exercise 7 on page 48, you are modeling the kind of response called for by the instruction Say the whole thing.

- Maintain a one-second pause after saying, I can say the whole thing and Listen again.

Remember that in step b you are modeling the statement. You want the children to imitate your model, so it is important to say the statement at exactly the same rate you will say it in step c. The rate should be medium slow.

In step b,

- point to the picture before saying, Say the whole thing with me;

- pause after your instruction for the same length of time you paused in step b. Then touch the picture to signal that the children are to respond;

- lead the children at the same rate you used to model the statement;

- keep touching the picture as long as you and the children are making the statement. You want them to know that the entire statement is about that picture.

- lead the children through the statement until they are firm at saying each word and saying the words at an appropriate rate. You may need to lead them several times—as many as seven times for some lower-performing children. Praise the children who are saying it correctly, and encourage those who are trying hard.

In step d the children say the statement by themselves. Do not respond with them:

- If children are not responding correctly after seven trials, move to another exercise and return to the identification exercise later.

- Point before saying Your turn. . . .

- Maintain your one-second pause.

- Keep touching the picture as the children respond.

- Make sure they make an acceptable response. An acceptable response is one in which the children begin responding the instant you touch the picture and produce all the words in the statement at the rate you established in steps b and c.

Corrections

The children may leave out words or confuse the order of words in a statement.

If you hear mistakes at step c when you are leading the children, model the response for them. Say the statement several times so that the children operate from your lead and not from the lead of other children. Then repeat the step.

If the children are having a great deal of trouble producing the statement, you may be saying it too quickly. Return to step b and say it more slowly; you will be providing the children with a new model of how to say it. Maintain the same slower pacing when doing steps c and d. In subsequent lessons gradually increase the rate at which you model and lead the responses. Your goal is to get the children to respond at a normal speaking rate.

If children persistently omit one or more words from the statement, stress these words when you say the statements with them. You can also pat knees or clap the children's hands together as you emphasize those words.

EXERCISE 7   Identity Statements

1. We're going to talk about these things. When I touch something, you tell me about it.
   a. (Point to a.) What is this? (Touch.)
      A ball. ●
      Say the whole thing. (Touch.) *This is a ball.*
   b. (Point to b.) What is this? (Touch.)
      A banana.
      Say the whole thing. (Touch.) *This is a banana.*
   c. (Point to c.) What is this? (Touch.)
      A flower.
      Say the whole thing. (Touch.) *This is a flower.*
   d. (Point to d.) What is this? (Touch.) *A tree.*
      Say the whole thing. (Touch.) *This is a tree.*

2. Let's do that again.
   (Repeat part 1 until all children's responses are firm.)

Individual Turns
(Repeat part 1, calling on different children for each step.)

Corrections
EXERCISE 7
● **Error**
   (Children say the entire sentence.)
   Correction
   1. Stop. My turn. What is this? (Touch.) A ball.
   2. Your turn. What is this? (Touch.) *A ball.*
   3. Now say the whole thing. (Touch.) *This is a ball.*
   4. (Repeat part 1 until all children respond correctly.)

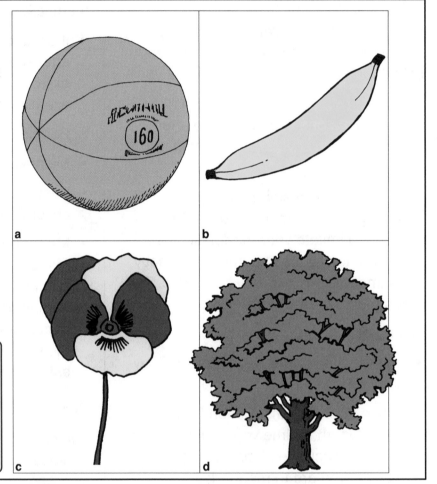

Lesson 8: Identity Statements

In the exercise above, the children again identify objects by giving two-word responses and then say the whole thing. The difference between this exercise and the preceding ones is that you do not model or lead any of the children's responses.

Teaching Techniques

• Make sure the children make the responses indicated in the exercise. These conventions of responding will be used throughout the program. The question What is this? is answered with a word or phrase. Say the whole thing indicates the children make an entire statement.

- The children are to respond at a normal or near-normal speaking rate—not in a drone or with a shout.

- In teaching the exercise it is important to establish a predictable and rhythmic pace for going from one picture to another. When the children make mistakes, you must slow down and correct them, but when they are performing well, you can move rapidly.

Corrections

If the children make the whole statement in response to the question What is this? follow the correction specified in the corrections box. Don't wait for them to complete the statement. As soon as you hear them say This, stop them. Then model the response called for. Say A ball. What is this? A ball. Your turn. What is this?

If children don't say the whole statement in step 3 of the correction, again stop them and model the kind of response called for: Stop. My turn to say the whole thing. Listen. This is a ball. Then say Your turn. Say the whole thing. Then repeat the correction.

If children produce drony statement responses, stop them and show them the rate at which you want them to say the statement: My turn to say the whole thing. This is a ball. Your turn to say the whole thing.

**EXERCISE 6   Yes-or-No Questions
and "Not" Statements**

1. We're going to talk about this picture. (Point to the cat.)
   a. Everybody, what is this? (Touch.) *A cat.*
      Is this a car? (Touch.) *No.*
      Is this a cat? (Touch.) *Yes.*
      Is this a dog? (Touch.) *No.*
      Is this a fish? (Touch.) *No.*
   b. What is this? (Touch.) *A cat.*
      Say the whole thing. (Touch.) *This is a cat.*
   c. Is this a fish? (Touch.) *No.*
      I can say the whole thing. This is not a fish.
      Listen again. This is not a fish.
   d. Say the whole thing with me. (Touch. Respond with the children.) *This is not a fish.*
      Again. (Touch.) *This is not a fish.*
      (Repeat step d until all children can make the statement with you.)
   e. All by yourselves. Say the whole thing. (Touch. Do not respond with the children.) *This is not a fish.* ●
      (Repeat steps d and e until all children can make the statement.)

2. Let's do that again.
   a. What is this? (Touch.) *A cat.*
      Say the whole thing. (Touch.) *This is a cat.*
   b. Is this a fish? (Touch.) *No.*
      Say the whole thing. (Touch.) *This is not a fish.*
   c. (Repeat part 2 until all children can make both statements.)

Individual Turns
(Repeat part 2, calling on different children for each step.)

Corrections

EXERCISE 6

● **Error**
(Children don't say the entire sentence or don't say it correctly.)

Correction
1. Listen. Not a fish. Say it with me. (Signal.)
   (Repeat until all children say *not a fish* with you.)
2. This is . . . (signal) *not a fish.*
   (Repeat until all children say *not a fish* by themselves.)
3. Say the whole thing. (Touch.) *This is not a fish.*
4. (Repeat part 1.)

Lesson 16: Yes-or-No Questions and "Not" Statements

This is one of the exercises that demonstrates the relationship between **yes** and positive identity statements and between **no** and negative identity statements. In this exercise the children will produce a **not** statement.

Teaching Techniques

- Pacing is important in presenting this exercise. Ask the questions quickly to keep the children's attention on the picture. But if they start making mistakes, slow the rate at which you ask questions.

- Be precise with your pointing and touching signals. Hold your finger about an inch from the picture as you ask a question. Then pause, lift your finger, and touch the picture. After the children respond, quickly lift your finger and point for the next question.

- When modeling the statement in part 1, step c, pause after the word **is** and stress the word **not.** This is (pause) not a fish. The pause shows the children that the first part of the statement is the same as the familiar This is a cat. Stressing the word **not** allows the children to focus on placing the word **not** appropriately in the sentence.

- In part 2 the children pair the response **a cat** with the statement *This is a cat* and pair the response **no** with the statement *This is not a fish.* The objective of this exercise is to have the children say the positive and negative statements in sequence and without error.

Corrections

In part 1, expect some children to have trouble saying the statement with you. If they do, follow the correction in the box.

If the children have trouble in step 3 of the correction, have them pause after **is** and stress **not.** Do this by holding up your finger after they say **is** and touching the picture again for the last part of the statement.

If the children make mistakes in part 2, firm their responses on both the answer **no** and the statement. Then present steps a and b in sequence until the children are firm on both steps.

**EXERCISE 6 Yes-or-No Questions
with "Not" Statements**

1. Let's look at this picture.
   a. (Point to the kite.) Everybody, what is this? (Touch.) *A kite.*
      Say the whole thing. (Touch.) *This is a kite.*
   b. Get ready to answer some questions.
      Is this a ball? (Touch.) *No.*
      Is this a bottle? (Touch.) *No.*
      Is this a kite? (Touch.) *Yes.*
      Is this a cat? (Touch.) *No.*
      (Repeat until all children's responses are firm.)
   c. One more time. Is this a kite? (Touch.) *Yes.*
      Say the whole thing. (Touch.) *This is a kite.*
      Is this a car? (Touch.) *No.*
      Say the whole thing. (Touch.) *This is not a car.* ●

2. Now look at this picture.
   a. (Point to the car.) Everybody, what is this? (Touch.) *A car.*
      Say the whole thing. (Touch.) *This is a car.*
   b. Get ready to answer some questions about this picture.
      Is this a kite? (Touch.) *No.*
      Is this a car? (Touch.) *Yes.*
      Is this a bottle? (Touch.) *No.*
      (Repeat until all children's responses are firm.)
   c. One more time. Is this a car? (Touch.) *Yes.*
      Say the whole thing. (Touch.) *This is a car.*
      Is this a kite? (Touch.) *No.*
      Say the whole thing. (Touch.) *This is not a kite.*

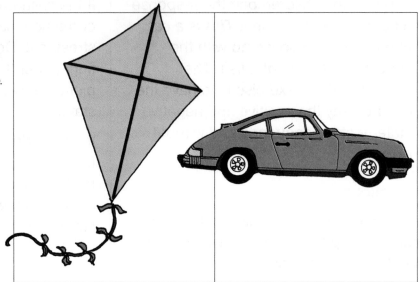

Corrections

EXERCISE 6

● **Error**
(Children say *This is a car.*)

Correction
1. We're talking about a kite.
2. Is this a car? (Touch.) *No.*

3. Let's say the whole thing. (Touch. Respond with the children.) This is not a car.
4. All by yourselves. (Touch. Do not respond with the children.) *This is not a car.*
5. (Repeat step 4 until all children's responses are firm.)
6. (Return to part 1.)

Lesson 18: Yes-or-No Questions with "Not" Statements

In this exercise the children say the *not* statement without the teacher first modeling and leading it.

Corrections

Sometimes children respond as follows at the end of step c in part 1. When you ask, Is this a car? they answer, *This is a kite.* What they are saying is correct, but repeating that statement will not give them the practice they need in making the *not* statement. Follow the correction specified in the exercise. Say, I asked about a car. So you have to tell me about the car. The idea is that they must learn that if you ask about a **car**, they must use the word **car** in their answer. This response convention is used throughout the program.

Remember to repeat part 1 after correcting the mistake. The children are considered firm on the exercise when they respond without error to the sequence of steps in each exercise.

EXERCISE 5 Common Objects

[**Note:** You will find a pointer helpful in this exercise. Touch the objects in any order that is convenient for you.]

1. I'm going to touch some objects in this room and tell you what they are.
  a. (Touch a chalkboard.) This is a chalkboard.
  What is this? (Touch.) *A chalkboard.*
  b. (Touch a door.) This is a door.
  What is this? (Touch.) *A door.*
  c. (Touch a window.) This is a window.
  What is this? (Touch.) *A window.*

2. Tell me what I touch.
  a. (Touch a chalkboard.) Everybody, what is this? (Signal.) *A chalkboard.*
  b. (Touch a door.) Everybody, what is this? (Signal.) *A door.*
  c. (Touch a window.) Everybody, what is this? (Signal.) *A window.*

3. (Repeat part 2 until all children's responses are firm.)

4. Let's do those objects again.
  a. (Touch a chalkboard.) Everybody, what is this? (Signal.) *A chalkboard.*
  Say the whole thing. (Signal.) *This is a chalkboard.*
  b. (Repeat step a until all children's responses are firm.)
  c. (Touch a door.) Everybody, what is this? (Signal.) *A door.*
  Say the whole thing. (Signal.) *This is a door.*
  d. (Touch a window.) Everybody, what is this? (Signal.) *A window.*
  Say the whole thing. (Signal.) *This is a window.*

5. (Repeat part 4 until all children's responses are firm.)

Individual Turns
(Repeat part 4, calling on different children for each step.)

Common Objects
Lessons 7–25

In the common objects exercises, children learn to identify and make statements about the various objects they see and use in the classroom. The children learn

1. the vocabulary of the classroom so that they can follow instructions;

2. that everything around them has a name. When they have this understanding, they will know how to ask questions about things they don't know about;

3. that the language in the exercises can be used to describe what they see and use in the classroom.

Lesson 7: Common Objects

Teaching Techniques

The first time you introduce an object, you should actually touch it, as the exercise specifies. Walking around your classroom to touch objects may be somewhat disruptive in your classroom, so after you have introduced an object and the children are familiar with its name, you can point to it with your finger or with a yardstick or pointer. But if the children are having trouble with a name, continue to actually touch the object.

You may vary the order of touching objects according to their location in your classroom. Initially, you might prefer to walk the children around the classroom to show them the objects. If this routine presents management problems, drop it.

Corrections

If children don't know the name of an object

1. tell them the name of the object: A chalkboard;

2. touch the chalkboard and repeat the question. If children are

mispronouncing the word, have them repeat the correct pronunciation until firm;

3. use a model-lead-and-test correction:
My turn. Chalk (pause) board.
Say it with me. (Signal.) Chalk (pause) board.
Repeat until all children's responses are firm.
All by yourselves. (Signal.) *Chalkboard.*

Repeat this procedure until all children can pronounce the word correctly. Then point to the chalkboard and present the original question.

The track is designed to teach children about missing objects so they can do a variety of workbook exercises that involve missing objects.

Lesson 18: Missing Objects

Teaching Techniques

If some children have trouble keeping their eyes closed when you are removing an object, direct children to Put your head down. Children are to maintain a face-down position so they can't see which object you remove.

EXERCISE 3   Missing Objects

[**Note:** You will need a ruler and a piece of chalk for this exercise.]

1. You're going to learn about missing objects.
   a. (Show ruler and chalk.) I have a ruler. I have chalk. Do I have the ruler? (Signal.) *Yes.*
   Point to the ruler. (Signal. The children point.)
   Do I have chalk? (Signal.) *Yes.*
   Point to the chalk. (Signal. The children point.)
   b. Let's do it again.
   (Repeat step a until all children's responses are firm.)

2. I'm going to try to fool you. I'm going to take away one of these objects. See if you can tell which object is missing.
   a. Everybody, close your eyes. Don't look. (Remove the ruler. Show chalk.)
   Everybody, open your eyes. What object do I have now? (Signal.) *Chalk.*
   Do I have the ruler anymore? (Signal.) *No.*
   b. I don't have the ruler anymore, so the ruler is missing. Which object is missing? (Signal.) *The ruler.*
   Yes, the ruler is missing.

3. Let's do it again. (Show the ruler and chalk.)
   a. Do I have the ruler? (Signal.) *Yes.*
   Do I have chalk? (Signal.) *Yes.*
   b. Close your eyes. (Remove chalk.) Open your eyes. What object do I have now? (Signal.) *The ruler.*
   Do I still have the chalk? (Signal.) *No.*
   c. I don't have the chalk anymore, so the chalk is missing. Which object is missing? (Signal.) *The chalk.*

4. Once more. (Show ruler and chalk.) I have the ruler, and I have chalk.
   a. Close your eyes. (Remove chalk.) Open your eyes.
   b. Which object do I still have? (Signal.) *The ruler.*
   Which object is missing? (Signal.) *The chalk.*

5. (Repeat exercise until all children's responses are firm.)

Lesson 18

If children have trouble identifying the missing object, ask these questions:

Do I have a ruler?
Do I have chalk?
I don't have _____. So which object is missing?

Opposites
Lessons 19–150

In *Reading Mastery Plus,* Level K, certain descriptive words that have clearly defined opposites are treated as polar concepts—the objects described are either **long** or **short, wet** or **dry, big** or **small.** Later, in the comparative track, the children build on this fundamental language structure to make judgments about things that are, for example, **bigger** or **taller** than other things.

In the first exercises in the opposites track, the children learn only one of the two opposite words that can be used to describe an object. For example, they do not learn **long** or **short** in the same lesson. Instead, instruction begins with **long** and **not long.** After they have practiced using **long** and **not long** for several lessons, they are introduced to a word that means the same as **not long— short.**

The presentation for each opposite concept is similar, with similar demonstrations and statements:

1. The children learn the word for one member of an opposite pair and demonstrate the meaning of that word;

2. The children generate statements using opposites: for example, the woman is tall; the woman is not tall;*

3. After the children are firm on the first member of the opposite pair, they learn the opposite word.**

In addition, the children practice a variety of opposite pairs in different exercises that run to the end of the program.

A list of the opposites the children learn is shown below, along with the number of the lesson where each opposite first appears.

Opposites*	Lesson
full/not full	19
wet/not wet	25
big/not big	32
long/not long	45
old/not old	53

Opposites**	Lesson	Opposites**	Lesson
full/empty	36	awake/asleep	125
big/small	38	late/early	127
wet/dry	40	fast/slow	129
long/short	48	sick/well	131
old/young	56	hard/soft	136
tall/short	86	daytime/nighttime	140
hot/cold	118	clean/dirty	143
sad/happy	120	lose/win	147
open/closed	123	quiet/noisy	149

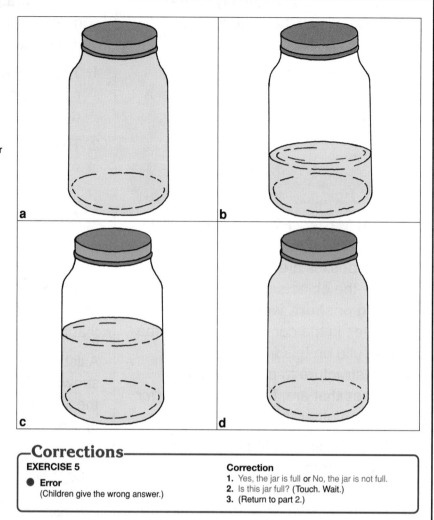

EXERCISE 5 Opposites—Full/Not Full

1. Look at these jars.
   (Point to a.) What is this?
   (Signal.) *A jar.*
   (Point to b.) What is this?
   (Signal.) *A jar.*

2. We'll talk some more about these jars.
   a. (Point to a.) This jar is full.
   b. (Point to b.) This jar is not full.
   c. Your turn. (Point to each jar and ask:)
   Is this jar full? (The children are to answer *yes* or *no.*) ●
   d. (Repeat steps a through c until all children's responses are firm.)

3. Now we're going to say the whole thing.
   a. (Point to a.) Is this jar full? (Touch.) *Yes.*
   My turn to say the whole thing. This jar is full.
   b. (Point to b.) Is this jar full? (Touch.) *No.*
   Say the whole thing. (Signal.) *This jar is not full.*
   c. (Point to c.) Is this jar full? (Touch.) *No.*
   Say the whole thing. (Signal.) *This jar is not full.*
   d. (Point to d.) Is this jar full? (Touch.) *Yes.*
   Say the whole thing. (Signal.) *This jar is full.*

4. Let's do that again.
   (Repeat part 3 until all children's responses are firm.)

Individual Turns
(Repeat part 3, calling on different children for each step.)

Corrections

EXERCISE 5

● **Error**
(Children give the wrong answer.)

Correction
1. Yes, the jar is full **or** No, the jar is not full.
2. Is this jar full? (Touch. Wait.)
3. (Return to part 2.)

Lesson 20: Opposites—Full/Not Full

The first concept, **full** and **not full,** is introduced in lesson 19. The first exercise (not shown here) is a demonstration in which you fill an empty glass with water to show the difference between a "not full" glass and a full glass. Be sure that you have the real objects necessary for the demonstration. Your demonstration should go very quickly—the quicker the better.

The second exercise (shown above) is the picture presentation of the same concept.

In this exercise, the children use the word **full** in statements.

Teaching Techniques

- In part 2, step c, point quickly to each jar in turn and ask, Is this jar full?

- In part 3, allow the children to examine each picture as you ask, Is this jar full? Then pause a second and touch the picture. After the children answer *yes* or *no,* quickly give the instruction Say the whole thing.

EXERCISE 6   Opposites—Full/Empty

1. We're going to talk about full and empty.
   a. (Point to a.) Is this wastebasket full? (Touch.) *Yes.*
   b. (Point to b.) Is this wastebasket full? (Touch.) *Yes.*
   c. (Point to c.) Is this wastebasket full? (Touch.) *No.*

2. Listen. This wastebasket is empty. Everybody, say the whole thing about this wastebasket. (Touch.) *This wastebasket is empty.*
   (Repeat until all children's responses are firm.)

3. I'll point to each wastebasket. Say **full** if it is full. Say **empty** if it is empty.
   a. What are you going to say if it is full? (Signal.) *Full.*
      What are you going to say if it is empty? (Signal.) *Empty.*
   b. (Point to each wastebasket. The children are to say *full* or *empty*.)

4. (Repeat part 3 until all children's responses are firm.)

Individual Turns
(Repeat the exercise, calling on different children for each step.)

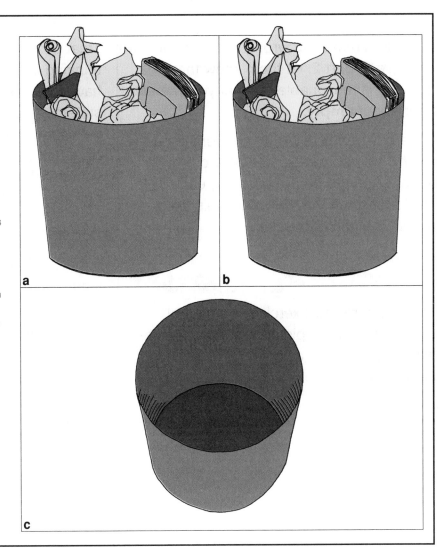

Corrections

If the children were firm on preceding exercises, they should have no problems with exercise 5. If they have trouble with the *not* statement, use the model-lead-and-test correction.

Lesson 36: Opposites—Full/Empty

After six opposite words have been introduced and practiced, the children are introduced to the first opposite pair exercise in Lesson 36. This exercise shows them that an object that is not full can be called **empty.**

Teaching Techniques

- When a new opposite word is introduced, give the children thinking time for steps that involve that word. In part 2 the children "say the whole thing" about an empty wastebasket.

- When presenting part 3, ask the two questions and then point to one of the wastebaskets. Pause before touching it. This will help the children think about what they must say; without the pause, they may make mistakes.

Corrections

If children make the wrong statement in exercise 6, part 2, let them know that what they say is reasonable but that you want to hear about **empty.**

If the children give wrong answers in part 3 *(This wastebasket is not full.),* pause for a longer period before touching each wastebasket. If they still make mistakes, repeat the entire exercise.

Lesson 96: Opposites

This is the review exercise—a series of questions without pictures using opposite words to describe a variety of objects, animals, and people.

EXERCISE 4   Opposites

1. Listen.
   a. If something is not old, it is the opposite of old, so it's young. If something is not wet, it's the opposite of wet, so it's dry. If something is not big, it's the opposite of big. So what do you know about it? (Signal.) *It's small.*
   b. Listen. I'm thinking about a television set that is not big. It's the opposite of big. So what do you know about it? (Pause. Signal.) *It's small.*
   c. Listen. I'm thinking about frogs that are not young. They're the opposite of young. So what do you know about them? (Pause. Signal.) *They're old.*
   d. Listen. I'm thinking about windows that are not dry. They're the opposite of dry. So what do you know about them? (Pause. Signal.) *They're wet.*

2. (Repeat part 1 until all children's responses are firm.)

Individual Turns
(Repeat part 1, calling on different children for each step.)

Teaching Techniques

Treat this exercise as a game. You are thinking of something and the children have to figure out what it is. Read each statement forcefully, emphasizing the words at the end (not big, not young, not dry). Ask the question quickly. Hold up your hand, pause, and signal. The children should respond together.

Corrections

If the children say *small* instead of *It's small,* say, That's right. It's small. Let's all say that. It's small. Then repeat step a until all children are saying, *It's small.*

If the children give a wrong answer or no answer, tell them the correct answer (It's small.) immediately. Then repeat the step. Repeat the exercise until they can answer each question correctly and on signal.

Plurals
Lessons 46–74

Children must understand the difference between references to singulars and plurals if they are to follow instructions accurately and fully understand demonstrations. The only difference between the two instructions Circle the word and Circle the words is the ending **-s** on **words.** Some children have not learned to attend to the noun endings and possible verb variations that indicate whether the speaker is referring to one object or more than one.

Plurals are introduced with actions exercises. After the children have learned to distinguish between the words used to describe singular and plural actions, picture exercises are introduced.

In the plurals track, the children learn

1. to attend to the endings of matched singular and plural nouns: *Touch your ears. Touch your ear;*

2. to make action statements that contain singular and plural words: *I am touching my knees. I am touching my knee;*

3. to learn singular and plural nouns and statements that describe pictures of objects: for example, *You are touching the dogs. These are dogs. These are not dogs. These dogs are sleeping. These dogs are not sleeping.*

EXERCISE 2   Actions—Plurals

[Note: Pronounce ssss as zzzz.]

1. Let's find out if you can really listen.
   a. My turn. I'll tell you if I hold up fingerssss or a finger. Listen carefully.
   b. (Hold up two fingers.) Fingerssss.
      (Hold up three fingers.) Fingerssss.
      (Hold up your index finger.) Finger.
      (Hold up four fingers.) Fingerssss.
      (Hold up your little finger.) Finger.

2. Your turn. Tell me if I hold up fingerssss or a finger. ●
   a. (Hold up three fingers.) Is this fingerssss or finger? (Signal.) *Fingers.*
   b. (Hold up two fingers.) Is this fingerssss or finger? (Signal.) *Fingers.*
   c. (Hold up one finger.) Is this fingerssss or finger? (Signal.) *Finger.*
   d. (Hold up four fingers.) Is this fingerssss or finger? (Signal.) *Fingers.*
   e. (Hold up one finger.) Is this fingerssss or finger? (Signal.) *Finger.*

Individual Turns
(Repeat part 2, calling on different children for each step.)

Lesson 46: Actions—Plurals

This introductory exercise gives children practice in hearing and saying singular and plural nouns. Children who aren't used to saying the **ssss** or **zzzz** sound at the end of words often have difficulty hearing the difference between singular and plural nouns in instructions.

Teaching Techniques

- Exaggerate the **zzzz** sound in **fingers.**

- Make sure that the children are saying the final **zzzz** sound in the word **fingers.**

- Have the children repeat the exercise several times. The more practice they receive at the beginning of the track, the less they will need in subsequent exercises.

Corrections

If some children answer the first question in part 2 incorrectly, follow the model-lead-and-test correction.

1. Model the response: fingerssss. Exaggerate the final sound of the word.

2. Lead the children: Say it with me. Fingerssss. Repeat until firm.

3. Test the children: Repeat the instruction.

4. Call on individual children. Praise those who are saying the endings correctly.

EXERCISE 2 Actions—Plurals

1. Watch what I do. Let's see if I can fool you. Listen carefully.
   a. Hold up your hands. (Pause. Signal. Wait.) Put your hands down.
   b. Hold up your hand. (Pause. Signal. Wait.) Put your hand down.
   c. Hold up your hand. (Pause. Signal. Wait.) Put your hand down.
   d. Hold up your hands. (Pause. Signal. Wait.) Put your hands down.
   e. (Repeat part 1 until all children's responses are firm.)

2. Watch me again. See if I can fool you. Listen carefully.
   a. Touch your ears. (Pause. Signal. Wait.) Put your hands down.
   b. Touch your ears. (Pause. Signal. Wait.) Put your hands down.
   c. Touch your ear. (Pause. Signal. Wait.) Put your hand down.
   d. (Repeat steps a through c until all children's responses are firm.)

Individual Turns
(Repeat parts 1 and 2, calling on different children for each step.)

Lesson 51: Actions—Plurals

In this exercise in the plurals track, the children respond to instructions that require them to hold up or touch one or more than one thing. Their actions will be correct only if they can hear the difference between singular and plural nouns.

Teaching Techniques

Notice that the exercise calls for you to pause between the instruction and the signal calling for the children's response. Your pause must be long enough to give the children time to think about their responses. Pausing will reduce the number of errors. As the children become more proficient at distinguishing between plural and singular endings, you can reduce the length of the pause.

Corrections

Expect some children to have trouble with this exercise. If you think some of your children are going to make the mistake of touching only one ear when you say Touch your ears, follow this pre-correction procedure before step b.

1. Listen. Earssss. Say it. (Signal.) *Earssss.*

2. Ear. Say it. (Signal.) *Ear.*

3. Touch your ears. Do it. (Signal. Wait.)

4. Touch your ear. Do it. (Signal. Wait.)
   Then start step b.

If they make the mistake of touching both ears when you instruct them to touch your ear, say:

1. Ear. Just one ear. Touch your ear.

2. Now touch your earssss. (Signal.)

If children make more than one or two errors on the exercise, repeat the entire exercise. (A good idea is to go on to another exercise in the lesson, then return to this exercise before the end of the lesson.)

If the children are weak in these plurals exercises, make sure that they practice plurals at other times of the day. For example, when they are leaving for recess, present an exercise to each child: Hold up your handssss or Hold up your hand. Present the instructions in random order, sometimes giving the singular instruction two or three times in a row. Don't alternate singular and plural instructions from child to child, or some children will learn that every **other** time you ask the questions, both hands should be held up.

EXERCISE 2 Plurals

1. Tell me if I touch carsssss.
   a. (Touch one car.) Am I touching carsssss? (Signal.) *No.*
   b. (Touch two cars at the same time.) Am I touching carsssss? (Signal.) *Yes.*
   c. (Touch three cars at the same time.) Am I touching carsssss? (Signal.) *Yes.*
   d. (Touch one car.) Am I touching carsssss? (Signal.) *No.*
   e. (Touch two cars at the same time.) Am I touching carsssss? (Signal.) *Yes.*
   f. (Repeat part 1 until all children's responses are firm.)

2. Watch.
   a. (Touch one car.) Am I touching carsssss? (Signal.) *No.*
      What am I touching? (Signal.) *A car.*
      Say the whole thing about what I am doing. (Signal.) *You are touching a car.*
   b. (Touch two cars.) Am I touching carsssss? (Signal.) *Yes.*
      What am I touching? (Signal.) *Cars.*
      Say the whole thing about what I am doing. (Signal.) *You are touching cars.*
   c. (Repeat part 2 until all children's responses are firm.)

Individual Turns
(Repeat the exercise, calling on different children for each step.)

Corrections

EXERCISE 2

[**Note:** Use this correction for all wrong responses.]

Correction
1. (Tell the correct answer.)
2. (Have the children say it with you.)
3. (Repeat the exercise from the beginning.)

Lesson 49: Plurals

Teaching Techniques

In the first picture exercise you touch either a car or cars. The children are to respond by saying *car* or *cars.* At the end of part 2 you touch some cars and ask, Am I touching cars? After the children answer, you say, Say the whole thing about what I am doing. The children are to say, *You are touching cars.* They should have no trouble with this statement, because they practiced a similar statement, *I am touching my ears,* in the preceding exercise.

EXERCISE 8 Plurals

1. (Point to all pigs at the same time.) Listen.
   These are pigs. What are these? (Signal.)
   Pigs.
   a. Yes, these are pigs.
      Say the whole thing. (Signal.)
      These are pigs.
   b. (Repeat part 1 until all children's
      responses are firm.)
2. Some of these pigs are on the car.
   a. (Point to each pig and ask:) Is this pig on
      the car? (The children are to answer *yes*
      or *no*.)
   b. (Repeat part 2 until all children's
      responses are firm.)
3. (Point to the pigs in the car.)
   a. What are these? (Touch.) *Pigs.*
      Where are these pigs? (Touch.) *In the car.*
   b. Say the whole thing. (Touch.) *These pigs
      are in the car.*
   c. (Repeat part 3 until all children's
      responses are firm.)
4. (Point to the pigs on the car.)
   a. Where are these pigs?
      (Touch.) *On the car.*
   b. Say the whole thing about these pigs.
      (Touch.) *These pigs are on the car.*
   c. (Repeat part 4 until all children's
      responses are firm.)
5. Let's talk about the car and the pigs one more
   time.
   a. (Point to pigs on the car.) Where are these
      pigs? (Signal.) *On the car.*
      Say the whole thing about these pigs.
      (Signal.) *These pigs are on the car.*
   b. (Point to pigs in the car.) Where are these
      pigs? (Signal.) *In the car.*
      Say the whole thing about these pigs.
      (Signal.) *These pigs are in the car.*

   c. (Repeat part 5 until all children's
      responses are firm.)

Individual Turns
(Repeat the exercise, calling on different
children for each step.)

Lesson 61: Plurals

In this exercise the children are
introduced to the plural statement form
"These are pigs."

Teaching Techniques

Expect some children to have trouble
saying the statement *These are pigs.*
Typical mistakes include adding words
and omitting the word **are,** and saying **or**
instead of **are.** You can help reduce errors
by emphasizing the word **are** in step 1
and by saying the statement in a rhythm
that has three distinct beats: These
(pause) are (pause) pigs.

Corrections

If children have trouble making the
statement, repeat the model-lead-and-test
procedure until the children's responses
are firm. With some groups you may have
to provide many repetitions before the
children are saying the statement
appropriately.

EXERCISE 4 Comparatives

1. Look at the picture.
   a. (Point to a.) What is this? (Touch.) *A ball.*
   b. (Point to b, c, and d.) What are these? (Touch.) *Apples.*
      Say the whole thing. (Signal.) *These are apples.*
   c. (Point to e.) What is this? (Touch.) *A cup.*
   d. (Point to a and e.) Which is bigger, the ball or the cup? (Touch.) *The ball.*
      Yes, the ball is bigger than the cup. Say that. (Signal.) *The ball is bigger than the cup.*
   e. (Repeat part 1 until all children's responses are firm.)

2. One of these apples is bigger than the ball. I'll point to the apples. You tell me which apple is bigger than the ball.
   a. (Point to b.) Everybody, is this apple bigger than the ball? (Touch.) *Yes.*
   b. (Point to c.) Everybody, is this apple bigger than the ball? (Touch.) *No.*
   c. (Point to d.) Everybody, is this apple bigger than the ball? (Touch.) *No.*
   d. (Repeat part 2 until all children's responses are firm.)

3. (Point to b.) Listen. This apple is bigger than the ball. Say that. (Touch.) *This apple is bigger than the ball.*
   (Repeat part 3 until all children can make the statement.)

Individual Turns
(Repeat parts 2 and 3, calling on different children for each step.)

Comparatives
Lessons 126–148

Comparatives are an extension of opposites. In the opposites track, the children describe pairs of objects as, for example, big and small. In the comparatives track, the children learn to compare two objects by using the words **bigger** or **smaller,** for example. They learn the conventional way of stating the comparison: This object is bigger (smaller) than that object.

The objectives of the comparatives track are

1. to teach comparative forms of familiar opposites words: **bigger, smaller, taller, shorter, longer;**

2. to teach the statements for comparing two objects: The rock is bigger than the box; the box is smaller than the rock.

Lesson 126: Comparatives

Comparatives are introduced in lesson 126. The children compare objects and then "say the whole thing," using the word **bigger.**

Teaching Techniques

• Remember to stress the word **bigger** in the statement.

Corrections

The children may have trouble saying the statement. Use this procedure to help them:

1. Listen. Bigger than. Everybody, say it with me. Bigger than. Again. All by yourselves. **(Signal.)**

2. Listen. The rock is bigger than the box. Say the whole thing. **(Signal.)**

3. If the children have trouble, lead them on the whole statement. Then test them by having them say it by themselves.

Information and Background Knowledge

The objectives of the information and background knowledge tracks are

1. to make sure that the children have the basic information that relates to school routines, their names, the names of their teacher and school, the days of the week, and the months and seasons of the year;

2. to teach the children the relationship between objects and their parts, the names of parts of the body, and the names and functions of the parts of some common objects—a table, a toothbrush, an umbrella, and so forth;

3. to teach the children to identify the materials of which common objects are made;

4. to present background knowledge about some occupations, natural phenomena, and locations.

The tracks that relate to basic school information are

Names (of children)	Lessons 1–18
Information (about school and community)	Lessons 1–29
Days of the Week	Lessons 30–149
Months	Lessons 87–149
Seasons	Lessons 123–149

In these tracks, the children learn

1. the first names and whole names of each child in the group and the difference between their first name and whole name;

2. the name of their teacher, the name of their school, and the name of the city or county where they live;

3. the number and names of the days of the week, the months of the year, and the seasons of the year;

4. the meanings of **today** and **tomorrow;**

5. some of the characteristics of the four seasons.

Names
Lessons 1–18

EXERCISE 2   Information—Names

1. We're going to learn names.
   a. (Ask one child to stand up. Say the child's whole name—John Jones, for example.)
   _____ _____, stand up. Your first name is _____. What's your first name? (The child responds.)
   b. Everybody, what's his/her first name? (Signal. The children say the child's first name.) Good. _____, sit down.

2. (Repeat part 1 with several children.)

Lesson 1: Information—Names

Teaching Techniques

This is a simple but important exercise. If some children have trouble learning names, do only three or four names the first day and the rest in the second lesson. By the fourth day, every child should know the name of every other child in a group of six to eight children.

Corrections

1. If children give their whole name when asked for their first name, say, You're telling me your whole name. I want just your first name.

   Listen. Your first name is _____. What's your first name?

2. When the child responds correctly, go to step b.

If children are not firm on first names, they will have trouble with the exercises in which they use whole names. If they need help, try to present games during other parts of the day that incorporate children's names. These games require a child to

call on another by name. Praise children who correctly use the names of other children in these games.

School Information
Lessons 1–29

EXERCISE 3   Information—School

1. Here are some things you should know.
   a. Listen. I'm your teacher. My name is _____. Everybody, what's your teacher's name? (Pause. Signal. The children say the teacher's name.)
   b. (Repeat step a until all children's responses are firm.)
   c. Listen. You go to _____ School. Everybody, what's the name of the school you go to? (Pause. Signal. The children say the name of their school.)
   d. (Repeat step c until all children's responses are firm.)

2. Let's try those questions again.
   a. Everybody, what's your teacher's name? (Pause. Signal.)
   b. What's the name of the school you go to? (Pause. Signal.)

3. (Repeat part 2 until all children's responses are firm.)

Individual Turns
(Repeat part 2, calling on different children for each step.)

Lesson 1: Information—School

Teaching Techniques

- If there is more than one adult in the classroom, teach the children the name of each adult.

- Be sure the children are looking at you as you start the exercise. After you ask the question in part 1, pause for about a second and then use a hand-drop signal. Let the children know they are to respond to your signal. Repeat step a until all children answer correctly and on signal. Follow the same procedure for step c.

- In later lessons the children are asked, What city do you live in? If the children live in a rural area, substitute, What county do you live in?

Corrections

If the children confuse the two answers in exercise 3, part 2,

1. help them by pointing to yourself and to the classroom.

2. pause between the two questions and stress the words **school** and **teacher.**

When the children are able to answer the two questions correctly, stop pointing.

> **EXERCISE 2   Information—Days of the Week**
>
> 1. Let's do the days of the week.
>   a. There are seven days in a week. How many days are there in a week? (Signal.) *Seven.*
>   b. My turn. I'll say the days of the week. Listen. Sunday, Monday, Tuesday, Wednesday, Thursday, Friday, Saturday. I said the days of the week.
>   c. Listen. Sunday, Monday. Say those days with me. (Signal. Respond with the children.) Sunday, Monday.
>   d. Again. (Signal. Respond with the children.) Sunday, Monday.
>
> 2. All by yourselves.
>   a. Say those days of the week. (Signal. Do not respond with the children.) *Sunday, Monday.*
>   b. (Repeat step a until all children can say the days.)
>   Good. Tomorrow we'll say the days of the week again.

Lesson 30: Information—Days of the Week

The children learn to name the days of the week over a seven-lesson period. In this first exercise, they listen to the sequence of days and learn to say the first two days in order.

Teaching Techniques

- In step a, you ask how many days there are in a week. Make sure all the children answer.

- In step b, you say the names of all the days in the week. Make it sound interesting by giving a definite cadence to the sequence. For example, you might clap three times to establish a cadence, then say, Sunday, Monday, **Tuesday** (pause) Wednesday, Thursday, **Friday** (pause) Saturday. The more distinctive you make the name of some of the days, the easier it will be for the children to learn the sequence.

• For some children, this may be new learning. Do not try to teach more than what each exercise requires. But if the children already know some of the days, you can do these exercises quickly.

• It is important for the children to say new days by the end of the exercise in which they are introduced. This will require increasing practice as more days are included. If too many repetitions seem necessary, give the children additional practice at other times of the school day.

Months of the Year
Lessons 87–149

EXERCISE 2   Information—Days, Months

1. We're going to talk about days and months.
   a. Everybody, how many days are in a week? (Signal.) *Seven.*
      Name them. (Signal.) *Sunday, Monday, Tuesday, Wednesday, Thursday, Friday, Saturday.*
   b. Listen. **There are twelve months in a year.** Listen again. There are twelve months in a year. How many months in a year? (Signal.) *Twelve.* ●
      Say the whole thing. (Signal.) *There are twelve months in a year.*
   c. (Repeat step b until all children's responses are firm.)

2. I'll name some months of the year.
   a. Listen to the first three months: January, February, March. Everybody, say the first three months of the year with me. (Signal. Respond with the children.) January, February, March.
      (Repeat step a until all children's responses are firm.)
   b. All by yourselves. Say the first three months of the year. (Signal.) *January, February, March.*
      (Repeat step b until all children's responses are firm.)
   c. Listen. How many months are in a year? (Signal.) *Twelve.*
      Say the whole thing. (Signal.) *There are twelve months in a year.*
   d. Everybody, say the first three months of the year. (Signal.) *January, February, March.*
      (Repeat step d until all children's responses are firm.)

Corrections

EXERCISE 2

● **Error**
   (The children say *Seven.*)
   Correction
   1. You're telling how many days there are in a week. I want to know how many months in a year.

2. How many months in a year? (Signal.) *Twelve.*
3. How many days in a week? (Signal.) *Seven.*
4. Again.
   (Return to the beginning of step a.)

Lesson 87: Information—Days, Months

Teaching Techniques

- On different days the order *Days—Months* is reversed. It is important to let the children know that they must listen carefully to the beginning question of each exercise. To prevent errors, stress the critical words in the question about **days** of the week and the question about **months** of the year.

- As with the days of the week, recite the months so that you give some of them a distinctive personality.

Corrections

Follow the corrections in the box if children confuse the numbers of days and months.

If the children have not learned the days of the week when they start work on months, they may become confused. If your children start making mistakes, firm them on the days of the week and the answer to the question How many days are in a week? Then ask how many months in a year.

If children continue to have trouble, change the form of the instructions:

1. Say, Listen. Tell me how many **days** are in a **week.** Then say, Get ready. Pause three seconds to allow children time to think. Then signal. The children respond *Seven.*

2. Say, Listen. Tell me how many **months** are in a **year.** Then say, Get ready. Pause three seconds. (Signal.) The children respond *Twelve.*

By using this procedure you are providing the children with thinking time and correcting these information mistakes immediately.

EXERCISE 5 Seasons

1. These pictures show the same place at different seasons of the year.

　a. (Point to a.) This picture shows winter. Snow is on the ground. Snow is on the mountain. There are no plants in the field. Look at the tree. There are no leaves on the tree.

　b. (Point to b.) This picture shows spring. Spring comes after winter. Say that. (Signal.) *Spring comes after winter.* See the little plants coming up in the field? The tree has little leaves. There is still snow on the mountain.

　c. (Point to c.) This picture shows summer. Summer comes after spring. Say that. (Signal.) *Summer comes after spring.* Look at the plants in the field. They're big. The tree has leaves. There is no snow on the mountain.

　d. (Point to d.) This picture shows fall. Fall comes after summer. Say that. (Signal.) *Fall comes after summer.* The plants in the field are dead. The leaves on the tree are falling. There is some snow on the ground.

2. My turn. I'll touch the picture and say the seasons. Here I go.

　a. (Point to a.) Winter.
　　(Point to b.) Spring.
　　(Point to c.) Summer.
　　(Point to d.) Fall.

　b. Say the seasons with me. (Touch each picture in order and say the seasons with the children.)

　c. Your turn. All by yourselves. Say the seasons. (Touch each picture in order. The children are to say the seasons.)

　d. (Repeat part 2 until all children can say the four seasons.)

Seasons
Lessons 123–149

Lesson 123: Seasons

Teaching Techniques

In part 1 point to and quickly describe each of the pictures. Don't drag out the descriptions. Make sure the children are looking at the picture you're talking about.

Part 2 contains the critical steps. When presenting part 2, say the names so that each has a personality. For example: Wiinter, **spring** (pause) sssummer, **fall.**

Corrections

Correct mistakes in part 2 by modeling and leading (using the cadence you have worked out).

Lesson 124: Seasons

In the next seasons exercise, beginning at lesson 124 (not shown here), the children are introduced to the rule There are four seasons in a year. Emphasize the words **four** and **seasons** so that the children will understand that this rule differs from the ones for days of the week and months of the year.

After you review the names of the seasons, ask the children about each of the four pictures in turn, calling on individuals to make observations about the picture and discuss the characteristics of the seasons in their own communities. Having the entire group repeat each child's good observations will help children remember the characteristics of the different seasons.

Part/Whole
Lessons 23–147

Some children have trouble with the idea that an object can be described in more than one way. These children seem to think that, after the object has been labeled, nothing more can be said about it. Yet that object is an example of hundreds of different concepts. A pencil is an example not only of **pencil** but also of something yellow, a writing instrument, a hard object, something with a point, and so forth.

One primary purpose of the part/whole track is to show the children that we can do a "double-take" with objects. We can identify the whole object; we can also name the parts of the object. This double-take idea is further amplified as children do exercises with opposites, colors, shapes, and classification in which attention is called to some other property of an object after it has been identified.

In the first exercise of the part/whole track the children learn the parts of the head through actions exercises. Next they identify parts of the head in a picture. Starting in lesson 25 they learn the parts of a common object—a table. Below is a list of the objects presented, with the number of the lesson where each first appears.

head	23	body	81
table	25	house	86
pencil	27	shoe	91
toothbrush	30	nail	96
elephant	36	pin	97
wagon	39	window	99
tree	43	chair	101
umbrella	54	cabinet	106
car	60	saw	107
flower	63	hammer	111
coat	74	broom	112
		belt	112

The part/whole track provides the children with practice in organizing information. The important thing is that children learn **how** to learn new names, to remember them so they aren't confused with other names, and to use them. Because some of the vocabulary taught in the track is used in other tracks, it is important for children to learn the vocabulary used in the part/whole exercises.

EXERCISE 1   Actions—Parts of the Body

[**Note:** If children make a mistake, demonstrate the correct action and have the children do it. Then return to step a in part 2 and repeat the exercise.]

1. It's time for some actions.
   a. I can touch my chin. Watch. (Touch your chin.)
   b. What am I doing? (Signal.) *Touching your chin.*

2. Now it's your turn.
   a. Everybody, smile. (Signal. Wait.)
   What are you doing? (Signal.) *Smiling.*
   Say the whole thing. (Signal.) *I am smiling.*
   b. Everybody, touch your chin. (Signal. Wait.)
   What are you doing? (Signal.) *Touching my chin.*
   Say the whole thing. (Signal.) *I am touching my chin.*
   c. Everybody, touch your leg. (Signal. Wait.)
   What are you doing? (Signal.) *Touching my leg.*
   Say the whole thing. (Signal.) *I am touching my leg.*
   d. Everybody, touch your head. (Signal. Wait.)
   What are you doing? (Signal.) *Touching my head.*
   Say the whole thing. (Signal.) *I am touching my head.*
   e. Everybody, touch your hand. (Signal. Wait.)
   What are you doing? (Signal.) *Touching my hand.*
   Say the whole thing. (Signal.) *I am touching my hand.*
   f. Put your hand down. (Signal.)

3. Let's do that again.
   (Repeat part 2 until all children's responses are firm.)

Lesson 22: Actions—Parts of the Body

Parts of the body are introduced in an actions exercise.

Teaching Techniques

If children already know the names of the parts of the body introduced in part 1, move quickly to part 2. Some children, however, will need to be taught carefully from the beginning. You may have to repeat some of the part names more often than is indicated in the exercise.

Corrections

If the children have trouble with any step, either show or tell them the answer. Then repeat the step. Then repeat the entire exercise. Be sure to present some individual turns.

EXERCISE 7 Part/Whole

1. Today we're going to learn the parts of a table. (Circle the top table with your finger.)
   a. Everybody, what is this? (Touch.) *A table.*
   b. Say the whole thing. (Touch.) *This is a table.*

2. (Point to the bottom table.) Here's a table that is in parts. I'll name the parts.
   a. (Point to the legs.) These are legs. (Point to the top.) This is a top.
   b. (Point to the legs.) What are these parts called? (Touch.) *Legs.* (Point to the top.) What is this part called? (Touch.) *A top.*
   c. (Repeat steps a and b until all children's responses are firm.)

3. (Point to the top table.) Let's see if you can name the parts of the other table.
   a. (Point to the legs.) What are these parts called? (Touch.) *Legs.*
   b. (Point to the top.) What is this part called? (Touch.) *A top.*
   c. (Circle the table.) Legs and a top are parts of a . . . (touch) *table.* Yes. What's the whole object called? (Touch.) *A table.*
   d. (Repeat part 3 until all children's responses are firm.)

4. (Point to a table in the room.)
   a. Now let's name the parts of this table. (The children are to name each part as you point to it.)
   b. What's the whole object called? (Touch.) *A table.*

5. (Call on different children.) What do you do on a table? (Praise reasonable responses.)

Lesson 25: Part/Whole

Most part/whole objects are introduced by means of an "exploded" picture. This is the first such exercise. It gives the children a vivid demonstration of the separate parts of a table. Later in the exercise the children work from a picture of the whole object. They see that the part names they have learned can also be used in describing the whole object.

Teaching Techniques

- Do part 1 quickly. In part 2 point to the parts and name them in an important-sounding way. Emphasize the words **legs** and **top.**

- Repeat part 3 until the children can respond correctly. Make sure that your signals are precise so that the children will know what part you are asking about so that they will be able to respond together.

- In part 3 the children must identify the whole object. This step is important. The children must be able to give the object's name as well as the names of its parts.

- Looking at and naming the parts of a real table demonstrates that the part names can be used with real objects.

- Move at a brisk pace through this exercise but, where necessary, allow the children some thinking time. At the end of each part/whole exercise, the children should be able to respond perfectly to each step.

Corrections

If the children have trouble, tell them the answer. Then return to the beginning of the exercise and present the remaining steps in sequence.

Review Exercises

All of the objects introduced in the track are presented again in review exercises. If the children are firm on the part/whole exercises, they will be able to do the review exercises quickly. You will find that they enjoy "rattling off" these answers.

The question What do we usually do with a . . . ? appears at the end of most of the review exercises. Call on different children to answer this question. The question is designed to start the children thinking about how different objects are used.

Whenever the children forget the name of a part, give them the correct answer. Then repeat the exercise.

Materials
Lesson 57–148

In the materials track, children learn to identify common materials. This information is important because it shows children a new aspect of objects and, in this way, helps them to build their fund of information. For some of the exercises, you will need to bring objects made of different materials to the lesson.

A list of the materials the children learn is shown below, along with the number of the lesson where each material first appears.

Material	Lesson
cloth	57
paper	57
plastic	57
wood	59
rubber	59
glass	67
metal	78
leather	80
concrete	84
paper	116
brick	121

Lesson 57: Materials

For exercise 6 on page 77, you will need a cloth shirt with plastic buttons.

This exercise is particularly important because it helps the children differentiate between the name of a part and the material that part is made of.

Teaching Techniques

- Let the children feel the parts of the shirt you use in the task before you begin.

- Present the steps in part 2 until the children are firm. You should do these steps very quickly.

Corrections

If the children name a material when they should name a part, correct them by saying, You told me the **material** of this part. But I asked for the **name** of this part. What's the name of this part? If children fail to respond correctly, tell them the answer and repeat the question.

EXERCISE 6   Materials

[**Note:** You will need a cloth shirt with plastic buttons.]

1. We're going to talk about this shirt.
   a. (Hold up a shirt or point to a child's shirt. Point to the collar.) A shirt has a collar.
   b. (Point to the front.) A shirt has a front.
   c. (Point to a button.) A shirt has buttons.

2. Now it's your turn.
   a. (Hold up the shirt or point to it.) Everybody, get ready to name each part of this shirt. (Touch the collar.) What is the name of this part? (Signal.) *The collar.*
   b. (Touch the front.) What is the name of this part? (Signal.) *The front.*
   c. (Touch a button.) What is the name of this part? (Signal.) *A button.*

3. Listen carefully.
   a. (Touch a button.) What part am I touching? (Signal.) *A button.*
      Listen. The button is made of plastic. What's it made of? (Signal.) *Plastic.*
   b. (Touch the front.) What part am I touching? (Signal.) *The front.*
      Listen. The front is made of cloth. What's it made of? (Signal.) *Cloth.*
   c. And what's the button made of? (Signal.) *Plastic.*
      And what's the front made of? (Signal.) *Cloth.*
   d. (Repeat the exercise until all children's responses are firm.)

For exercise 5, you will need to prepare three circles, each the same size and ideally the same color. One should be plastic, one paper, and the third cloth.

EXERCISE 5   Materials—Demonstration

[**Note:** Prepare three circles, each approximately 5 inches in diameter. One is to be made of plastic, one of paper, and one of cloth. You should have a lapboard or a large book on which to put the three circles.]

1. We're going to learn what things are made of.
   a. (Point to the circles.) Everybody, what are these? (Signal.) *Circles.*
      Yes, circles.
   b. (Point to the paper circle.) This circle is made of paper. What is it made of? (Touch.) *Paper.*
   c. (Point to the cloth circle.) This circle is made of cloth. What is it made of? (Touch.) *Cloth.*
   d. (Point to the plastic circle.) This circle is made of plastic. What is it made of? (Touch.) *Plastic.*
   e. (Repeat part 1 until all children's responses are firm.)

2. I'll point to each circle. You tell me what it is made of.
   a. (Point to the plastic circle.) What is this circle made of? (Signal.) *Plastic.*
      (Point to the cloth circle.) What is this circle made of? (Signal.) *Cloth.*
      (Point to the paper circle.) What is this circle made of? (Signal.) *Paper.*
   b. Let's do those again.
      (Repeat step a until all children's responses are firm.)

Individual Turns
(Repeat part 2, calling on different children.)

Teaching Techniques

- Display the three circles on a flat surface. Point to each circle and identify the material.

- If the children have trouble in exercise 5, part 1, repeat part 1, presenting the circles in a different order.

- You may want to have the children hold or touch each of the circles.

Corrections

If the children make mistakes in part 2, tell them the correct answer and then repeat part 2.

EXERCISE 6   Materials

1. Look at the objects in this picture. All of these objects are made of plastic. When I touch each object, you name it. (Point to each object. The children are to respond *a bag, a bottle, a comb, a tablecloth, a wastebasket, a purse.*)

2. Take a good look at the objects and see how many you can remember. (Let the children look at the book for about ten seconds.)

3. (Remove the picture from the children's view.) See if you can name at least three things in the picture that are made of plastic. (Call on three or four children to name different objects made of plastic. Each child should name at least three things.)

4. Can anyone think of anything else made of plastic? (Accept all good answers.)

Lesson 65: Materials

This is an exercise that children find enjoyable. They first identify the objects made of a specific material in a picture. Then they see how many objects they can name when the picture is not visible. Similar exercises are used with all the materials taught in the program.

Teaching Techniques

- Present exercise 6 as a challenge. After the children have identified the objects, put down the book and say,

Now you get to see how many things you can remember.

- Praise the children who name at least three objects. Act astonished if a child can name five or all six objects.

Corrections

- If a child is unable to name three objects, say, I'll let you look at the picture again, but then you'll have to name **four** things in the picture. Allow the child to examine the picture for about five seconds. Then remove it and ask the child to name four objects that are made of plastic.

- If the child names objects that are made of plastic but are not in the picture, say, That is made of plastic, but it isn't in the picture. Name only objects that are in the picture.

- If most of the children do not do well, show the entire group the picture again. Call on several children to tell what they see. Then say, I'll come back to this picture later. I'll see who can remember at least three objects in this picture. Do the next exercise in the lesson, and then return to the materials exercise. Ask the question again, without showing the picture. Praise children who can name three objects from the picture.

Lesson 70: Materials

EXERCISE 3   Materials

1. Think of things that are made of wood. Let's see who can name at least three things made of wood.
   (Call on different children to name objects made of wood. Each child should name at least three things.)

2. Think of things that are made of cloth. Let's see who can name at least three things made of cloth.
   (Call on different children to name objects made of cloth. Each child should name at least three things.)

3. Think of things that are made of plastic. Let's see who can name at least three things made of plastic.
   (Call on different children to name objects made of plastic. Each child should name at least three things.)

This review exercise appears frequently throughout the program. It requires the children to name objects made of different materials.

Teaching Techniques

Call on two or three children for each part. Move quickly from one child to another. Praise all appropriate responses.

Corrections

- If children name only objects that have appeared in picture exercises, say, You can name **any** object that is made of wood. I'll name some—fence, tent stake, boat, window frame, pencil shaft, cane, chair, table. Your turn. When I call on you, name at least three things made of wood.

- If children name only those objects that somebody has just named, say, Yes, those are good objects. But see if you can name some new ones.

Praise children who name novel things. However, do not accept questionable items. For example, if a child says that a boot is made of wood, say, I guess somebody could make a boot of wood, but I don't think that boots are made of wood. Name something else that is made of wood.

Common Information
Lessons 66–150

In the common information track the children learn about a variety of occupations, places, and natural phenomena. Information is presented both through pictures and through simple explanations. New words are introduced in the track every two to seven lessons. Every word is reviewed at least five times. These are the words introduced and the lesson where each word first appears.

dentist	66	driver	112
city	66	passenger	113
farm	68	beach	115
store	69	ship	116
land	70	thermometer	116
sky	70	grocery store	117
sun	70	painter	120
clouds	70	airport	126
firefighter	74	pilot	127
teacher	75	fire station	128
Earth	78	lumberjack	129
forest	80	library	131
ocean	82	librarian	132
orchard	89	restaurant	134
carpenter	90	customer	135
doctor	103	waiter	136
nurse	103	engine	143
patient	104	mechanic	145
medicine	107	garage	147
police officer	108		
jungle	111		

EXERCISE 3   Common Information

1. Get ready for some new information.
   a. Listen. A dentist is a person who fixes teeth. What do we call a person who fixes teeth? (Signal.) *A dentist.*
      Say the whole thing about a dentist. (Signal.) *A dentist is a person who fixes teeth.*
   b. Again. (Signal.) *A dentist is a person who fixes teeth.*
      (Repeat step b until all children can make the statement.)
   c. Listen. A city is a place with lots of people. What do we call a place with lots of people? (Signal.) *A city.*
      Say the whole thing about a city. (Signal.) *A city is a place with lots of people.*
   d. Again. (Signal.) *A city is a place with lots of people.*
      (Repeat step d until all children can make the statement.)

2. Let's see how much information you remember.
   a. What do we call a person who fixes teeth? (Signal.) *A dentist.*
      Say the whole thing about a dentist. (Signal.) *A dentist is a person who fixes teeth.*
   b. What do we call a place with lots of people? (Signal.) *A city.*
      Say the whole thing about a city. (Signal.) *A city is a place with lots of people.*
   c. (Repeat part 2 until all children's responses are firm.)

3. I'll turn the page and we'll see a picture of a dentist.
   (Turn the page quickly.)

4. (Show the picture to the children. Ask
different children the following questions.)
What do you see in this picture?
What else do you see in this picture?
How do you think the man in the chair feels?
What do you think the dentist will do?
(Praise all good responses.)

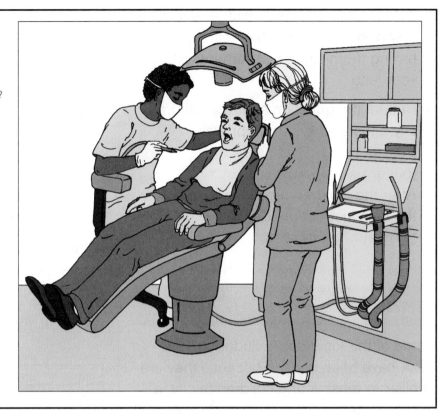

Lesson 66: Common Information

The exercise presents information about
the concepts **dentist** and **city.** This
information is presented on the first page
of the exercise. The children then identify
a picture of a dentist on the next page.

Teaching Techniques

The children may have to practice the new
statements introduced. After they have
learned to make the statements, return to
the beginning of the exercise and present
the entire routine briskly. Do not accept
slow, draggy responses.

- Don't leave a common information
  exercise until you are sure that every
  child can answer correctly at every
  step. Every statement taught in the
  track is reviewed many times in
  subsequent lessons. If you leave an
  exercise before the children's
  responses are firm, they will have
  problems in later lessons. If they
  perform well every day, the exercises
  will be more enjoyable as they progress
  through the program.

- Many of the common information
  exercises have a picture on the second
  page. Have fun with the children as
  they answer your questions and
  discuss what they see in the picture.

Corrections

Some children may have trouble making
the statements. These procedures will
make it easier for them:

1. As you ask the questions in part 1,
   stress the words that they will use in
   the response: What do we call (pause)
   a person who fixes teeth?

2. If necessary, lead the children until their responses are firm. Then test them by having them say the statement without your lead.

3. Repeat the question after the children say the statement appropriately: Yes, a dentist. Listen again. What do we call (pause) a person who fixes teeth? After the children reply move quickly to the next instruction: Say the whole thing about a dentist.

Locations
Lessons 124–150

Some of the locations included in this track have been chosen because they are familiar to most young children (a city, a grocery store). Others have been chosen because they may be unfamiliar to the children (a jungle, an airport) but important to their general knowledge. Most of the locations that are taught have been previously introduced in the common information track.

In the locations track the children learn

1. the name and primary function of thirteen locations;

2. the names of some things that are observed in each location;

3. the names or titles of people often found in these locations;

4. the function of some of the things and people found in these locations.

These are the locations taught and the lesson in which each is introduced.

city	67	jungle	136
farm	68	airport	140
grocery store	124	fire station	144
dentist's office	127	library	146
doctor's office	128	garage	147
ocean	126	restaurant	149
forest	133		

EXERCISE 6   Locations

1. Today we're going to learn about a grocery store. What do we call a place where we buy food? (Signal.) *A grocery store.*

2. Here's a picture of a grocery store. I'll name some of the things you see in a grocery store. Watch.
   (Point to each item in turn.)
   a. These are shelves. What are these? (Touch.) *Shelves.*
      The shelves hold the food that people buy.
   b. This is a customer. What is this? (Touch.) *A customer.*
      She is going to buy things in the store.
   c. She is pushing a grocery cart. What is she pushing? (Touch.) *A grocery cart.*
      She puts things she wants to buy in the grocery cart.
   d. Here's a cash register. What is this? (Touch.) *A cash register.*
      It holds the money that people pay to buy things.
   e. This man is a checker. What is this man? (Touch.) *A checker.*
      He takes money from the customers and puts their groceries into bags.

3. Let's see if you remember the names of those things.
   a. (Point to the shelves.) What are these? (Touch.) *Shelves.*
   b. (Point to the customer.) What is she called? (Touch.) *A customer.*
   c. (Point to the grocery cart.) What is this? (Touch.) *A grocery cart.*
   d. (Point to the cash register.) What is this? (Touch.) *A cash register.*
   e. (Point to the checker.) What is he called? (Touch.) *A checker.*

   f. (Repeat steps a through e until all children's responses are firm.)

4. What else do you see in the picture? (Call on different children.)
   a. (Circle the entire picture.) What do we call the place you see in this picture? (Touch.) *A grocery store.*
   b. Can you think of something else you would see in a grocery store? (Accept reasonable responses.)

Lesson 124: Locations

Teaching Techniques

- Make sure you are pointing so that the children can see which part of the picture you are asking about.

- Go over part 2 until the children can identify all the objects without error.

- In part 4 you ask the children to name the **place** where these objects are found. You are no longer asking them to name the objects. When you ask the question, emphasize the word **place.** Pause a moment to give the children a chance to "switch gears." Then touch the picture.

Corrections

Immediately correct any errors in part 2. Tell the children the correct answer, repeat the question, then return to the beginning of part 2.

If the children identify one of the objects in the picture when asked about the place, say, You're telling me about the. . . . I want to know the name of the **place.** What do we call the **place** we see in this picture?

Signs
Lessons 131–136

Children are introduced to signs in lesson 131. They learn about signs that have words and signs that have icons or symbols. The exercises from lesson 131 and 136 are on page 85.

Teaching Notes: Children are not held accountable for sounding out the words. They have not learned enough about sounds to sound out the words **danger** and **stop.** If children make mistakes, simply tell them the word and repeat the task they missed.

New signs are introduced in lessons 133 and 134. Here are the additional signs that children learn.

EXERCISE 1 Signs

a. These are signs. I'll tell you what each sign says.

b. (Point to the danger sign.) This sign says **danger.** What does it say? (Signal.) *Danger.* You may see this sign near places where a bridge is out or where workers are building something and a person could get hurt.

c. (Point to the stop sign.) This sign says **stop.** What does it say? (Signal.) *Stop.* A stop sign tells a driver not to keep on going. The driver has to stop at the stop sign and look for other cars before going on again.

d. (Point to the no smoking sign.) This sign doesn't have any words, but the line through it is just like a cross-out mark. The line through the sign means don't do this. This sign tells you **no smoking.** What does it tell you? (Signal.) *No smoking.*

e. (Point to the no bike sign.) This sign tells you **no bike riding.** What does this sign tell you? (Signal.) *No bike riding.*

f. (Point to the no dogs sign.) What does this sign tell you? (Signal.) *No dogs.*

g. Let's go over the signs again. I'll point to each sign. You tell me what it tells you or what it says.
(Point to the danger sign.) What does this sign say? (Signal.) *Danger.*
(Point to the stop sign.) What does this sign say? (Signal.) *Stop.*
(Point to the no smoking sign.) What does this sign tell you? (Signal.) *No smoking.*

(Point to the no bike riding sign.) What does this sign tell you? (Signal.) *No bike riding.*
(Point to the no dogs sign.) What does this sign tell you? (Signal.) *No dogs.*

h. (Repeat step g until firm.)

Here's the review exercise from lesson 136:

EXERCISE 1 Signs

a. You've seen all these signs before. You'll tell me what each sign says or what it tells you.

b. (Point to the stop sign.) What does this sign say? (Signal.) *Stop.*
(Point to the no smoking sign.) What does this sign tell you? (Signal.) *No smoking.*
(Point to the no dogs sign.) What does this sign tell you? (Signal.) *No dogs.*
(Point to the exit sign.) What does this sign say? (Signal.) *Exit.*
(Point to the no swimming sign.) What does this sign tell you? (Signal.) *No swimming.*

c. (Repeat step b until firm.)

Instructional Words and Problem-Solving Concepts

The purpose of this group of tracks is to teach the meanings and uses of a number of words and concepts important to following instruction, solving logical problems, and answering questions. Below is a list of the tracks with the lesson in which each one starts.

Track	Lesson
Spatial and Temporal Relations	13–43
Prepositions	22–82
And—Actions	55–61
Same/Different	84–150
Some, All, None	87–100
Actions—Or	97–110
Before, After	95–115
Where, Who, When, What	116–150
If-Then Rules	120–150

The program presents these important concepts in many contexts. In all but one track the concepts are first introduced in actions exercises. They appear in later actions reviews. The concepts also appear in picture exercises and later in track reviews and in applications and absurdities exercises. Most of these concepts also appear as workbook activities.

Spatial and Temporal Relations
Lessons 13–43

Children learn a variety of temporal sequencing skills and vocabulary. Early in the program, they learn **first** and **next** as words that describe temporal events— what somebody does first, what the person does next. Later, children learn how to apply those words to "static" pictures, for instance a picture of three dogs in line walking toward a door. The dog that is first in line is the dog that will reach the door first. Children do a variety of worksheet activities that require knowledge of first, next, and last. (See pages 87–88 in this guide.)

Much later in the program, starting with lesson 98, children are introduced to **before** and **after.** These words parallel **first** and **next.** If a person smiles and then claps, the clapping occurs after the person smiles. The smiling occurs before the person claps.

The sequencing-events track begins in lesson 13, with the introduction of **first** and **next.**

EXERCISE 3   Actions—First, Next

1. Listen. Here's a new game.
- **a.** First I'm going to clap. Next I'm going to smile. Once more. First I'm going to clap. Next I'm going to smile.
- **b.** What am I going to do first? (Signal.) *Clap.* What am I going to do next? (Signal.) *Smile.*
- **c.** (Repeat step b until all children's responses are firm.)
- **d.** My turn. Here I go. (Clap. Pause. Smile.) What did I do first? (Signal.) *Clapped.* What did I do next? (Signal.) *Smiled.*
- **e.** Your turn. First you'll clap. Next you'll smile.
  Show me what you'll do first. Get ready. (Signal. Children clap.)
- **f.** Show me what you'll do next. Get ready.
  (Signal. Children smile.)
  Good. First you clapped. Next you smiled.
- **g.** I'll tap two times. Show me the thing you do first and the thing you do next. Get ready. (Tap two times. Children clap, then smile.)

2. (Repeat part 1 until all children's responses are firm.)

Lesson 13: Actions—First, Next

Teaching Techniques

In steps e and f the children are to show you what they do first and next. Be careful that some of the children don't lead the others and show them what to do. All together. Wait for my signal. Show me what you do first.

    Get ready. (Signal.)

    Good. Now show what you do next. Get ready. (Signal.)

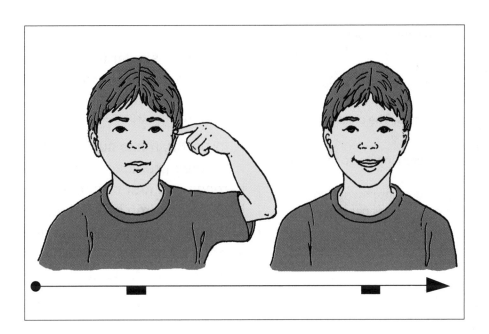

Lesson 19: Actions—First, Next

After the children have worked on exercises like this one for several lessons, they will do worksheet activities that apply **first** and **next** to illustrations of actions. For these exercises, children follow the arrow and identify what to do **first** and what to do **next.** Note that **first** and **next** are related to pictures that are not actually ordered in time; the boys are both present at the same time. But by following a sequencing rule (following the arrow), one of the objects becomes the first one you'll touch. The other object becomes the next one you'll touch. This notion is important for reading where the first letter is not really temporally first. It is first only if you follow the sequencing rule of moving from left to right as you identify the letters.

EXERCISE 2 Actions—First, Next, Last

[**Note:** You will need a chair for this exercise.]

1. We're going to do first, next, and last.
   (Ask three children to stand in front of
   the group. Place a chair to the right of the
   children and stand at the other end of the
   children. Direct the children in line to turn
   and face the chair.)
   a. Everybody, if these children walk to the
      chair, who will get to the chair first?
      (Signal. The children respond.)
      So, who is first in line now? (Signal. The
      children respond.)
   b. Who is next? (Signal. The children
      respond.)
      Who is last? (Signal. The children
      respond.)

2. (Ask the three children to turn so they face
   you.)
   a. Everybody, if these children stay in line
      and walk to me, who will get to me first?
      (Signal. The children respond.)
   b. So, who is first in line? (Signal. The
      children respond.)
      Who is next in line? (Signal. The
      children respond.)
      Who is last? (Signal. The children
      respond.)

3. You said that _____ will get to me first
   if the children walk toward me. Let's see if
   you are right.
   a. [Name the three children], stay in line
      and walk toward me.
   b. So, who got to me first? (Signal. The
      children respond.)
      Who got to me next? (Signal. The
      children respond.)
      Who got to me last? (Signal. The
      children respond.)

Later, children do an expanded version of
the **first-next** exercises that incorporates
last. The expanded version helps the
children learn more about the relationship
between sequencing events in space and
sequencing events in time. For these
activities, several children line up. You ask
which child would reach the door first if
the line moved toward you. This type of
activity is similar to arrow exercises except
the line actually moves.

Teaching Techniques

In part 2, make sure that children are firm
on their prediction about which child will
reach you first before you present part 3.
Once children see the relationship
between standing in line and reaching a
point by moving, they should have no
trouble with this activity.

A more advanced version of this exercise
starts in lesson 35. It requires children to
analyze **first, next,** and **last** from pictures.

Prepositions
Lessons 22–82

On, in, over, and **under** are words that frequently occur in directions. If children are to understand and follow directions, they need a precise understanding of prepositions.

The objectives of the prepositions track are

1. to demonstrate the meanings of prepositions with real objects;

2. to teach children to perform actions that involve prepositions: Put your hand over your head;

3. to teach children to use prepositions to describe the relationship of objects in a picture.

Each preposition is introduced in a demonstration or actions exercise, then presented in picture exercises. Here is a schedule of the prepositions taught in the program.

Prepositions	Lesson
on	22
over	25
in front of	30
in	41
in back of	52
under	62
next to	71
between	82

**EXERCISE 4   Prepositions—On
(Demonstration)**

[**Note:** You will need a pencil and a table for this exercise.]

1. We're going to talk about a pencil and a table.
   a. (Hold up the pencil.) What is this? (Signal.) *A pencil.*
   b. (Point to the table.) What is this? (Signal.) *A table.*

2. My turn. I'll tell you if I hold the pencil **on** the table.
   a. (Hold the pencil on the tabletop.) Is the pencil **on** the table? Yes.
   (Hold the pencil on another part of the tabletop.) Is the pencil **on** the table? Yes.
   (Hold the pencil over the tabletop.) Is the pencil **on** the table? No.
   (Hold the pencil next to the table.) Is the pencil **on** the table? No.
   (Hold the pencil near the floor.) Is the pencil **on** the table? No.
   b. Your turn. Tell me if the pencil is on the table.
   (Repeat step a, with the children answering the questions.)

3. Now we're going to say the whole thing. Watch. (Put the pencil on the table.)
   Is the pencil on the table? (Signal.) *Yes.*
   Say the whole thing with me. (Signal.) The pencil is on the table.
   All by yourselves. Say the whole thing about where the pencil is. (Signal.) *The pencil is on the table.*

4. (Repeat part 3 until all children can make the statement.)

Lesson 22: Prepositions—On

(Demonstration)

In this first exercise, the children learn the difference between **on** and **not on.**

Teaching Techniques

For demonstrations of this kind to be successful, you must move very quickly. In part 2a you are showing the children the difference between **on** and **not on.** If your pacing is slow, they will tend to forget what you have just shown, and they will make mistakes.

Study the instructions so that you can present exercise 4, part 2 without having to read from the book. For your first two demonstrations, you will position the pencil on different parts of the tabletop. You will present three demonstrations of **not on;** your pencil will be **over, next to,** and **near** the table. For each demonstration, first position the pencil and then quickly ask the question Is this pencil on the table? **Answer each of the questions** yes or no. **Your answer must follow your question quickly to keep the children from responding. Make it clear that step a is your turn. Then at step b repeat step a with the children answering the questions.**

When all the children respond correctly, move quickly to statement production in part 3. Lead the children through the statement in a natural tone of voice, but emphasize the word **on.**

Corrections

Some children have trouble saying preposition statements. Often they omit the word **is.** They may also slur the preposition word—which may mean that they will later confuse **on** and **under.**

To firm the children on saying the statement in part 3, say it with a pause: The pencil is **(pause) on** the table. The pause helps the children see that the first part of the statement is similar to familiar statements, such as, The boy is running. By stressing **on,** you help the children place the word in the sentence.

If children have trouble saying the statement with you,

Model the response:

My turn. The pencil is **(pause) on** the table.

Lead the response:

Say the whole thing with me. The pencil is **(pause) on** the table.

Test the response:

All by yourselves. Say the whole thing about where the pencil is. **(Signal.)** *The pencil is on the table.*

By stressing the first words the children will say in their response, you make it easier for them to respond correctly.

The children must be firm on saying these statements and all the subsequent preposition statements. If you are not sure of some of the children's responses, test them individually.

EXERCISE 5   Prepositions—On/Over

1. We're going to talk about this picture.
(Point to a leaf.) What is this? (Touch.) *A leaf.*
(Point to the dog.) What is this? (Touch.)
A dog.

2. One of these leaves is over the dog.
(Point to each leaf and ask:) Is this leaf over the dog? (The children answer *yes* or *no.*) ●
(Repeat until all children's responses are firm.)

3. (Point to a.)
Everybody, where is this leaf? (Touch.) *Over the dog.*
Say the whole thing about where this leaf is.
(Touch.) *This leaf is over the dog.*
(Repeat until all children can make the statement.)

4. One of these leaves is on the dog. (Point to each leaf and ask:) Is this leaf on the dog? (The children answer *yes* or *no.*) ●
(Repeat until all children's responses are firm.)

5. (Point to b.) Everybody, where is this leaf? (Touch.) *On the dog.*
Say the whole thing about where this leaf is.
(Touch.) *This leaf is on the dog.*
(Repeat until all children can make the statement.)

Individual Turns
(Repeat parts 3 through 5, calling on different children.)

Corrections

EXERCISE 5

● **Error**
(The children give the wrong answer.)

Correction
1. (Give the correct answer.)
2. (Repeat the step.)

Lesson 26: Prepositions—On/Over

This first picture exercise follows the introduction of **on** and **over** in actions exercises. For the first time, the children discriminate between two prepositions. The picture shows a dog and some leaves—two on the ground, one on the dog's back, and one hovering over it.

In parts 2 and 3 the children work on the preposition **over** by answering a series of yes/no questions and then making a statement about the leaf that is **over** the dog. In parts 4 and 5 the children work on the preposition **on.**

EXERCISE 4   Actions—Prepositions: In Front Of

[Note: You will need a chair for this exercise.]

1. I'm going to put a chair in front of me.
   a. (Place the chair directly in front of you.) The chair is in front of me. Where is the chair? (Signal.) *In front of you.*
   b. (Turn so that the chair is to your right.) Is the chair in front of me now? (Signal.) *No.*
   c. (Turn so the chair is to your left.) Is the chair in front of me now? (Signal.) *No.*
   d. (Turn so the chair is directly in front of you.) Is the chair in front of me now? (Signal.) *Yes.* Where is the chair now? (Signal.) *In front of you.*

2. (Repeat part 1 until all children's responses are firm.)

3. Let's do something harder.
   a. (Call on a child.) Put the chair in front of me. (The child responds.) Everybody, where is the chair? (Signal.) *In front of you.* Say the whole thing. (Signal.) *The chair is in front of you.*
   b. (Turn so the chair is in back of you. Call on a child.) Put the chair in front of me. (The child responds.) Everybody, where is the chair? (Signal.) *In front of you.* Say the whole thing. (Signal.) *The chair is in front of you.*
   c. (Turn so the chair is to your side. Call on a child.) Put the chair in front of me. (The child responds.) Everybody, where is the chair? (Signal.) *In front of you.* Say the whole thing. (Signal.) *The chair is in front of you.*

4. (Repeat part 3 until all children's responses are firm.)

Lesson 30: Actions—Prepositions:

In Front Of

In front of is introduced with a demonstration. It is always used with objects that have fronts and backs.

Teaching Techniques

Practice this exercise before presenting it to the children so that it will go smoothly.

- In part 1, place a chair in front of you. Then turn different ways and ask the children, Is this chair in front of me now? Move quickly through this series of steps.

- In part 3, call on different children to place the chair in front of you. These steps should be done rapidly. Don't let a child take too long to place the chair, or the attention of the group will stray.

Corrections

If children have trouble making the statement, follow the statement correction procedure. Pause after **is** and stress the prepositional words **in front of.**

If the children have trouble in part 2.

1. show them your front and say, Here is my front;

2. point straight ahead and say, Here's in front of me;

3. say, Put the chair so that it is in front of me. Put it so that I am pointing to it;

4. after the child places the chair appropriately, say, Let's do another one. Turn so that the chair is no longer in front of you and say, Put the chair in front of me. Do not point unless the child has trouble.

EXERCISE 4 Prepositions—In Front Of, On, Over

1. One of these dogs is **in front of** the bike. One of these dogs is **on** the bike. One of these dogs is jumping **over** the bike.

2. Get ready to tell me where each dog is.
   a. (Point to a.) Everybody, where is this dog? (Touch.) *Over the bike.*
   b. (Point to b.) Everybody, where is this dog? (Touch.) *On the bike.*
   c. (Point to c.) Everybody, where is this dog? (Touch.) *In front of the bike.*
   d. (Repeat until all children's responses are firm.)

3. We're going to talk about one of the dogs. (Point to b.)
   a. Where is this dog? (Touch.) *On the bike.*
      Say the whole thing about where this dog is. (Touch.) *This dog is on the bike.*
   b. Is this dog in front of the bike? (Touch.) *No.*
      Say the whole thing. (Touch.) *This dog is not in front of the bike.* ● ■

4. Now we'll talk about another dog. (Point to c.)
   a. Where is this dog? (Touch.) *In front of the bike.*
      Say the whole thing about where this dog is. (Touch.) *This dog is in front of the bike.*
   b. Is this dog on the bike? (Touch.) *No.*
      Say the whole thing. (Touch.) *This dog is not on the bike.*

Individual Turns
(Repeat parts 3 and 4 until all children can make the statements.)

Corrections

EXERCISE 4

● **Error**
(The children respond incorrectly.)
Correction
1. Is the dog in front of the bike? (Touch.) *No.*
2. Say the whole thing. (Touch.) *This dog is not in front of the bike.*
3. (Repeat until the children respond correctly.)

■ **Error**
(The children say *This dog is on the bike.*)
Correction
1. We're talking about **in front of.**
2. Is the dog **in front of** the bike? (Touch.) *No.*
3. Let's say the whole thing. (Touch. Respond with the children.) *This dog is not in front of the bike.*
4. All by yourselves. (Touch. Do not respond with the children.) *This dog is not in front of the bike.*
5. (Repeat part 4.)

Lesson 34: Prepositions—In Front Of, On, Over

When this exercise appears, the children have had **on, over,** and **in front of** in both actions and picture exercises. This picture exercise consolidates what they have learned. A similar exercise is used with other prepositions in later lessons.

Teaching Techniques

Children sometimes confuse the responses called for by the questions What is this? and Where is this? To reduce errors, it is important to stress the words **what** and **where** whenever they appear in the exercise.

The pacing in this exercise is important. Move very quickly when presenting the yes/no questions. But do not hurry the children when asking the **what** question or the **where** question.

In parts 3 and 4 the children should be able to answer each question and make each statement without error. Don't let them shout the statements or make them in a droning manner. This part of the exercise should be done quickly, and the children's responses should be confident and natural-sounding.

Corrections

If the children make mistakes on **in front of,** follow the correction used when **in front of** was introduced:

1. Show me the front of the bike.

2. Now show me what's in front of the bike.

3. Repeat the questions.

EXERCISE 4   Actions—And

1. It's time for some actions.
   a. Everybody, stand up. (Signal. Wait.)
      What are you doing? (Signal.) *Standing up.*
      Say the whole thing. (Signal.) *I am standing up.*
      Sit down.
   b. Everybody, stand up **and** touch your head.
      Get ready. (Signal. Wait.)
      What are you doing? (Signal.) *Standing up and touching my head.*
      (Repeat step b until all children can make the statement.)
   c. Say the whole thing with me. (Signal. Respond with the children.)
      I am standing up and touching my head.
      (Repeat step c until all children's responses are firm.)
   d. All by yourselves. Say the whole thing. (Signal. Do not respond with the children.)
      I am standing up and touching my head.
   e. Again. (Signal.) *I am standing up and touching my head.*
      (Repeat step e until all children can make the statement.)
      Sit down.

2. Let's do that again.
   a. Everybody, stand up and touch your head.
      Get ready. (Signal. Wait.)
      What are you doing? (Signal.) *Standing up and touching my head.*
   b. Say the whole thing. (Signal.) *I am standing up and touching my head.*

3. Here's another one.
   a. Everybody, sit down and touch your nose.
      Get ready. (Signal. Wait.)
      What are you doing? (Signal.) *Sitting down and touching my nose.*
      Say the whole thing. (Signal.) *I am sitting down and touching my nose.*
   b. (Repeat step a until all children's responses are firm.)

Actions—And
Lessons 55–61

The meaning and use of the word **and** is taught in two actions exercises and used in a variety of exercises throughout the program.

The particular usage of **and** emphasized in the program is illustrated by this example: The ball is little and green. The same meaning could also be phrased as The ball is green and little. The word **and** joins the two descriptive terms; the order in which the terms are mentioned doesn't matter.

Lesson 55: Actions—And

Teaching Techniques

Note that the instructions for these tasks don't involve things that happen first and next. If, for example, the instruction says, Touch your foot and touch your wrist, the child must be touching his foot and his wrist at the same time. It doesn't matter which he touched first.

The children are to continue performing the actions until you present the next instructions. Watch them carefully to make sure they are not copying responses from other children. If in doubt, call on individual children.

Corrections

Expect some children to have trouble with the statements. For example, to firm their responses in part 3,

1. model: Sitting down (pause) and touching my nose. Note the pause and the emphasis on the word **and;**

2. lead: Say it with me. Sitting down (pause) **and** touching my nose. The lead should contain the same pause and emphasis as the model. Repeat the lead until the children's responses are firm;

3. test: Your turn. The children are to make the response with the pause and emphasis;

4. call on individual children. If any children have trouble, return to the lead step and repeat the lead and test until all the children's responses are firm.

Same/Different Lessons 84–150

Typically, early school exercises refer to things as being the same only when they are identical. The problem with limiting the concept **same** to "identical" is that **same** is frequently used in other senses, such as "the same color," "the same shape," or "the same size." In these exercises the children learn that **same** can mean that something about two or more things is identical but that it is not necessary that everything be identical.

The concept of same involves comparing objects. When we say, for example, that two boys are doing the same thing, we are not making a statement about what either boy is doing; we are simply saying that if you observe the actions of both boys, you will be able to make the same observations about them. Similarly, when we say that two girls are wearing something that is the same, we are not saying what they are wearing; we are simply calling attention to the fact that some article of clothing worn by one girl is also worn by the other.

In the same/different track the children learn

1. to perform the **same** action the teacher performs;

2. to identify, in pictures, the **same** action performed by different characters;

3. the concept that things with the same label are the same. For example, all birds can be the same because all are labeled **birds;**

4. that people and animals may be "the same" in many ways: Two elephants may be the same because they both have hats, because they are both sitting, and because they are both elephants;

5. that objects can be described as "the same" because they have the same function, because they are found in the same place, because they have the same parts, or because they do the same thing;

6. that **different** is the opposite of **same;**

7. to compare objects, people, and animals and make observations about how they are the same and how they are different.

In the same/different track, children first learn to apply the concepts **same/not same.** Later they learn **different** as a word that means **not same.**

EXERCISE 1   Actions—Same

1. We're going to play a game.
  a. Everybody, I'm going to do something. Then you're going to do the **same thing.** My turn. (Tap your head once.) I did it.
  b. Your turn. Do the **same thing** I did. Get ready. (Signal. The children tap their head once.)
  Good. You did the **same thing** I did.
  c. (Repeat part 1 until all children's responses are firm.)

2. Here's another one.
  a. I'm going to do something. Then you're going to do the **same thing.**
  My turn. (Clap your hands twice.) I did it.
  b. Your turn. Do the **same thing** I did. Get ready. (Signal. The children clap their hands twice.)
  Good. You did the **same thing** I did.
  c. (Repeat part 2 until all children's responses are firm.)

3. New game.
  a. Your turn. Get ready to touch the floor. (Signal. The children are to touch the floor.)
  Stop touching the floor.
  b. Watch me. Tell me if I do the **same thing** you did. (Touch your nose.)
  Am I doing the **same thing** you did? (Signal.) *No.*
  c. Tell me what to do. (Signal.) *Touch the floor.*
  (Touch the floor.)
  Now am I doing the **same thing** you did? (Signal.) *Yes.*
  (Keep touching the floor.)
  d. What did you do? (Signal.) *Touched the floor.*
  What am I doing? (Signal.) *Touching the floor.*
  (Lift your hand from the floor.)
  e. We did something that was the same. Tell me what we did that was the same. (Signal.) *Touched the floor.*
  Yes, we touched the floor.
  f. (Repeat part 3 until all children's responses are firm. Then praise the children.)

Individual Turns
(Repeat the exercise, calling on different children for each step.)

Lesson 84: Actions—Same

The first exercise in the track introduces the idea of doing the same thing.

Teaching Techniques

Like other actions exercises that teach concepts, the demonstrations in parts 1 and 2 must be executed smoothly. Watch your pacing. Make sure that you can present the steps without looking at the book.

Go very rapidly in part 3 to keep the children from forgetting what they did that you are trying to match. The slower you go, the greater the possibility that the children will make mistakes in this part of the exercise.

Ignore any wording errors, such as children saying *touch the floor* instead of *touched the floor.* You are teaching **same.** Don't confuse the children with corrections on other details.

Corrections

If the children make mistakes in part 2, tell them the answer, then return to the beginning of part 2. Let's do that last part again. Your turn. . . .

EXERCISE 4 Same

1. Look at these boys.
   (Point to each boy and ask:) What is this boy doing? (Touch. The children are to answer *running, climbing, running, swinging.*)

2. We'll talk about each boy.
   a. (Point to a.)
   Is this boy tall? (Touch.) *Yes.*
   What is this boy doing? (Touch.) *Running.*
   One of the other boys is doing the same thing. We're going to find out which boy is doing the same thing.
   b. (Point to b.)
   Is this boy doing the same thing the tall boy is doing? (Touch.) *No.* ●
   c. (Point to c.)
   Is this boy doing the same thing the tall boy is doing? (Touch.) *Yes.*
   d. (Point to d.)
   Is this boy doing the same thing the tall boy is doing? (Touch.) *No.*

3. Look at this boy again.
   a. (Point to a.)
   What is this boy doing? (Touch.) *Running.*
   b. (Point to a and c.)
   What are they doing that is the same? (Touch.) *Running.*
   c. These boys are the same because they are running. Why are these boys the same? (Touch.) *Because they are running.*
   d. (Repeat part 3 until all children's responses are firm.)

4. Let's say the whole thing about why these boys are the same. (Signal. Respond with the children.) These boys are the same because they are running.

Your turn. Let's say the whole thing about why these boys are the same. (Signal. Do not respond with the children.) *These boys are the same because they are running.*

5. (Repeat part 4 until all children's responses are firm.)

┌─ Corrections ─
EXERCISE 4

● **Error**
   (The children say *Yes.*)
   Correction
   1. What's the tall boy doing? (Touch.) *Running.*
   2. Is this boy running? (Touch.) *No.*
      So this boy is not doing the same thing the tall boy is doing. Climbing is not the same as running.
   3. (Repeat step b.)

Lesson 87: Same

This is the first picture exercise in the same/different track. It is similar to the actions exercises in that it focuses on "doing the same thing."

Teaching Techniques

The children will catch on to this exercise more easily if you move quickly from step to step. If the children don't make any mistakes, you shouldn't have to slow down until part 4, where they make the statements.

Corrections

If children make mistakes in step b, follow the correction in the corrections box.

Expect some children to have some trouble saying the statements in part 4. You can help them by presenting the statement in this way: These boys are the same (pause) because they are running. You can say the first part of the statement, These boys are the same. . . . Then have them say the second part, *because they are running,* until their responses are firm. Then have them say the entire statement.

EXERCISE 7   Same

1. (Point to the cups.) Look at the picture.
   (Point to each cup and ask:) What is this?
   (Touch. The children are to answer *a cup*.)

2. I know why these things are the same.
   Because they are cups.
   a. Everybody, why are these things the
      same? (Touch.) *Because they are cups.*
      Yes, they are the same because they are
      cups.
   b. Say the whole thing about why they are
      the same. (Signal.) *They are the same
      because they are cups.*
   c. (Repeat until all the children can make the
      statement.)

3. (Point to the children.) Look at the picture.
   (Point to each child and ask:) What is this?
   (Touch. The children are to answer *a boy*
   or *a girl*.)

4. I know why these children are the same.
   Because they are standing.
   a. Everybody, why are these children the
      same? (Touch.) *Because they are
      standing.*
      Yes, they are the same because they are
      standing.
   b. Say the whole thing about why they are
      the same. (Signal.) *They are the same
      because they are standing.*
   c. (Repeat until all the children can make the
      statement.)

5. Let's do it again.
   a. (Point to the cups.) Everybody, why are
      these things the same? (Touch.) *Because
      they are cups.*
   b. (Point to the children.) Everybody, why are
      these children the same? (Touch.)
      Because they are standing.

   c. (Repeat part 5 until all the children can
      make the statement.)

Individual Turns
(Repeat the exercise, calling on different
children for each step.)

Lesson 88: Same

This is the second same/different exercise
introduced in lesson 88. It teaches the
children that things can be labeled "the
same" if they have the same name.

Corrections

In part 2, the children may respond by
saying, *They are cups.* To correct, say,
Yes, **because** they are cups. Let's say
"because they are cups."

EXERCISE 5 Same

1. Two of these elephants are wearing the same thing.
   a. (Point to a.)
      What is this elephant wearing? (Touch.) *A hat.*
   b. (Point to c.)
      What is this elephant wearing? (Touch.) *A hat.*
   c. Everybody, what are they wearing that's the same? (Touch.) *A hat.*
      So why are these elephants the same? (Touch.) *Because they're wearing hats.*
   d. Say the whole thing about why these elephants are the same. (Signal.) *These elephants are the same because they're wearing hats.*

2. Two of these elephants are holding the same thing.
   a. (Point to a and b.)
      These animals are holding the same thing.
   b. (Point to a.)
      What is this elephant holding? (Touch.) *Flowers.*
   c. (Point to b.)
      What is this elephant holding? (Touch.) *Flowers.*
   d. Everybody, what are they holding that's the same? (Touch.) *Flowers.*
      So why are these elephants the same? (Touch.) *Because they are holding flowers.*
   e. Say the whole thing about why these elephants are the same. (Signal.) *These elephants are the same because they're holding flowers.*

3. Two of these elephants are doing the same thing.
   a. (Call on a child.) Point to those elephants.
      Everybody, what are they doing that's the same? (Signal.) *Sitting.*

   b. (Point to b and c.)
      Everybody, what are they doing? (Touch.) *Sitting.*
      So why are these elephants the same? (Touch.) *Because they're sitting.*
   c. Say the whole thing about why these elephants are the same. (Signal.) *These elephants are the same because they're sitting.*

4. (Repeat the exercise until all children's responses are firm.)

Lesson 91: Same

In this exercise the children make observations about different ways that things are "the same."

Teaching Techniques

• When presenting part 1, point to the hats. When presenting part 2, point to the flowers. When presenting part 3, point to the back legs of each elephant to prompt the correct responses.

• The quicker you move through these steps, the greater the chance that the children will see the basis for judging why each pair of elephants is the same.

EXERCISE 4 Same—Class

I'm going to name some things that are in the
same class. You're going to tell me the class.

a. Listen. Bucket, glass, package. They're in
the same class. Everybody, what class are
they in? (Signal.) *Containers.*
(Repeat until all children's responses are
firm.)

b. Listen. Tricycle, motorboat, taxi. They're in
the same class. Everybody, what class?
(Signal.) *Vehicles.*
(Repeat until all children's responses are
firm.)

c. Listen. Banana, toast, potato. They're in
the same class. Everybody, what class?
(Signal.) *Food.*
(Repeat until all children's responses are
firm.)

d. Listen. Monkey, pig, rabbit. They're in the
same class. Everybody, what class?
(Signal.) *Animals.*
(Repeat until all children's responses are
firm.)

e. Listen. Cabinet, cup, bag. They're in the
same class. Everybody, what class?
(Signal.) *Containers.*
(Repeat until all children's responses are
firm.)

Lesson 94: Same—Class

The exercise above is the first of a series
of exercises that teaches the children
about objects that are in the same class,
objects that do the same thing, objects
that are found in the same place, and
objects that have the same parts. Treat
these exercises as games. In the
classification game the teacher says, I'm
going to name some things that are in the
same class. You're going to tell me the
class. The teacher names several vehicles
and then asks, What class are they in?
The children operate from words only—
there are no pictures.

Teaching Techniques

- You may wish to pause after naming
  the objects. This pause is critical and
  should last at least two seconds. Some
  children need this thinking time. Later
  you can reduce the length of the pause.
  If you hurry the children too much, they
  will begin to guess.

- It is important that you acknowledge all
  appropriate responses. For example, if
  you ask what chalk and a pencil do that
  is the same, a child might say, *You
  draw with them.* Accept the response:
  Yes, you draw with them. Let's say that
  they write. Listen. Chalk and a pencil
  (pause). What do they do that's the
  same?

Corrections

If children have trouble with more than
one step, repeat the entire exercise until
they can respond correctly.

Lesson 109: Actions—Same/Different

In this actions exercise, the word **different** is introduced.

Teaching Techniques

Move quickly through each of the steps. Make sure the children are watching you. When you ask, Am I doing the same thing or something different? emphasize the word **different.**

Make sure the children keep touching their nose from step a through step b. At the end of step b, tell them to put their hands down.

Corrections

The children may have difficulty saying "something different." Repeat the words with them several times. If children don't answer a question correctly, tell them the answer. Then return to the beginning of part 1.

EXERCISE 1 Actions—Same/Different

1. Here's our first game for today.
   a. Everybody, touch your nose. (Signal.) Keep touching it. What are you doing? (Signal.) *Touching my nose.*
   b. Tell me if I do the same thing you're doing. Watch. (Touch your nose. Keep touching it.)
   Am I doing the same thing you're doing or am I doing something different? (Signal.) *The same thing.*
   (Repeat until all children's responses are firm.)
   c. Now watch. (Touch the floor.)
   Am I doing the same thing you're doing or am I doing something different? (Signal.) *Something different.*
   d. Watch again. (Touch your nose.)
   Am I doing the same thing you're doing or am I doing something different? (Signal.) *The same thing.*
   e. Watch again. (Touch your chair.)
   Am I doing the same thing you're doing or am I doing something different? (Signal.) *Something different.*
   f. Yes, I am doing something different. Everybody, say the whole thing. (Signal.) *You are doing something different.*

2. Here's a new game.
   a. Everybody, point to the ceiling. (Signal.) Tell me if I do the same thing you're doing or something different.
   b. Watch. (Point to the wall.)
   Am I doing the same thing you're doing or am I doing something different? (Signal.) *Something different.*
   Say the whole thing. (Signal.) *You are doing something different.*
   c. Watch. (Point to the ceiling.)
   Am I doing the same thing you're doing or am I doing something different? (Signal.) *The same thing.*
   Say the whole thing. (Signal.) *You are doing the same thing.*
   d. (Repeat steps b and c until all children's responses are firm.)

Individual Turns
(Repeat the exercise, calling on different children for each step.)

EXERCISE 2   Same/Different—Class

1. We're going to talk about the classes things are in.
   a. Everybody, what class is soup in? (Signal.) *Food.*
   b. Everybody, what class is an apple in? (Signal.) *Food.*
   c. Everybody, what class is a tree in? (Signal.) *Plants.*
   d. Everybody, what class is a motorboat in? (Signal.) *Vehicles.*
      (Repeat until all children's responses are firm.)

2. Listen.
   a. Soup and an apple. (Pause.)
      Are they in the same class or in different classes? (Pause. Signal.) *The same class.*
      You're right. They are in the same class.
      What class is soup in? (Pause. Signal.) *Food.*
      Is an apple in the same class? (Pause. Signal.) *Yes.*
      Yes, soup and an apple are in the same class.
   b. Soup and a tree. (Pause.)
      Are they in the same class or in different classes? (Pause. Signal.) *Different classes.*
      You're right. They are in different classes.
      What class is soup in? (Pause. Signal.) *Food.*
      Yes, food.
      Is a tree in the same class? (Pause. Signal.) *No.*
      No, it's not in the same class.
      So soup and a tree are in different classes.
   c. Soup and a motorboat. (Pause.)
      Are they in the same class or in different classes? (Pause. Signal.) *Different classes.*
      You're right. They are in different classes.
      What class is soup in? (Pause. Signal.) *Food.*
      Yes, food.
      Is a motorboat in the same class? (Pause. Signal.) *No.*
      No, it's not in the same class.
      So soup and a motorboat are in different classes.

Lesson 112: Same/Different—Class

In this exercise the children apply the concept of **same and different** to what they have learned about classes.

Teaching Techniques

The pauses indicated in the exercise are important. Give the children ample thinking time before signaling for their response.

Corrections

If the children answer the first question in part 2 incorrectly, say, Listen. What class is soup in? The children say *Food.* Then say, So are soup and an apple in the same class? The children say *yes.* Then return to the beginning of part 2. Adapt this correction for questions about objects in a different class.

EXERCISE 2   Same/Different

1. We're going to tell why things are the same and why they are different.
   A bird and an airplane. Think of them. Why are they the same? (Call on a child. Accept reasonable responses such as *Because they both fly*.)

2. My turn. I'm going to name some ways that they are different.
   a. Listen. A bird is alive, but an airplane is not alive. Everybody, say that. (Signal.) *A bird is alive, but an airplane is not alive.*
      That's one way they are different.
   b. Listen. A bird is an animal, but an airplane is not an animal. Everybody, say that. (Signal.) *A bird is an animal, but an airplane is not an animal.*
      That's another way they are different.

3. Now it's your turn.
   a. Raise your hand if you can name a way that a bird and an airplane are different. (Call on a child. If the child gives an appropriate response, say:) Everybody, say that. (Signal.) ●
   b. Name another way that a bird and an airplane are different.
      (Call on another child. If the child gives an appropriate response, say:) Everybody, say that. (Signal.)
   c. (Repeat step b until all the children who have raised their hands have responded.)

─ **CORRECTIONS** ─

EXERCISE 2

● **Error**
(The child cannot give an appropriate response.)

Correction
(If necessary, prompt the child with these questions.)
Is a plane a vehicle?
Does a bird have windows?
Does an airplane have feathers?
Does an airplane breathe?
Is a bird made of metal?

Lesson 113: Same/Different

In this exercise the children make observations about how two objects can be different. You give them two examples of how two objects are different, then they make observations of their own. They have to name ways in which the objects are different.

Teaching Techniques

- In part 3, the children are to name ways in which an airplane and a bird are different. Acceptable responses include any that you have provided as examples in part 2.

- Have the children repeat acceptable responses, then call on other children to name additional ways the two objects differ.

- Listen carefully to all responses and praise children who give unique responses.

Corrections

If the children do not produce any responses in part 3, repeat part 2. Then present part 3 again. Praise the children even if they repeat only the responses you specified. Then suggest another response. Keep prompting the children until they begin to give good responses.

Have fun with these exercises. Accept all reasonable answers. If the children come up with many different responses, have the group repeat only two or three. But do have everyone complete the statement You told me how a bird and an airplane are. . . . (signal).

If all the previous same/different exercises have been well taught, the children should do well on these review exercises. If you don't get any answers after a couple of seconds, give an example. This procedure will usually get the children started.

Some, All, None
Lessons 87–100

The words **some, all,** and **none** are used in many teacher instructions and written directions. The objective of this track is that the children will learn the precise meaning of each of these words. The meaning of each word is first demonstrated in an actions exercise: **All** is introduced first, then **some** and how it differs in meaning from **all. None** is taught last, in exercises that contrast its meaning to **all** and **some.**

In lesson 91 (not shown), the children learn to use **some** and **all** in picture exercises. Later in the program, **some, all,** and **none** appear in the concept applications track.

Lesson 87: Actions—Some/All

In this first exercise the children learn the difference between **all** and **not all.**

Teaching Techniques

• Because you are sometimes holding up all your fingers, you cannot use the hand-drop signal in this exercise. You can signal by moving your hands up and down or by tapping your foot. In any case, be sure to maintain the same timing you use with the hand-drop signal.

• Keep the pacing brisk. Move from one step to another without pausing between steps. When the children are to repeat the statement, make the pause longer.

EXERCISE 1   Actions—Some/All

1. Look at my hands.
   a. My turn. I'm going to hold up all of my fingers. What am I going to hold up? (Signal.) *All of your fingers.*
   b. Here I go. (Hold up all ten fingers.) What am I holding up? (Signal.) *All of your fingers.*
      Say the whole thing. (Signal.) *You are holding up all of your fingers.*
   c. Your turn. Hold up all of your fingers. (Signal. Wait.)
      What are you holding up? (Signal.) *All of my fingers.*
      Say the whole thing. (Signal.) *I am holding up all of my fingers.*
   d. (Repeat part 1 until all children's responses are firm.)

2. Put your hands down. Watch me.
   a. (Hold up four fingers.) Am I holding up all of my fingers? (Signal.) *No.*
      (Hold up nine fingers.) Am I holding up all of my fingers? (Signal.) *No.*
      (Hold up three fingers.) Am I holding up all of my fingers? (Signal.) *No.*
   b. (Hold up ten fingers.) Am I holding up all of my fingers? (Signal.) *Yes.*
      What am I holding up? (Signal.) *All of your fingers.*
      Say the whole thing. (Signal.) *You are holding up all of your fingers.*
   c. (Repeat part 2 until all children's responses are firm.)

Individual Turns
(Repeat part 2, calling on different children for each step.)

• Make sure the children correctly say the statements in the exercise, pronouncing each word and maintaining an appropriate rate.

EXERCISE 1   Actions—Some/All

1. Look at my hands.
   a. (Hold up four fingers.) Am I holding up **all** of my fingers? (Signal.) *No.*
   I'm not holding up **all** of my fingers. I'm holding up **some** of my fingers.
   b. (Hold up eight fingers.) Am I holding up **all** of my fingers? (Signal.) *No.*
   I'm holding up **some** of my fingers.
   c. (Hold up nine fingers.) Am I holding up all of my fingers? (Signal.) *No.*
   I'm holding up **some** of my fingers.
   d. (Repeat part 1 until all children's responses are firm.)

2. Watch me. Tell me if I hold up **all** of my fingers or **some** of my fingers.
   a. Watch. (Hold up ten fingers.) Is this all of my fingers or some of my fingers? (Signal.) *All of your fingers.*
   b. Watch. (Hold up nine fingers.) Is this all of my fingers or some of my fingers? (Signal.) *Some of your fingers.*
   c. Watch. (Hold up six fingers.) Is this all of my fingers or some of my fingers? (Signal.) *Some of your fingers.*
   d. Watch. (Hold up ten fingers.) Is this all of my fingers or some of my fingers? (Signal.) *All of your fingers.*
   e. (Repeat steps a through d until all children's responses are firm.)
   f. (Hold up four fingers.) Is this **all** of my fingers or **some** of my fingers? (Signal.) *Some of your fingers.*
   Say the whole thing about what I am holding up. (Signal.) *You are holding up some of your fingers.*
   g. (Repeat step f until all children's responses are firm.)

3. Now it's your turn.
   a. Hold up all of your fingers. (Signal.) What are you holding up? (Signal.) *All of my fingers.*
   b. Put your fingers down.
   Hold up **some** of your fingers. (Signal. Quickly point to each child who is holding up some of his/her fingers. Say:) _____ is holding up some of his/her fingers. Put your hands down.
   c. (Repeat steps a and b until all children's responses are firm.)
   d. Everybody, hold up some of your fingers. (Signal.)
   What are you holding up? (Signal.) *Some of my fingers.*
   Say the whole thing. (Signal.) *I am holding up some of my fingers.*
   e. (Repeat step d until all children's responses are firm.)

Lesson 88: Actions—Some/All

This exercise introduces the word **some.**

Teaching Techniques

First you demonstrate what **some** means, then you present a series of examples. Go through these quickly. In part 3, the children must follow your instructions, holding up some or all of their fingers. If a child holds up one finger, say, Yes, that's some of your fingers. Step b demonstrates the idea that **some** is not a specific number of fingers.

In lesson 94 (not shown), a similar exercise introduces the word **none.**

EXERCISE 4   Some/All

[**Note:** You will need an extra piece of paper for this exercise.]

1. Look at the boys. Tell me if I cover up some of the boys or all of the boys.
   a. (Cover two boys.) Did I cover up some of the boys or all of the boys? (Signal.)
      Some of the boys.
      Say the whole thing about what I did. (Signal.) *You covered up some of the boys.*
   b. (Cover all the boys.) Did I cover up some of the boys or all of the boys? (Signal.)
      All of the boys.
      Say the whole thing about what I did. (Signal.) *You covered up all of the boys.*
   c. (Cover three boys.) Did I cover up some of the boys or all of the boys? (Signal.)
      Some of the boys.
      Say the whole thing about what I did. (Signal.) *You covered up some of the boys.*

2. (Repeat part 1 until all children's responses are firm. Praise the children.)

Lesson 91: Some/All

The first picture exercise appears at lesson 91, after **some** and **all** have been introduced in actions exercises. The picture exercises should be easy if the children's responses were firm on the actions exercises.

Teaching Techniques

- In part 1 you hold a piece of paper over the pictures of the boys. Ask the question, Did I cover up some of the boys or all of the boys? Signal the response using the hand-drop signal or a foot tap, and then quickly move to the next step.

- You should be able to do the steps in quick succession.

Corrections

If the children make a mistake on either the **all** question or the **some** question, stop them and lift up the paper. Say, Watch me. Then slowly cover the same number of boys as before. Ask, Did I cover **some** or **all** of the boys? Repeat the entire sequence until the children are responding correctly.

Actions—Or
Lessons 97–110

This track has only actions exercises, although the concept **or** appears in the concept application track.

The concept **or** is one of the most important in logical reasoning. When children are able to figure out alternative possibilities, they can work a large range of logical problems. If they are to have an adequate idea of possibilities and know how to express them, they must be able to use statements containing **or.**

Young children, however, often have trouble saying the word **or** in a statement such as "She will go on the swing **or** the slide." They may say **and** or **are** or omit the word. The actions exercises in this track demonstrate the meaning of the word and give children practice in using it.

The objectives of the track are that the children learn

1. how to talk about more than one possibility, using **or;**

2. the relationship between **or** alternatives and the word **maybe;**

3. to give oral responses that contain the word **or.**

EXERCISE 2   Actions—Or

1. I'm going to do something. See if you can figure out what I'm going to do.
   a. Listen. I'm going to frown or smile. What am I going to do? (Signal.) *Frown or smile.* (Repeat step a until all children's responses are firm.)
      Yes, **maybe** I'll frown **or maybe** I'll smile.
   b. Listen. I'm going to frown or smile. Am I going to drink juice? (Signal.) *No.*
      Am I going to frown? (Signal.) *Maybe.*
      Am I going to smile? (Signal.) *Maybe.*
      (Repeat step b until all children's responses are firm.)
   c. I'm going to frown or smile. What am I going to do? (Signal.) *Frown or smile.*
      Here I go. (Smile.) Did I frown? (Signal.) *No.*
      Did I smile? (Signal.) *Yes.*
   d. What did I do? (Signal.) *Smiled.*
      Say the whole thing. (Signal.) *You smiled.*
      (Repeat step d until all children's responses are firm.)

2. (Repeat part 1 until all children's responses are firm.)

Lesson 97: Actions—Or

Teaching Techniques

- In part 1 make sure that the children are actually saying **or** when they make the response *frown or smile.* (They may become confused and actually be saying **are.**) Listen carefully to their responses.

- Pause before each question. If you rush the children, they may make mistakes.

- Exaggerate your action at step c, then quickly ask the questions Did I frown? Did I smile?

Corrections

To correct mistakes in pronouncing **or,**

1. say the word. Listen. **Or.** Everybody say that. Repeat until responses are firm.

2. present the phrase "frown or smile." Listen. Frown **or** smile. Everybody, say that. Make sure that the children are saying **or** and are stressing the word.

3. repeat step a. Listen. I'm going to frown or smile. What am I going to do? Repeat this sequence until all the children's responses are firm.

If children say yes to the question Am I going to frown? in step b, correct in this manner: **Maybe** I'll frown and maybe I'll smile. My turn. I'm going to frown **or** smile. Am I going to frown? **Maybe.** Am I going to drink juice? **No.** Your turn. Am I going to frown? **The children respond** *maybe.*

Expect to repeat this correction a few times. Make sure that the children are responding *maybe* to the questions Am I going to frown? and Am I going to smile?

If the children miss the questions in step c, ask, What did I do? Then ask either Did I frown? or Did I smile?

If the children make mistakes in steps b or c, repeat the exercise from step a.

Before and **after** are used to relate events on a time scale. When a child goes down a slide, he first climbs the ladder, then slides down the slide, then stands up on the ground. When you ask the child questions about this series of events— what happened **before** what—you are asking him to remember the order of events and then to specify which event preceded another.

The concept **after** is easier for children than **before** because children are dealing with events in a normal order when using **after.** To talk about an event that occurred before, they must take one step back in time.

The objectives of the Before/After track are

1. to relate the words **first** and **next** to the words **before** and **after;**

2. to teach the meaning of the word **after** and to demonstrate its relationship to **next;**

3. to teach **before** as the opposite of **after;**

4. to apply both **before** and **after** to comic-strip picture sequences.

EXERCISE 2 Actions—First, Before, After

1. It's time for some actions.
   a. Listen. **First** you're going to stamp your foot. **Then** you're going to touch your nose. What are you going to do **first?** (Signal.) *Stamp my foot.*
      What are you going to do **after** you stamp your foot? (Signal.) *Touch my nose.*
   b. (Repeat step a until all children's responses are firm.)
   c. Everybody, show me what you do **first**. (Signal. The children stamp their foot.) What are you doing? (Signal.) *Stamping my foot.*
   d. What are you going to do **after** you stamp your foot? (Signal.) *Touch my nose.*
      Do it. (Signal. The children touch their nose.)
      What are you doing? (Signal.) *Touching my nose.*
   e. What did you do **before** you touched your nose? (Signal.) *Stamped my foot.*
      Yes, you stamped your foot.
      (Repeat step e until all children's responses are firm.)

2. (Repeat part 1 until all children's responses are firm.)

3. Let's do another one.
   a. Listen. **First** you're going to clap. **Then** you're going to wave. **Then** you're going to touch the floor.
   b. What are you going to do first? (Signal.) *Clap.*
      What are you going to do **after** you clap? (Signal.) *Wave.*
      What are you going to do **after** you wave? (Signal.) *Touch the floor.*
      (Repeat step b until all children's responses are firm.)
   c. Everybody, show me what you do **first**. (Signal. The children clap.) What are you doing? (Signal.) *Clapping.*
   d. What are you going to do **after** you clap? (Signal.) *Wave.*
      Do it. (The children wave.)
      What are you doing now? (Signal.) *Waving.*
      What did you do before you waved? (Signal.) *Clapped.*
   e. Listen. What are you going to do after you wave? (Signal.) *Touch the floor.*
      Do it. (Each child is to touch the floor.)
      What are you doing now? (Signal.) *Touching the floor.*

4. (Repeat part 3 until all children's responses are firm.)

Individual Turns
(Repeat parts 1 and 3, calling on different children for each step.)

Lesson 98: Actions—First, Before, After

Starting in lesson 98 children learn **before.** In this exercise, the meaning of **before** is related to **after.** In part 1 the children do a two-part action routine, answering **before** and **after** questions. Part 3 involves a three-part exercise (clap, wave, touch the floor). The pattern of both parts of the task is the same; first the children work on **after,** then on **before.**

Teaching Techniques

Make sure the children can respond to the questions in part 1 before proceeding to part 3.

Corrections

Expect the children to have trouble with **before** questions. For example, in part 3, when they answer the question What did you do before you waved? they may say *Touch the floor.* To correct, say, You told me what you did **after** you waved. I want to know what you did **before** you waved. Repeat the question. If children still have trouble, show the action sequence and point out when you clap That's what I do **before** I wave. Then return to part 3 and repeat all of the steps.

EXERCISE 1   Actions—Before

1. Here's the first game.

  a. Watch me. (Clap your hands.) What am I doing? (Signal.) *Clapping.*
  (Touch your knees and keep touching them.) What am I doing now? (Signal.) *Touching your knees.*

  b. What did I do **before** I touched my knees? (Signal.) *Clapped.*
  Yes, I clapped.
  (Repeat until all children's responses are firm.)

  c. Let's say the whole thing about what I did before I touched my knees. (Signal. Respond with the children.) *You clapped before you touched your knees.*

  d. All by yourselves. Say the whole thing about what I did before I touched my knees. (Signal. Do not respond with the children.) *You clapped before you touched your knees.*

  e. (Repeat steps c and d until all children can make the statement.)

  f. What am I doing now? (Signal.) *Touching your knees.*
  Say the whole thing about what I am doing. (Signal.) *You are touching your knees.*
  (Repeat until all children's responses are firm.)

2. Here's a new one.

  a. Watch me. (Touch your elbow. Keep touching it.) What am I doing? (Signal.) *Touching your elbow.*
  (Stop touching your elbow. Touch your head and keep touching it.) What am I doing now? (Signal.) *Touching your head.*

  b. What did I do **before** I touched my head? (Signal.) *Touched your elbow.*
  Yes, I touched my elbow.
  (Repeat until all children's responses are firm.)

  c. Say the whole thing about what I did before I touched my head. (Signal. Do not respond with the children.) *You touched your elbow before you touched your head.*
  (Repeat until all children's responses are firm.)

  d. What am I doing now? (Signal.) *Touching your head.*
  Say the whole thing about what I am doing. (Signal.) *You are touching your head.*
  (Repeat until all children's responses are firm.)

Individual Turns
(Repeat the exercise, calling on different children for each step.)

Lesson 103: Actions—Before

In this exercise, the children make complete statements using the word **before.** They make complete statements with **after** in later exercises.

Teaching Techniques

In steps c and d the children make the **before** statement. Be sure the children's responses are firm before going to the next steps.

Corrections

If the children have trouble making the statements, use the model-lead-and-test procedure to help them.

EXERCISE 4   After

1. These pictures tell a story about what a man did.
   a. (Point to a.)
      First the man got out of the car. What did he do? (Touch.) *Got out of the car.*
   b. (Point to b.)
      Then he changed the tire. What did he do? (Touch.) *Changed the tire.*
   c. (Point to c.)
      Then he got in the car. What did he do? (Touch.) *Got in the car.*
   d. (Point to d.)
      Then he drove away. What did he do? (Touch.) *Drove away.*

2. Let's make it a little harder. Look at the pictures. ●
   a. (Point to a.) What did the man do first? (Touch.) *Got out of the car.*
   b. (Point to b.) What did he do **after** he got out of the car? (Touch.) *Changed the tire.*
   c. (Point to c.) What did he do **after** he changed the tire? (Touch.) *Got in the car.*
   d. (Point to d.) What did he do **after** he got in the car? (Touch.) *Drove away.*

3. (Repeat part 2 until all the children's responses are firm.)

4. Let's do it again. This time I'm not going to point to the pictures.
   a. What did the man do first? (Signal.) *Got out of the car.*
   b. What did he do **after** he got out of the car? (Signal.) *Changed the tire.*
   c. What did he do **after** he changed the tire? (Signal.) *Got in the car.*
   d. What did he do **after** he got in the car? (Signal.) *Drove away.*

5. (Repeat part 4 until all children's responses are firm.)

CORRECTIONS

EXERCISE 4

● **Error**
(Use the following correction for any error the children make in part 2.)

Correction
1. (Touch the appropriate picture.) Here's what he did after he . . .
2. What did he do after . . . ?
3. (Repeat part 2.)

Lesson 101: After

Starting in lesson 101, the children work from picture sequences in the before/after exercises. The first exercises are only with **after;** a similar exercise in lesson 105 combines **before** and **after.**

Teaching Techniques

In part 2 you should touch the pictures in the following way to signal responses: 1) Touch picture a to signal response to the question What did the man do first? 2) Keep touching picture a as you ask the question What did he do after he got out of the car? 3) Then touch picture b and keep touching it as you ask, What did he do after he changed the tire? 4) Touch picture c and keep touching it as you present the next question.

Practice this touching procedure. It helps the children see how the progression from picture to picture relates to the series of **after** questions.

Note that you are not to point or touch in part 4. The children must be firm before you present the final series of questions.

Corrections

Expect the children to give responses other than those called for by the exercise. Instead of saying *Changed the tire,* they may say, *He is pumping up that tire.* Instead of saying *Got in the car,* they may say *Get in the car.* Instead of saying *Drove away,* they may say *Droved away* or *Drived away.*

Accept these answers if they express the correct idea and are consistent with what is shown in the picture. Then tell the children the response in the book: Let's say **drove away.** Say it. Repeat the question until the children's responses are firm. Then continue the exercise.

If–Then Rules
Lessons 120–150

This track introduces the children to deductive reasoning. An **if-then** "rule" is actually a statement with a premise and a conclusion. The initial rules that the children work with do not refer to real life *(if it rains, the flowers will grow)* but to made-up situations *(if a door is striped, it has a lion behind it).* This tactic forces the children to focus on the information in the

statement rather than on knowledge they already have or on intuition. The skill of applying specific information (deductive reasoning) is very important in working mathematical and scientific problems, where the answers are not obvious but are predictable from **if-then** rules.

The **if-then** statements, or rules, have two parts—the **if** part and the **then** part: *If a dog is fat,* (then) *he has a bone.* The key to understanding this statement is to focus on the first part. If the dog is fat, the second part of the statement will be true. The statement does not say anything about dogs that are not fat. They may or may not have a bone.

In this track the children will learn

1. the meaning of **if-then** by means of a game in which the children respond to a command **only if** a specified condition is fulfilled *(if the teacher says "go," touch your head);*

2. to apply an **if-then** rule by selecting from a group of pictures the picture or pictures that fulfill the condition in the **if** part of the rule;

3. to make up **if-then** rules based on features of objects illustrated.

EXERCISE 1   Actions—If-then Rules

1. Get ready to learn a rule and play a game.
  a. Listen to this rule: If the teacher says "Go," touch your head.
  b. Listen again. If the teacher says "Go," touch your head.
  c. Everybody, say the rule with me. **(Signal.)** *If the teacher says "Go," touch your head.*
  d. All by yourselves. Say the rule. **(Signal.)** *If the teacher says "Go," touch your head.*
  e. (Repeat steps a through d until all children can say the rule.)

2. Tell me.
  a. What are you going to do if the teacher says "Go"? **(Signal.)** *Touch my head.* ● ◆
  b. Are you going to touch your head if the teacher says "Go"? **(Signal.)** *Yes.*
  c. Are you going to touch your head if the teacher says "Touch your head"? **(Signal.)** *No.*
  d. Are you going to touch your head if the teacher says "Stand up"? **(Signal.)** *No.*

3. Now we're going to play a game. Remember—if the teacher says "Go," touch your head. Wait for my signal.
  a. Let's see if I can fool you. Get ready. (Pause.) **Go.** (Signal. The children touch their head.) ▲
  b. Let's see if I can fool you. Get ready. (Pause.) **Clap.** (Signal. The children should not do anything.) ■
  c. Let's see if I can fool you. Get ready. (Pause.) **Stand up.** (Signal. The children should not do anything.)
  d. (Repeat steps a through c until all children correctly perform the action.)

CORRECTIONS

EXERCISE 1

● **Error**
(Children don't say *Touch my head.*)
Correction
  1. What's the rule? (Signal.) *If the teacher says "Go," touch your head.*
  2. So, what are you going to do if the teacher says "Go"? You're going to touch your head.
  3. (Repeat part 2, step a.)

◆ **Error**
(Children perform the action.)
Correction
  1. I said **tell** me what you're going to do if I say "Go."
  2. Tell me what you're going to do if I say "Go." (Signal.) *Touch my head.*

  3. Yes, you have to wait until I say "Go" to do it.
  4. (Repeat part 2, step a.)

▲ **Error**
(Children don't perform the action.)
Correction
  1. Everybody, what did I just say? (Signal.) *Go.*
  2. And what's the rule? (Signal.) *If the teacher says "Go," touch your head.*
  3. So, what do you do when I say "Go"? (Signal.) *Touch my head.*
  4. Let's try the game again. (Repeat part 3, step a.)

■ **Error**
(Children perform the action.)
Correction
  1. Everybody, what's the rule? (Signal.) *If the teacher says "Go," touch your head.*
  2. Did I say "Go"? (Signal.) *No.*
  3. So, should you touch your head? (Signal.) *No.*
  4. Let's try the game again. (Repeat part 3, step b.)

Lesson 120: Actions—Rules

In this exercise the children play a game. They are to respond to a command **if** the teacher does the action specified in the first part of the rule. If the teacher does anything else, they are to do nothing.

Teaching Techniques

• In part 1, present the rule as follows: If the teacher says "go," **(pause)** touch your head.

• Make sure that all the children can say the rule before you move to part 2.

• Present part 3 of the exercise as a game—challenge the children. Let them know you would **like** to fool them.

Corrections

If the children have trouble saying the rule, repeat the model-lead-and-test procedure specified in part 1.

If the children make errors, follow the corrections specified in the box. You will need to practice these corrections, as you will probably have occasion to use all of them.

EXERCISE 5 Constructing Rules

Let's make up rules for these painters.

1. Look at the painters who are tall.
   a. Listen. If a painter is tall, what part of the room is he painting? (Signal.) *The ceiling.*
   b. You're going to say the rule. Start with "If a painter is tall" and tell what he is painting. (Signal.) *If a painter is tall, he is painting the ceiling.*
   c. (Repeat step b until all children can say the rule.)

2. Look at the painters who are short.
   a. Listen. If a painter is short, what part of the room is he painting? (Signal.) *The wall.*
   b. So what's the rule if a painter is short? (Signal.) *If a painter is short, he is painting the wall.*
   c. (Repeat step b until all children can say the rule.)

3. Let's say those rules again.
   a. What's the rule about a painter who is short? (Signal.) *If a painter is short, he is painting the wall.*
   b. What's the rule about a painter who is tall? (Signal.) *If a painter is tall, he is painting the ceiling.*

4. (Repeat part 3 until all children can say the rules.)

Individual Turns
(Repeat the exercise, calling on different children for each step.)

Lesson 132: Rules

In this exercise the children help make up the "rule" by observing features of the picture.

Teaching Techniques

Pause after the questions so that the children can consider their responses. When you ask what the rule is, emphasize the words **tall** and **short.**

Corrections

If the children do not respond to the first question, If a painter is tall, what part of the room is he painting? correct as follows:

1. Show me a painter who is tall.

   Show me another painter who is tall.

2. Point to the first tall man. What part of the room is this painter painting? *The ceiling.*

3. So, if a painter is tall, what part of the room is he painting? *The ceiling.*

Repeat this step with the second tall man.

If necessary, use the same procedure for the next questions. Then repeat the entire exercise.

Where, Who, When, What
Lessons 116–150

When this track begins, the children have already had experience with **where** questions (in the prepositions track) and with a variety of **what** questions and **who** questions (in the actions track). **When** questions are introduced in this track. Primary-grade teachers ask these types of questions when they ask children questions about their reading. Children who can accurately answer **where, what, who,** and **when** questions about pictures, spoken sentences, and paragraphs will be ready to deal with questions when they are asked about stories they read.

The objective of the track is to help the children learn to listen to and discriminate between questions that start with **who, what, where,** and **when,** and to respond to them.

EXERCISE 3   When

1. Listen.
   a. First the boy ran. Then the boy sat. Once more. First the boy ran. Then the boy sat.
   b. What did the boy do first? (Signal.) *Ran.* Then what did the boy do? (Signal.) *Sat.*

2. Listen.
   a. The boy sat after he ran. Say that. (Signal.) *The boy sat after he ran.*
   b. My turn. When did the boy sit? After he ran.
      Your turn. When did the boy sit? (Signal.) *After he ran.*

3. Listen.
   a. The boy ran before he sat. Say that. (Signal.) *The boy ran before he sat.*
   b. When did the boy run? (Signal.) *Before he sat.*

4. (Repeat parts 1 through 3 until all children's responses are firm.)

Individual Turns
(Repeat the exercise, calling on different children for each step.)

EXERCISE 5   Where, Who, When, What

1. These pictures tell a story about what an owl did.
   a. (Point to the ladder in picture a.)
      This ladder is next to the tree. Where is this ladder? (Touch.) *Next to the tree.*
      (Point to a.)
      First the owl climbed the ladder. Who climbed the ladder? (Touch.) *The owl.*
   b. (Point to b.)
      What is the owl doing in this picture? (Touch.) *Eating an apple.*
      (Repeat part 1 until all children's responses are firm.)

2. Now I'm not going to touch the pictures.
   a. Everybody, what did the owl do first? (Signal.) *Climbed the ladder.*
      Yes.
   b. My turn. When did it climb the ladder? Before it ate the apple.
      Your turn. When did it climb the ladder? (Signal.) *Before it ate the apple.*
   c. (Repeat part 2 until all children's responses are firm.)

3. Now answer these questions.
   a. What did the owl eat? (Signal.) *An apple.*
   b. Where was the ladder? (Signal.) *Next to the tree.*
   c. Who climbed the ladder? (Signal.) *The owl.*
   d. (Repeat part 3 until all children's responses are firm.)

4. Let's do those questions again.
   a. Who climbed the ladder? (Signal.) *The owl.*
   b. Where is the ladder? (Signal.) *Next to the tree.*
   c. When did the owl climb the ladder? (Signal.) *Before it ate the apple.*

d. (Repeat part 4 until all children's responses are firm.)

5. (Repeat parts 1 through 4 until all children's responses are firm.)

Individual Turns
(Repeat the exercise, calling on different children for each step.)

This exercise and the exercise on page 117 are the first two exercises in the **where, who, when,** and **what** track. In exercise 3 the children focus on **when** by responding to your questions about what a boy did and when he did what he did. In exercise 5, the children respond to a group of **who, what, where,** and **when** questions. The concepts **before** and **after** are also incorporated into these exercises.

Teaching Techniques

Starting in part 2 in exercise 5, you do not touch the pictures. You want the children to respond to the words in the questions. You also need to pause after each response before presenting the next question. Give the children time to think—if you rush them, they will make errors.

Corrections

To correct any mistake, tell the children the right answer. Then repeat the question. If they make more than one mistake in part 4, repeat the entire exercise. If the children start making mistakes, you should pause before signaling their response.

Classification

Classification Lessons 46–131

Children who are able to identify an object such as a car may not understand the relationship between a car and the broader class **vehicles,** which includes not only cars but also other objects that have a particular set of features. For example, when we say that a car is a vehicle, we indicate that it shares some features with trucks, boats, and other members of the class **vehicles.**

Classification concepts are important in logical reasoning for these reasons:

1. They prepare children to group objects in different ways (for example, as cars, as vehicles, as things made of metal).

2. They support the idea that there are many things we can say about a given object—including a statement of classification.

3. Finally, the understanding of classification is essential to reasoning from analogy and other higher-order thinking skills.

In this track, the children learn

1. common classification words;

2. the names of objects that are found in each class;

3. statements for describing objects and the classes they are in;

4. classification rules for some classes and the use of these rules to determine whether or not an object is in a given class.

Following is a list of the classification concepts taught in the program and the lesson where each word first appears:

vehicles	46	clothing	69	plants	106
food	56	animals	78	tools	117
containers	66	buildings	96	furniture	128

A similar sequence of exercises is used for each class. First the children are introduced to the class name (**vehicles,** for example) used to describe a group of objects (a car, a boat, an airplane, for example). They are then shown that different members of the class have different names—often these names are already familiar to the children; others may be new. For some of the classes, a rule (a vehicle is made to take you places, for example) is then introduced and the children practice applying the rule. They also practice statements that express the relationship between the class name and the names of members of the class. Finally, they play a classification game.

Classes are reviewed and integrated with other tracks. They appear in concept application as well as in location and same/different exercises.

Lesson 46: Classification

Vehicles, the first classification concept taught, is presented in a two-page exercise (see page 121). The first page shows pictures of objects that can be classified as vehicles and objects that cannot. The second-page pictures are all of vehicles.

Teaching Techniques

- When you identify each object on the first page of the exercise as a vehicle or not a vehicle, speak in such a way that the information sounds very important. Emphasize the word **not** when you talk about objects that are **not** vehicles.

- You are testing the children's understanding with the question Is this a vehicle? Ask these questions quickly.

- In part 4 the children establish the relationship between the word **vehicle** and the objects on the page. Stress the words **this vehicle.** If you don't, the children may produce the statement *This is a vehicle* instead of *This vehicle is a car.*

Corrections

On the first page, some children will answer the question Is this a vehicle? with *No, it's a car.* Follow the correction specified in the corrections box. Let the children know that what they are saying is reasonable, but do not labor the correction or get into lengthy explanations.

EXERCISE 4   Classification

1. We're going to talk about vehicles.
   (Point to a.) This is a vehicle.
   (Point to b.) This is not a vehicle.
   (Point to c.) This is not a vehicle.
   (Point to d.) This is a vehicle.
   (Point to e.) This is a vehicle.
   (Point to f.) This is a vehicle.

2. Get ready to tell me which objects are vehicles.
   (Point to each object and ask:) Is this a vehicle? ●
   (The children answer *yes* or *no*.)

3. Now let's look at some more vehicles.
   (Turn the page quickly.)

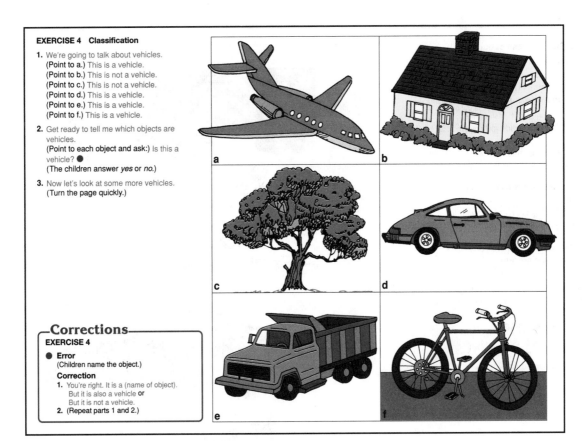

─Corrections─

EXERCISE 4

● **Error**
   (Children name the object.)
   Correction
   1. You're right. It is a (name of object).
      But it is also a vehicle **or**
      But it is not a vehicle.
   2. (Repeat parts 1 and 2.)

EXERCISE 4   Classification (cont.)

4. Let's talk about these pictures.
   a. (Point to a.) Is this a vehicle? (Touch.) *Yes.*
      Say the whole thing. (Touch.) *This is a vehicle.*
      What kind of vehicle is this? (Touch.) *A car.*
      Yes, this vehicle is a car.
      Say the whole thing about **this vehicle.**
      (Touch.) *This vehicle is a car.*
   b. (Repeat step a until all children's responses are firm.)
   c. (Point to b.) Is this a vehicle? (Touch.) *Yes.*
      Say the whole thing. (Touch.) *This is a vehicle.*
      What kind of vehicle is this? (Touch.) *A bike.*
      Yes, this vehicle is a bike.
      Say the whole thing about **this vehicle.**
      (Touch.) *This vehicle is a bike.*
   d. (Repeat step c until all children's responses are firm.)
   e. (Point to c.) Is this a vehicle? (Touch.) *Yes.*
      Say the whole thing. (Touch.) *This is a vehicle.*
      What kind of vehicle is this? (Touch.) *A truck.*
      Yes, this vehicle is a truck.
      Say the whole thing about **this vehicle.**
      (Touch.) *This vehicle is a truck.*
   f. (Repeat step e until all children's responses are firm.)
   g. (Point to d.) Is this a vehicle? (Touch.) *Yes.*
      Say the whole thing. (Touch.) *This is a vehicle.*
      What kind of vehicle is this? (Touch.) *An airplane.*
      Yes, this vehicle is an airplane.
      Say the whole thing about **this vehicle.**
      (Touch.) *This vehicle is an airplane.*

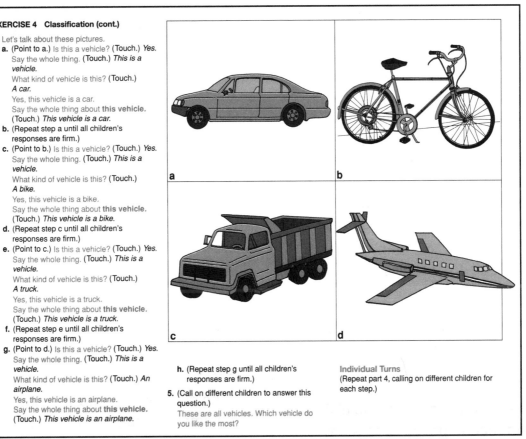

   h. (Repeat step g until all children's responses are firm.)

5. (Call on different children to answer this question.)
   These are all vehicles. Which vehicle do you like the most?

Individual Turns
(Repeat part 4, calling on different children for each step.)

EXERCISE 7 **Classification**

1. We're going to learn a rule about vehicles. (Point to each vehicle and ask:) What kind of vehicle is this? (The children are to answer *a truck, an airplane, a car, a canoe.*)

2. Here's a rule about all vehicles.
   a. Listen. If it is made to take you places, it is a vehicle.
   Listen again. If it is made to take you places, it is a vehicle.
   b. Everybody, say the rule with me. (Signal. Respond with the children.) If it is made to take you places, it is a vehicle.
   c. Again. (Signal. Respond with the children.) If it is made to take you places, it is a vehicle.
   d. (Repeat step c until all children's responses are firm.)

3. All by yourselves.
   Say the rule about vehicles. (Signal.) *If it is made to take you places, it is a vehicle.* Again. (Signal.) *If it is made to take you places, it is a vehicle.*

4. Now let's look at the objects on the next page.
   (Turn the page quickly.)

Lesson 51: Classification

The word "rule" as used in the classification exercises refers to a statement that is true of all the examples covered by the rule. Rules are taught for these classifications: vehicles, food, plants, containers, clothing, buildings, and tools. The rule for vehicles is *If it is made to take you places, it is a vehicle.*

The first page of the exercise in which the rule is introduced appears above.

Teaching Techniques

To make the rule easier for the children to hear and repeat, present it this way: **If** (pause) it is made to **take** you places (pause) it is a **vehicle.** You stress **if** when they try to say the statement. The pause helps them hear if it, which may be a tongue-twister for some children.

Stressing **-es** in **places** calls the children's attention to the last word in the phrase and also to the ending (which some children omit). The pause after **places** allows the children to say the second part of the sentence more easily: *it is a vehicle.*

Corrections

If the children have trouble saying the statement, break the statement into two

EXERCISE 7   Classification (cont.)

5. We'll talk about these pictures.
   a. (Point to a.)
   Can this take you places? (Touch.) *No.*
   A tree can **not** take you places. So what do you know about a tree? (Touch.) *It's not a vehicle.*
   Again. What do you know about a tree? (Touch.) *It's not a vehicle.*
   (Repeat step a until all children's responses are firm.)
   b. (Point to b.)
   Can this take you places? (Touch.) *Yes.*
   If it is made to take you places, it's a . . . (touch) *vehicle.*
   A boat can take you places. So what do you know about a boat? (Touch.) *It's a vehicle.*
   Again. What do you know about a boat? (Touch.) *It's a vehicle.*
   (Repeat step b until all children's responses are firm.)
   c. (Point to c.)
   Can this take you places? (Touch.) *Yes.*
   If it is made to take you places, it's a . . . (touch) *vehicle.*
   A taxi can take you places. So what do you know about a taxi? (Touch.) *It's a vehicle.*
   Again. What do you know about a taxi? (Touch.) *It's a vehicle.*
   (Repeat step c until all children's responses are firm.)

6. (Repeat part 5 until all children's responses are firm.)

Individual Turns
(Repeat part 5, calling on different children for each step.)

parts as described above. First have them say, *If* (pause) *it is made to take you places;* then have them say *it is a vehicle.* Finally, have them say the whole statement.

Some children will not need this help; they will say the statement after a few trials. Others, however, may require many corrected repetitions before producing the statement correctly.

Lesson 51: Classification (second page)

Teaching Techniques

Your presentation of the steps in part 5 should indicate that they go together. As soon as the children answer *no* to the first question, present the next line immediately. Pause a second before you touch the picture. After the children say, *It's not a vehicle,* ask the final question.

Corrections

In step b some of the children may respond to the question So what do you know about a boat? by saying *vehicle* or *vehicles.* Correct by saying, **It is** a vehicle. Then return to the beginning of step b. The reason for holding the children to the responses *it is a vehicle* (or *it's a vehicle*) is that the wording appears in the rule *If it is made to take you places, it is a vehicle.* The wording "it is" makes the relationship of the rule to the response more obvious.

If children have trouble answering any of the questions in part 5, repeat all the steps on the page until their responses are firm.

Lesson 74: Classification

This exercise is a word game that is used with different classes throughout the rest of the program.

To perform successfully in this exercise, the children must be able to keep in mind the class term being used, relate the objects you name to the term, and decide whether or not each object belongs in the class. Children like playing this game.

EXERCISE 3   Classification

1. Let's see if you remember the different rules we've learned.
   a. What's the rule about food? (Signal.) *If you can eat it, it is food.*
      What's the rule about clothing? (Signal.) *If you can wear it, it is clothing.*
      What's the rule about vehicles? (Signal.) *If it is made to take you places, it is a vehicle.*
      What's the rule about containers? (Signal.) *If you put things in it, it is a container.*
   b. (Repeat step a until all children's responses are firm.)

2. Listen. We're going to play a game about foods. I'm going to name some foods, but don't let me fool you.
   a. If I name something that is a food, you say **yes.**
      If I name something that is not a food, you say **no.**
   b. What are you going to say if it is a food? (Signal.) *Yes.*
      What are you going to say if it is not a food? (Signal.) *No.*

3. Remember, I'm going to name some foods, but I may fool you.
   a. Listen. (Pause.) Peanut. (Signal.) *Yes.*
      Cheese. (Signal.) *Yes.*
      Boy. (Signal.) *No.*
      Why did you say no? (Signal.) *Because a boy is not food.*
   b. Listen. (Pause.) Egg. (Signal.) *Yes.*
      Lettuce. (Signal.) *Yes.*
      Popcorn. (Signal.) *Yes.*
      Hammer. (Signal.) *No.*
      Why did you say no? (Signal.) *Because a hammer is not food.*
   c. Listen. (Pause.) Pie. (Signal.) *Yes.*
      Orange. (Signal.) *Yes.*
      Meat. (Signal.) *Yes.*
      Banana. (Signal.) *Yes.*
      Cup. (Signal.) *No.*
      Why did you say no? (Signal.) *Because a cup is not food.*
   d. Listen. (Pause.) Potato. (Signal.) *Yes.*
      Salad. (Signal.) *Yes.*
      Hamburger. (Signal.) *Yes.*
      Umbrella. (Signal.) *No.*
      Why did you say no? (Signal.) *Because an umbrella is not food.*
   e. (Repeat part 3 until all children's responses are firm.)

Teaching Techniques

Present this activity as a game—it's played according to rules and with the goal of winning. Act as if you enjoy the idea of being able to fool the children. When they respond correctly, act a little disappointed, saying, for example, You children are too smart for me.

Don't give away the correct response with your expression—don't smile when you name a food and frown when you name something else. If you want to make the game more fun for the children, smile for one food and frown for the next or maintain the same expression as you read each word on the list. Pause very briefly before you give the signal. The children must have a moment to relate the object you named to the class term—in this case, food.

Corrections

If the children don't say *no* for the non-food in the list, preface your correction by saying, I fooled you that time. **Then say,** A hammer is **not** food.

Rhyming

Rhyming
Lessons 55–73

Rhyming is particularly important in showing children the relationship between words. As a general rule, words that have the same ending and different beginnings rhyme. The words **at, fat, rat, mat, cat, bat, sat,** and **slat** all have the same ending and all rhyme. Rhyming also permits children to blend a beginning sound with the rest of the word. When a child puts the sound **c** and the ending **at**

together, the child creates a word that rhymes with **at.** That word is **cat.**

Rhyming is introduced as a language skill, starting with lesson 55. In the initial exercises, you specify words that rhyme. In later exercises, children generate words that rhyme.

Exercise 1 on page 126 is the first rhyming exercise, from lesson 55.

Teaching notes: In steps b and c, children may have some trouble saying the words **cake, lake, steak.** Don't go on until their responses are firm.

Expect some children to have trouble in step e. They may not understand at first that you want them to say the word that is appropriate for the sentence. Children generally catch on after you tell them the correct response for the sentence. If they continue to make mistakes, follow this correction procedure.

Listen and tell me if this is right. The girl had a piece of chocolate steak. Is that right? *No.*

Listen: The girl had a piece of chocolate lake? Is that right? (Signal.) *No.*

Listen: The girl had a piece of chocolate cake. Is that right? (Signal.) *Yes.*

Your turn. Say the whole thing. *The girl had a piece of chocolate cake.*

In step i, you present individual turns. Make sure that children's responses are firm.

The procedure followed in lesson 55 is repeated in subsequent lessons for different groups of rhyming words. The children say the words, then choose the correct word for different sentences.

Lesson 55

EXERCISE 1   Rhyming

a. I'm going to say three words. These words rhyme. What do they do? (Signal.) *Rhyme.* Listen: **cake, lake, steak.**

b. Listen again: **cake, lake, steak.**
Say those words. (Signal.) *Cake, lake, steak.*

c. (Repeat step b until firm.)

d. I'll say the first two words. See if **you** can say the last word. **Cake, lake** . . . Your turn. (Signal.) *Steak.*
I'll say the first word. See if you can say both the other words. Listen: **cake** . . . Your turn. (Signal.) *Lake, steak.*

e. I'll say things. When I stop, see if you can say the right rhyming word.
Listen. The girl had a piece of chocolate . . . (signal) *cake.*
Say the whole thing. (Signal.) *The girl had a piece of chocolate cake.*

f. Her dad was cooking a great big . . . (signal) *steak.*
Say the whole thing. (Signal.) *Her dad was cooking a great big steak.*

g. That girl went swimming in a . . . (signal) *lake.*
Say the whole thing. (Signal.) *That girl went swimming in a lake.*

h. Let's do those again.
Her dad was cooking a great big . . . (signal) *steak.*
Say the whole thing. (Signal.) *Her dad was cooking a great big steak.*
That girl went swimming in a . . . (signal) *lake.*
Say the whole thing. (Signal.) *That girl went swimming in a lake.*
The girl had a piece of chocolate . . . (signal) *cake.*
Say the whole thing. (Signal.) *The girl had a piece of chocolate cake.*

i. (Repeat step h, calling on different children for each sentence.)

j. You're using words that rhyme. Good for you.

In lesson 58, exercise 1, children discriminate between words that rhyme and those that don't.

The rhyming words for lesson 58 are in the same family as those introduced in lesson 55. You introduce the family then, say pairs of words. Children tell you whether or not the words rhyme.

Teaching notes: Follow the steps closely. It may not seem important to have the children say each pair of words before indicating whether the words rhyme. However, when children say words, they are learning how rhyming words are the same and learning how words that don't rhyme are different from rhyming words.

In step c, you call on different children to say words that rhyme with cake. Praise children who say more than one word.

Lesson 58

EXERCISE 1   Rhyming

a. You've learned some rhyming words. Here are words that rhyme.
Listen: **cake, bake, snake, take, shake, flake, make.**

b. I'm going to say words. You'll tell me if they rhyme.
Listen: **cake, bake.** Say those words. (Signal.) *Cake, bake.*
Do they rhyme? (Signal.) *Yes.*
Listen: **lake, snake.** Say those words. (Signal.) *Lake, snake.*
Do they rhyme? (Signal.) *Yes.*
Listen: **lake, look.** Say those words. (Signal.) *Lake, look.*
Do they rhyme? (Signal.) *No.*
Listen: **take, hat.** Say those words. (Signal.) *Take, hat.*
Do they rhyme? (Signal.) *No.*

c. Listen: **cake.** Say some words that rhyme with **cake.** (Call on different children. Repeat correct words and praise children who said them.)

Repeat correct words so that you're sure the others in the group hear the words.

Children work on exercises similar to the two exercises above through lesson 70. Children learn about new families of rhyming words **(old, gold; at, sat; sing, ring; pan, ran; clean, mean).** They also review the various families they have practiced in earlier lessons.

In lesson 71, children review sentences that they had constructed earlier to create a verse. Each verse they say has two sentences.

Here's exercise 5 from lesson 71.

Lesson 71

EXERCISE 5   Rhyming

a. Listen. She had a pretty ring. Say that. (Signal.) *She had a pretty ring.* Listen. She loved to dance and sing. Say that. (Signal.) *She loved to dance and sing.*

b. (Repeat step a until firm.)

c. Here's something that's hard. I'll say both things. See if you can say both of them just the way I do.

d. Listen. She had a pretty ring. She loved to dance and sing. Say both things. Get ready. (Signal.) *She had a pretty ring. She loved to dance and sing.*

e. (Repeat step d until firm.) You're saying sentences that rhyme.

f. Here's another one. Listen. The dog was dirty, but the cat was clean. Say that. (Signal.) *The dog was dirty, but the cat was clean.* Listen. They lived in the nicest house you've seen. Say that. (Signal.) *They lived in the nicest house you've seen.*

g. (Repeat step f until firm.)

h. I'll say both things. Listen. The dog was dirty, but the cat was clean. They lived in the nicest house you've seen. Say both things. Get ready. (Signal.) *The dog was dirty, but the cat was clean. They lived in the nicest house you've seen.*

i. (Repeat step h until firm.)

Individual Turns
(Repeat step f, calling on different children for each sentence.)

Teaching notes: In steps d and h, you say a pair of rhyming sentences that children are to repeat. Say the sentences rhythmically so the cadence is the same for both sentences and the rhyming words are stressed. You may want to clap hands or tap feet in cadence with the sentences. Make it sound like fun. Praise children who say the sentences just as you say them.

You may have to model the sentence pairs several times before all the children are firm in saying them. Provide children with the repetition they need. Once they learn the rhyming skills, they will have a very powerful tool that will help them in reading.

Problem-Solving Strategies and Applications

The tracks in this group are

Review	33–37
Concept Application	36–147
Absurdities	120–134
Inquiry	144–148

The purpose of these exercises is not to teach new concepts but to provide new contexts, new uses, and new statements for the concepts taught in the other tracks of the program.

The review exercises prepare children for the concept-application exercises. The primary activity of the concept application track is to provide children with a rule for a picture. In the concept-application exercises, a rule is a statement that is used to solve a problem. Children predict the outcome that is based on the rule. Then they receive confirmation in the form of a picture that shows the outcome.

Absurdities exercises provide an opportunity for children to use what they have learned to tell what is wrong with a picture and why it is wrong.

Inquiry activities present the children with a topic about which they are to gather information. For instance, to find out how many teeth a grown-up person should have, they identify an expert about teeth—a dentist. Then children specify the question or questions they would ask the dentist.

EXERCISE 6   Review

1. Let's look at this picture.
   a. (Point to the fence.) This is a fence. What is it? (Touch.) *A fence.*
   b. (Point to the ducks.) These are ducks. What are these? (Touch.) *Ducks.*
   c. (Point to the cow.) This is a cow. What is it? (Touch.) *A cow.*

[**Note:** Do not point to the pictures for the rest of the exercise.]

2. Look at the picture again.
   a. Someone is jumping over the fence. Who is jumping over the fence? (Signal.) *The boy.*
   Yes, the boy.
   (Call on a child.) Why is the boy doing that? (Signal. Idea: *The cow is chasing him.*)
   b. Someone is feeding the ducks. Everybody, who is feeding the ducks? (Signal.) *The woman.*
   Yes, the woman.
   c. Something is sitting on the fence. What is sitting on the fence? (Signal.) *A cat.*
   Yes, a cat.
   d. Look at the boy again. What is the boy doing? (Signal.) *Jumping over the fence.*
   Say the whole thing about what the boy is doing. (Signal.) *The boy is jumping over the fence.*
   e. Look at the woman again. What is the woman feeding? (Signal.) *The ducks.*
   Say the whole thing about what the woman is doing. (Signal.) *The woman is feeding the ducks.*
   f. Look at the cat again. What is the cat sitting on? (Signal.) *The fence.*
   Say the whole thing about what the cat is sitting on. (Signal.) *The cat is sitting on the fence.*

3. Let's do it again.
   (Repeat part 2 until all children's responses are firm.)

4. (Call on different children to answer these questions.)
   What would you do if a cow chased you?
   What would you feed the ducks?
   (Praise reasonable responses.)

Individual Turns
(Repeat part 2, calling on different children for each step.)

Review
Lessons 28–37

A primary focus of these exercises is the review of the concepts that will be used in the rules that follow in the concept-application exercises. As exercise 6 from lesson 33 shows, the children talk about the picture.

Teaching Techniques

- Do not point to the picture in part 2. The children must respond to your questions without any extra prompting.

- These exercises provide the children with a relatively easy context for practicing phrases and statements. Children may require some repetition on the phrases and the statements. Make sure that they are firm before proceeding to the next exercise, as statements of this type will occur later.

EXERCISE 5 Concept Application

1. Look at the picture. The man will kick only one of these boxes.
   Listen. The man will kick the empty box that is next to the log. Which box will he kick? (Signal. Respond with the children.) *The empty box that is next to the log.*
   Say the whole thing about the box he will kick. (Signal. Do not respond with the children.) *He will kick the empty box that is next to the log.*

2. Now we'll talk about each box.
   a. (Point to a.)
      Is this box empty? (Touch.) *Yes.*
      Is this box next to the log? (Touch.) *No.*
      So will the man kick this box? (Touch.) *No.*
      Why won't the man kick this box? (Touch.) *It isn't next to the log.*
   b. (Point to b.)
      Is this box empty? (Touch.) *No.*
      Is this box next to the log? (Touch.) *Yes.*
      So will the man kick this box? (Touch.) *No.*
      Why won't the man kick this box? (Touch.) *It isn't empty.*
   c. (Point to c.)
      Is this box empty? (Touch.) *Yes.*
      Is this box next to the log? (Touch.) *Yes.*
      So will the man kick this box? (Touch.) *Yes.*
      How do you know the man will kick the box? (Touch.) *It's empty and next to the log.*
   d. (Point to d.)
      Is this box empty? (Touch.) *No.*
      Is this box next to the log? (Touch.) *No.*
      So will the man kick this box? (Touch.) *No.*
      Why won't the man kick this box? (Touch.) *It isn't empty and it isn't next to the log.*

3. (Repeat part 2 until all children's responses are firm.)

4. Say the whole thing about what the man will do. (Signal.) *The man will kick the empty box that is next to the log.*
   Let's see if you are right.
   (Turn the page quickly.)

Concept Applications
Lessons 36–147

The man will kick only one of these boxes is the rule for the concept-application exercise from lesson 87. Children say the rule, observe each box to determine whether it is empty and next to the log, and then make a prediction about the box the man will kick. The illustration on the next page confirms the prediction. It shows the man kicking the box next to the log. The rule says nothing about the other boxes.

The concepts the children must use to solve the problem are taught in different tracks—future tense, actions, opposites, and parts. What is new is the process of combining two descriptive attributes. The problem is, Which box will the man kick? The rule is, The man will kick the empty box next to the log.

To apply the rule about the box the man will kick, the children must look at each box and answer the two questions Is this box empty? and Is this box next to the log? The box for which each question is answered *yes* satisfies the conditions laid down by the rule, and the children can predict which box the man will kick. The teacher then turns the page and the children see a picture of the man kicking a box. This picture confirms their

EXERCISE 5 Concept Application (cont.)

5. Look at the picture. (Point.)
   Which box is the man kicking? (Touch.) *The empty box that is next to the log.*
   a. (Point to a.)
      Why didn't the man kick this box? (Touch.) *It isn't next to the log.*
   b. (Point to b.)
      Why didn't the man kick this box? (Touch.) *It isn't empty.*
   c. (Point to d.)
      Why didn't the man kick this box? (Touch.) *It isn't empty and it isn't next to the log.*
   d. (Repeat part 5 until all children's responses are firm.)

6. We'll talk some more about the boxes.
   a. (Point to a.)
      Where is this box? (Touch.) *Next to the ladder.*
      Say the whole thing about where this box is. (Touch.) *This box is next to the ladder.*
   b. (Point to b.)
      What is in this box? (Touch.) *Cats.*
      Where is this box? (Touch.) *Between the ladder and the log.*
      Say the whole thing about where this box is. (Touch.) *This box is between the ladder and the log.*

7. (Ask different children the following questions.)
   Do you like to play in boxes?
   Would you like a box of puppies?
   What would you do with a ladder?
   Would you like a box of kittens?

Individual Turns
(Repeat parts 5 and 6, calling on different children for each question.)

prediction. They have used the rule to come up with the correct solution to the problem.

Concept-application exercises are a central feature in the program for the following reasons:

1. Each exercise provides children with a new problem and shows that the concepts learned earlier can be used in problem-solving situations.

2. Each of the exercises presents different sentence structures, which ensures that the children will develop a facility for using two concepts in different contexts. Children won't be locked into one sentence structure for handling a particular concept. Rather, they will have a more flexible understanding of each concept and how it can be used.

3. The exercises provide a continuous review of the concepts taught in the program. After plurals have been taught, for example, they are reviewed in the concept-application track. This review is helpful to all the children but particularly valuable for lower-performing children because it provides them with extra practice with the concepts they have been learning.

4. Each exercise provides practice both in repeating new statements that involve familiar concepts and in applying problem-solving skills.

5. The exercises contain questions that allow children to express their feelings and observations about the situations depicted in the pictures.

6. The exercises are enjoyable. The children enjoy being challenged to solve the problems and the sense of accomplishment that comes from doing them correctly.

After a concept has been taught in some other track, it often appears in a concept-application exercise. At least one concept-application exercise appears in almost every lesson, starting with lesson 38. This means that children receive substantial practice in applying concepts to different types of problems.

A list of the different concept-application exercise types appears on this page. It shows a sample rule for applying concepts and the concepts the children use in working the problems.

The exercise type changes from day to day. In lesson 79, for example, the children do one type of exercise; in lesson 81 they do another.

Sample Rule	Principal Concepts
The black dog will run.	Color Actions
The boy wearing a hat is big.	Opposites Actions
The small monkey will climb up a table leg.	Opposites Actions Parts
The goats with spots will eat the grass.	Descriptive Terms Future Tense Actions
The vehicle with wheels will get stuck.	Classification Parts Future Tense Plurals
The rabbit will eat the big apple that has leaves.	Future Tense Actions Multiple Descriptive Terms Opposites Parts
The man will push the vehicle with four wheels.	Classification Multiple Descriptive Terms Parts Future Tense
Only the boys wearing hats will do the same thing.	Same Only Future Tense Descriptive Terms
The boys who will go swimming are wearing hats.	Future Tense Plurals Actions
Every boy is smiling.	Every Actions Descriptive Terms
The rabbit will eat a potato or eat a carrot.	Or Classification Future Tense Actions
A rabbit will jump into the can or the bowl.	Future Tense Actions Prepositions Or
All of the petals are on the flower.	All Part/Whole Prepositions
The rabbit will sit next to the plant that is smaller.	Prepositions Classification Comparatives
The man chopped down (all, some, none) of the trees.	All, Some, None Tense Plurals

Teaching Concept-Application Exercises

Only two of the concept-application exercises appear in this teacher's guide. The teaching techniques and corrections that are described for these two exercises can be applied to any of the other concept-application exercises.

Study the exercises before you present them. Anticipate the errors the children will make. They may have trouble repeating the rules. The children must be able to state the rules in order to work the problems; they must know the meaning of any new words to understand what the problems are about.

Present these exercises as "tough problems." When the children solve them, praise them for "good thinking."

Precise pointing and touching signals are important to the proper pacing of concept-application exercises. Be sure to keep touching the picture as long as the children are responding. Proceed quickly through each page of the exercise. Good pacing will not only help the children solve the problems—it will also make the exercises a lot more fun for them.

Lesson 38: Concept Application

Here is the concept-application exercise from lesson 38. The color **black** and the action **run** are used in this exercise.

In the early concept-application exercises, the children practice saying the rule before they see the picture.

Make sure the children can say the rule before you turn the page.

Teaching Techniques

Present each part as a unit. Present the steps in each of these parts so that they go together. In this way the children will

EXERCISE 3   Concept Application

1. We're going to solve a problem about dogs. Only one dog will run. You're going to figure out which dog will run.
   a. Listen. The black dog will run. Listen again. The black dog will run. Everybody, say the rule about the black dog. (Signal.) *The black dog will run.*
   b. Again. (Signal.) *The black dog will run.* (Repeat step b until all children can say the sentence.)
   c. Let's use the rule. Remember, only one of these dogs will run. Which dog will run? (Signal.) *The black dog.*
   Yes, the black dog will run.
   (Turn the page quickly.)

EXERCISE 3   Concept Application (cont.)

2. Look at the picture of the dogs.
   a. (Point to a.) Is this dog black? (Touch.) *No.* So will this dog run? (Touch.) *No.* ●
   b. (Point to b.) Is this dog black? (Touch.) *Yes.* So will this dog run? (Touch.) *Yes.* This dog is black, so it will run.
   c. (Point to c.) Is this dog black? (Touch.) *No.* So will this dog run? (Touch.) *No.*

3. Let's talk some more about these dogs.
   a. (Point to dog b.) This dog is black. So, what else do you know about this dog? (Touch.) *This dog will run.* Yes, this dog will run.
   b. (Point to dog a.) This dog is not black. So, what else do you know about this dog? (Touch.) *This dog will not run.* Yes, this dog will not run.
   c. (Point to dog c.) This dog is not black. So, what else do you know about this dog? (Touch.) *This dog will not run.* Yes, this dog will not run.

4. We'll do some more.
   a. (Call on a child.) Show me the dog that will run. (The child should point to the black dog.)
   b. Let's see if you are right. (Turn the page quickly.)

Corrections

EXERCISE 3

● **Error**
(Children say *Yes.*)

Correction
Remember the rule: The black dog will run. (Point to a.) Is this a black dog? (Touch.) *No.* This dog is not black, so it won't run.

EXERCISE 3 Concept Application
(cont.)

5. (Do not point to the picture.)
    a. Everybody, look at the picture. Tell me which dog is running. (Signal.) *The black dog.*
    b. Say the whole thing. (Signal.) *The black dog is running.*

6. Listen.
    a. (Point to a.) Is this dog running? (Touch.) *No.*
    b. (Point to b.) Is this dog running? (Touch.) *Yes.*
    c. (Point to c.) Is this dog running? (Touch.) *No.*

7. Listen again.
    a. (Point to dog a.) What is this dog doing? (Touch.) *Sleeping.*
       Say the whole thing. (Touch.) *This dog is sleeping.*
    b. (Point to c.) What is this dog doing? (Touch.) *Eating.*
       Say the whole thing. (Touch.) *This dog is eating.*

8. (Call on different children.)
    Do you like dogs?
    What kind of trick would you teach a dog?
    (Praise reasonable responses.)

Individual Turns
(Repeat parts 5 through 7, calling on different children for each step.)

more easily understand how the rule relates to the questions.

In part 4, you call on a child to **show** you the dog that will run. If the child points to the right dog, say, Let's see if that dog will run, and turn the page.

The answers to the questions in part 6 show the children that the color of the other dogs did not satisfy the rule. Ask the questions in part 7 as you point to and touch each dog. Be sure to lift your finger after each answer, then point to the next dog while you ask the next question. Keep touching the picture until the children finish responding.

The questions at the end of the exercise are very important. They encourage the children to use language in a freer and more personal way.

Have fun with these questions. If you wish, you can add one or two more. Praise good answers, and especially encourage children who give original responses.

Corrections

If the children have trouble saying the rule,

1. model the statement;

2. lead the children: Say it with me. The black dog (pause) will run. Repeat until their responses are firm;

3. test the children. All by yourselves. Say the rule.

If the children make mistakes with any question that follows the rule, use a correction that relates the rule to the problem:

1. Remember, only one of these dogs will run.
2. Which dog is that?
3. Repeat the question that was missed.

If the children are weak on any step within a part, correct that step and repeat the part until the children's responses are firm.

If they make more than one mistake on any page of the exercise, repeat the entire page. Remind them again about the rule.

If the children don't respond in part 5, quickly call on two other children to find the dog that will run. If they respond with the wrong dog, repeat the entire exercise, saying, I think we'd better try this again.

Absurdities
Lessons 120–134

The exercises in this track give the children an opportunity to apply what they have learned in another context. They decide, on the basis of what they have learned about objects and events, that certain situations are absurd, and they figure out why they are absurd.

An understanding of absurdity is useful not only in situations that call for logical analysis but in everyday life. Humor is often based on appeals to our understanding of the absurd.

Three kinds of absurdities are introduced in the program:

1. Absurdities of function—an object is put to an absurd use

2. Absurdities of parts—an object has absurd parts

3. Absurdities of location—something is in an absurd location

All the parts, locations, and objects that appear in the absurdities exercises have been taught in other tracks. These exercises, therefore, provide the children with a good review of these concepts.

Lesson 120: Absurdity—Function

The first page of this exercise is followed by a second page with a picture.

Teaching Techniques

In part 2 ask one or two children the questions. Accept and praise any reasonable responses.

Ask the remaining questions quickly, but before signaling the response, pause long enough for the children to consider the question.

Turn the page. Why is it absurd to eat with a pencil? is the critical question. The child's response must indicate a problem that would result if you tried to eat with a pencil (the pencil wouldn't pick up the food, it would hurt your mouth, it would taste funny). If the response does not describe a problem, the child has not answered the question. Do not leave the questions until the children have given at least three reasons why eating with a pencil is absurd.

EXERCISE 5 Absurdity—Function

1. It's time for an absurdity.
   a. Listen. If something is absurd, it is very silly. What do we call something that is very silly? (Signal.) *Absurd.*
   b. (Repeat step a until all children's responses are firm.)

2. Now answer these questions.
   a. Everybody, why do we need pencils? (Praise appropriate responses such as *To write with; to do our lessons with.*)
   b. Why do we need forks? (Praise appropriate responses such as *To eat with; to pick up our food.*)
   c. Would you use a pencil to brush your teeth? (Signal.) *No.*
      That would be absurd.
   d. Would you use a pencil to write your name? (Signal.) *Yes.*
   e. Would you use a pencil to put things in? (Signal.) *No.*
      That would be absurd.

3. On the next page we're going to see a picture with a pencil in it. See if you can find something in the picture that is absurd. (Turn the page quickly.)

EXERCISE 5 Absurdity—Function (cont.)

4. Look at the picture.
   a. The boy is doing something absurd with the pencil. What is he doing that is absurd? (*Call on a child. Idea: Eating with it.*)
   Yes, he is eating with it.
   b. Why is it absurd to eat with a pencil? (*Call on different children. Praise acceptable observations such as The pencil wouldn't pick up the food; the point would hurt your mouth; the pencil would write on you.*)
   c. What should the boy do with the pencil? (*Praise acceptable answers.*)
   What should the boy use to eat? (*Call on a child. Ideas: A fork; a spoon.*)

5. (*Ask different children the following questions.*)
   Would you eat with a pencil?
   What do you really use to eat with?
   Would you write your name with a fork?
   What would you use to write your name?

Call on different children for the questions in part 5. Have fun with these questions.

The children enjoy these exercises. You will find them using the concept **absurdity** in their conversations outside of the language lessons.

Corrections

If the children don't come up with good answers to the questions in part 2, help them and then repeat the questions. The children must be firm on these questions before you proceed.

If the children give wrong answers in step b, tell them right away they are wrong and why they are wrong. For example, if the children say *yes* in response to the last question, say, No, you can't put things in a pencil. It's too small. Then repeat the series. The children should correctly answer all the questions in part 2 before you turn the page.

If the children don't produce acceptable answers in part 4, say, My turn. Here's why it's absurd. The pencil wouldn't pick up the food. Here's another one. The point would hurt your mouth. Your turn. Tell me why it's absurd to eat with a pencil. Praise children who repeat any of the reasons you gave. Provide lavish praise for any children who give additional reasons. Do not accept responses that have been given by other children. That one has been said, Tom. Think of another one.

Lesson 134: Absurdity—Location

The absurdity—location exercise is similar to the absurdity—function exercises. The children first review the information about what would be and what would not be absurd to find in a grocery store. Then the children look at the picture on the next page and tell what they see in the picture that is absurd and why it is absurd.

EXERCISE 5 Absurdity—Location

We're going to talk about a grocery store.
- **a.** Name some things you would find in a grocery store. (Call on different children. Praise appropriate observations. Have the group repeat each good observation. For example:) Right. We find shelves in a grocery store. Let's all say that. (Signal.) We find shelves in a grocery store.
- **b.** Would you find an elephant in a grocery store? (Signal.) *No.*
  It would be absurd to see an elephant in a grocery store.
- **c.** Would you find a checker in a grocery store? (Signal.) *Yes.*
  Yes, you find a checker in a grocery store.
- **d.** Would you find a swimming pool in a grocery store? (Signal.) *No.*
  That would be absurd.
- **e.** Would you find an airplane in a grocery store? (Signal.) *No.*
  That would be absurd.

Inquiry
Lessons 144–148

A different type of problem-solving activity appears near the end of the program. For this activity, children are presented with a problem. They identify people who could provide them with the information they need to solve the problem. Children generate questions they would ask the person about the problem. They also indicate other questions they would like to ask the person.

Lesson 144: Inquiry

Teaching notes: Make sure that children are asking the questions. In step 2, page 140, children tell what question they would ask. If they have trouble, go back to step 1. Tell them what they are trying to find out, then repeat step 2.

In step 7, children are to generate other questions they would like to have answered. If children generate only a few questions, prompt them. For instance, ask questions like these:

Didn't you ever wonder what a farmer does in the winter?

Didn't you ever wonder what farmers do if their tractor breaks down?

EXERCISE 3 Inquiry

1. You've learned a lot of facts about different places and different kinds of jobs. You're going to tell me where you could go to find out the answers to some questions. Let's say you want to find out how many teeth a grown-up person should have.
   a. Everybody, what do you want to find out? (Signal.) *How many teeth a grown-up person should have.*
   b. You learned about people who really know a lot about teeth. Those are the people you could ask. Who would you ask to find out how many teeth a grown-up person should have? (Signal.) *A dentist.*
   c. And when you talk to a dentist, what would you ask? (Call on a child. *How many teeth should a grown-up person have?*)

2. Everybody, say that question. (Signal.) *How many teeth should a grown-up person have?* (Repeat part 2 until all children's responses are firm.)

3. Let's say you wanted to find out what cows like to eat most. You learned about people who really know a lot about cows. Everybody, who would you ask to find out what cows like to eat most? (Signal.) *A farmer.*
   And when you talk to a farmer, what would you ask? (Call on a child. *What do cows like to eat most?*)

4. Everybody, say that question. (Signal.) *What do cows like to eat most?* (Repeat part 4 until all children's responses are firm.)

5. Let's say you wanted to find out what paint is best for concrete. Everybody, what do you want to find out? (Signal.) *What paint is best for concrete.*
   a. You learned about people who know a lot about paint. Who are those people? (Signal.) *Painters.*
   b. And when you talk to a painter, what would you ask? (Call on a child. *What paint is best for concrete?*)

6. Everybody, say that question. (Signal.) *What paint is best for concrete?* (Repeat part 6 until all children's responses are firm.)

7. What are some other things you could ask a painter? (Praise good questions.)
   a. What are some other things you could ask a dentist? (Praise good questions.)
   b. What are some other things you could ask a farmer? (Praise good questions.)

What else did you wonder about? **Praise children who respond.**

Another good plan is to have the group repeat good questions.

Don't accept responses that are not questions. If children don't state a question, help them rephrase their response.

For example, a child says, *I'd like to know why cows don't get too cold in the wintertime.*

Say, So pretend that I'm the farmer and ask me the question about the cows.

Language Worksheet Activities

Worksheet activities are a part of each lesson, starting with lesson 1. The worksheet activities of *Reading Mastery Plus,* Level K have the following objectives:

1. **To expand upon what the children learn in other parts of the lessons** For example, after children learn prepositions, they do worksheet activities that require them to apply their knowledge of prepositions in another context. After children learn about different classes, they do worksheet activities that require them to identify objects in one or more of these classes. Nearly every concept the children learn in the exercises, from plurals to locations, also appears as a worksheet activity.

2. **To introduce new concepts** The children learn colors and shapes through the worksheet activities. In addition, they learn to do a variety of matching and picture-completion activities that involve skills that are particularly suited to a worksheet format. For example, they learn to complete and draw shapes, to draw lines that show where pictured objects belong, and to arrange things in sequence. In the temporal first-next activities, the children learn to follow an arrow and to sequence events that are illustrated on the shaft of the arrow.

3. **To provide practice in following directions** The worksheet activities provide children with a good foundation for following directions. Much of what children will do in school involves their knowing how to follow directions. Learning how to follow directions is important to school learning.

As the children do their worksheet activities, you will get valuable feedback regarding how individual children are progressing. In a sense, worksheet activities are like individual turns that are presented at the same time to different children. You can watch what individual children are doing and can readily identify any problems they may be having. You can repeat directions that give them problems. And, you can let them know when they are doing well.

4. **To provide the children with practice in performing the motor skills associated with many classroom activities (coloring, marking, matching, circling, and drawing)** The worksheet activities give children practice in staying within the lines of what they are coloring, following the dots, and drawing shapes and pictures. The children also learn to keep track of their crayons and papers. These motor and organizational skills are also important to success in school.

Presenting the Worksheet Activities

The directions for presenting the worksheet activities appear on the final pages of each lesson in the teacher's presentation book. The title, *Worksheet,* appears in the upper left-hand corner of these pages. A sentence under the title indicates what crayons and other materials the children will need for that day's set of activities. The directions follow the same conventions as the exercises in the main part of the lesson.

The first few times a new worksheet activity appears, it is teacher-directed. Only when the children know how to do the activity on their own should they be allowed to do so. If the children have trouble with a particular activity, show them what they should have done. Then reproduce the activity and have the children do it again under your direction. Do not permit the children to make the same mistakes from lesson to lesson. If individual children tend to make the same type of mistakes in a certain part of an activity, alert them to what they should do and provide lots of praise when they do it correctly.

Children can take home their completed worksheet pages. This can be a daily event or, preferably, one that occurs after the children have completed the activities in five or ten lessons. The pages can be stapled together as a language booklet for the children to take home and show their parents.

The Content of the Worksheet Activities

The major worksheet activities of the program are discussed in this section. The worksheet scope and sequence chart on page 239 displays the worksheet tracks in the program as well as the starting and ending lessons for each track.

As the chart shows, three activities appear in lesson 1. These are simple activities that introduce the children to the kind of work they will do on their worksheets and the kind of directions they will follow.

The three activities introduced in lesson 1 are touching, coloring, and making cross-out marks.

Touching

The purpose of these activities is for the children to learn to follow the direction "Touch the _____." Here are the teacher directions and student material for the touching exercise in lesson 1.

Worksheet

[**Note:** Each child will need a black, a red, and a brown crayon.]

Touching

1. (Hold up worksheet. Point to each object.) What is this? (Touch. The children respond.)
   a. I'll show you how to touch things. My turn to touch the dog. (Touch.) I touched the dog.
   b. My turn to touch the girl. (Touch.) I touched the girl.

2. (Distribute worksheets for lesson 1 to the children.)
   a. Your turn. Everybody, touch the dog. Get ready. (Signal. The children touch the dog.) ✓
      Fingers up.
   b. Again, everybody touch the dog. Get ready. (Signal. The children touch the dog.) ✓
      Fingers up.
      (Repeat until all children's responses are firm.)
   c. This time you're going to touch the girl. Everybody, touch the girl. Get ready. (Signal. The children touch the girl.) ✓
      Fingers up.
      (Repeat until all children's responses are firm.)

This direction will be used in a variety of other worksheet activities throughout the program. For example, you will give directions such as Touch the tall boy or Touch the box next to the suitcase.

Colors

Color activities begin on lesson 1 and continue throughout the program. The activities introduce the children to nine common colors. The schedule for their introduction appears below:

Color Introduced	Lesson
Yellow	11
Red	14
Blue	18
Black	34
Purple	35
Orange	42
Green	46
Brown	57
Pink	78

Children also follow coloring "rules" in a number of different worksheet activities. For example, the instructions for one classification exercise direct the children to Make each food red and Make each vehicle green.

Cross-Out Marks

Children learn to make cross-out marks (**X**s) so that they can follow a variety of directions that require them to cross out particular pictures of groups. In lesson 44, for example, the children apply what they learned to this direction: Cross out each box that does not have a car and a ball.

In the first 14 lessons, the children learn to make cross-out marks. The worksheet pages present rows of cross-out marks that are dotted or partially dotted. Here is the student material from lesson 8.

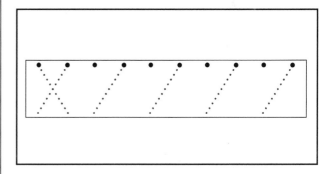

The children trace the cross-out marks and then complete them with a crayon.

A cross-out and circle activity is introduced in lesson 18 after the children have learned to make both cross-out marks and circles. The teacher directions and student material from lesson 29 are shown on page 144.

The children follow the "rule." The crossed-out object shows what should be crossed out. The circled object shows what should be circled.

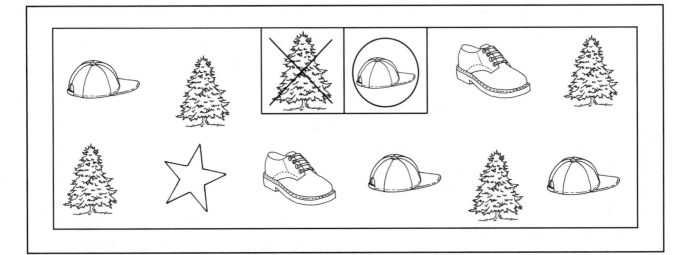

Matching

Matching activities begin in lesson 6. In the early lessons, the children draw a line from an object in the first column to an identical object in the second column. Here is the student material from lesson 7.

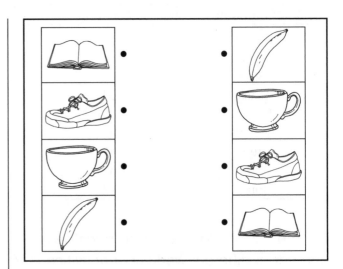

In a later variation of this activity, the children learn to match, for example, animals that are not identical. They match a horse with a horse, but one of the horses is standing and the other is sleeping. Here is the student material from lesson 23.

In another variation, not all of the objects are shown. Children first draw lines between the objects that are the same. Then they draw a line from the remaining object to an empty box. Finally, they draw the missing object in the empty box. Here is the student material from lesson 51.

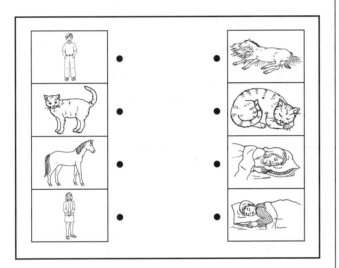

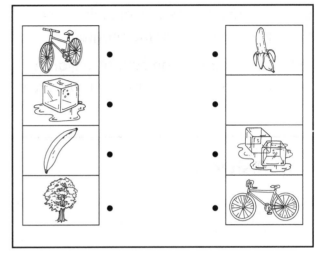

Pair Relations

In the pair relations activities, the children learn to match pairs of objects that are ordered in a particular way. This is an important reading skill because it requires the children to analyze the left-to-right relationship of the elements in the pair. Relations activities begin in lesson 31 and continue in activities of increasing difficulty to the end of the program.

In the first pair relation activity, children learn to circle each box that follows a rule and to cross out each box that does not follow the rule. Here are the teacher directions and student material from lesson 34.

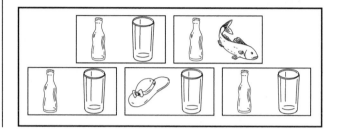

Worksheet 34

Pair Relations

1. Find the bottle. You're going to circle and cross out boxes.
   a. Here's the rule about the boxes: Each box should have a bottle and a glass.
   What should each box have? (Signal.)
   A bottle and a glass.
   b. Touch the first box. ✓
   Does that box have a bottle? (Signal.) *Yes.*
   Does that box have a glass? (Signal.) *Yes.*
   Listen. Does that box have a bottle and a glass? (Signal.) *Yes.*
   That's what the box should have.
   c. The next box has a bottle and a fish. Touch that box. ✓
   That box should have a bottle and a glass.
   Does that box have a bottle? (Signal.) *Yes.*
   Does that box have a glass? (Signal.) *No.*
   That box does not have a bottle and a glass, so that box is wrong.

   d. The next box has a bottle and a glass. Touch that box. ✓
   Does that box have a bottle? (Signal.) *Yes.*
   Does that box have a glass? (Signal.) *Yes.*
   So that box has a bottle and a glass.
   e. The next box has a hat and a glass. Touch that box. ✓
   That box should have a bottle and a glass.
   Does that box have a bottle? (Signal.) *No.*
   Does that box have a glass? (Signal.) *Yes.*
   Listen. Does that box have a bottle and a glass? (Signal.) *No.*
   That box does not have a bottle and a glass, so that box is wrong.
   f. The last box has a bottle and a glass. Touch that box. ✓
   Does that box have a bottle? (Signal.) *Yes.*
   Does that box have a glass? (Signal.) *Yes.*
   Listen. Does that box have a bottle and a glass? (Signal.) *Yes.*

2. Here's the circling rule: Circle each box that has a bottle and a glass.
   a. What are you going to do to each box that has a bottle and a glass? (Signal.) *Circle it.*
   b. Do it. Circle each box with a bottle and a glass. ✓

3. Here's the cross-out rule: Cross out each box that does not have a bottle and a glass.
   a. What are you going to do to each box that does not have a bottle and a glass? (Signal.) *Cross it out.*
   b. Do it. Cross out each box that does not have a bottle and a glass. ✓

A later variation presents two boxes at the top of the student material. The children cross out any box that is not like one of the boxes at the top. Here is the student material from lesson 69.

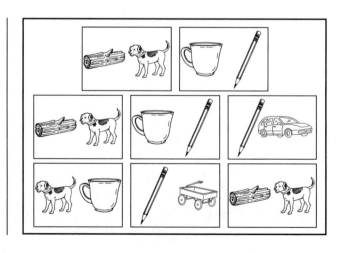

The next variation has two boxes at the top. All the other boxes have something missing. The children first circle the boxes that can be fixed up like one of the boxes at the top. The children cross out the boxes that cannot be fixed up. The children then fix up the circled boxes. Here are the teacher directions and student material from lesson 75.

Worksheet 75
SIDE 2

Pair Relations

1. (Hold up worksheet.) Find the box with the cake and the moon. ✓
   The boxes at the top show what the other boxes should look like.
   a. Touch the first box at the top. ✓
   What are the objects in that box? (Signal.) *A cake and a moon.*
   b. Touch the next box at the top. ✓
   What are the objects in that box? (Signal.) *A bike and a spoon.*

2. Listen. All the other boxes have something missing. You can fix up a box if the first object is either a cake or a bike.
   a. What does the first object have to be? (Signal.) *A cake or a bike.*

   b. Circle every box that has a cake or a bike as the first object. ✓
   c. Cross out every box that does not have a cake or a bike as the first object. Do it. ✓

3. Later you may fix up all the boxes you circled so they are like one of the boxes at the top.
   [Note: Present the Pre-Reading exercises for lesson 75.]

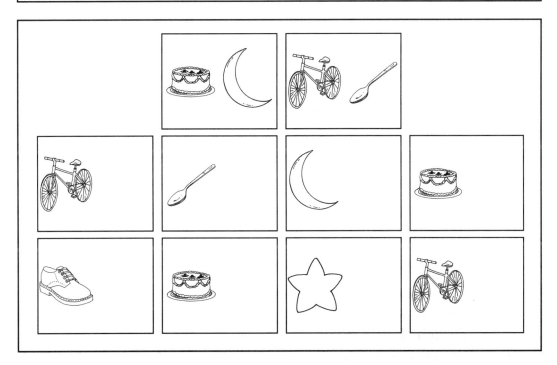

In later variations the children work with boxes that have three objects.

Picture Completion

Picture completion activities begin in lesson 37. The children follow the dots to complete a picture. Here is the student material from lesson 37.

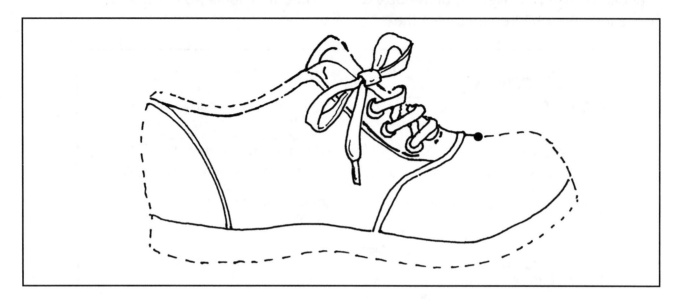

Spatial First

Spatial first activities are different from temporal first activities. In temporal first, something happens in time before something else happens. In spatial first, things are spatially arranged so that something is first if you follow a "rule." For example, the first letter in the word *bug* is *b*. The letter is first only if you know the rule of reading the letters from left to right.

Spatial first activities begin in lesson 44. Here is part of the teacher directions. Notice that the children use coloring rules to identify the car that is first in line, the car that is next in line, and the car that is last in line.

The first spatial first worksheet activity is preceded by a teacher demonstration. Three children line up in front of the group. You identify which child is first in line, next in line, and last in line. Then the children use these same first, next, and last concepts in their worksheet activities.

b. The car that is first in line will get to the stop sign first. Touch the car that is first in line. Get ready. (Signal.) ✓
Touch the car that is next in line. Get ready. (Signal.) ✓
Touch the car that is last in line. Get ready. (Signal.) ✓

c. (Repeat until all children's responses are firm.)

d. Here is the first coloring rule: Make the first car yellow.
Say the rule. (Signal.) *Make the first car yellow.*
Make a little yellow mark on the first car. ✓

e. Here's the next coloring rule: Make the next car blue.
Say the rule. (Signal.) *Make the next car blue.*
Make a little blue mark on the next car. ✓

f. Here's the last rule: Make the last car orange.
Say the rule. (Signal.) *Make the last car orange.*
Make a little orange mark on the last car. ✓

g. Later you may color the cars.

Top/Bottom

Another set of worksheet activities that involves teaching demonstrations is top/bottom, which begins in lesson 44. In the first demonstration, you show a cross-out mark at the top of a piece of paper. You then reorient the paper so that the mark is not at the top. Next, the children find the cross-out mark at the top of their worksheet.

In the later exercises, the children follow directions to cross out or circle the picture that is at the top of the worksheet.

Later in the program the children learn *middle* and *bottom*. They follow directions for circling or crossing out pictures that are at the middle or the bottom of the page. Here are the teacher directions and student material from lesson 56.

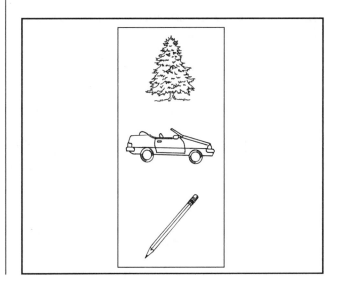

Worksheet 56 continued

SIDE 2

Top/Bottom/Middle

1. (Hold up worksheet.) Find the tree. ✓
   a. There are pictures in the box. One picture is at the top, one picture is at the bottom, and one picture is in the middle.
   b. Listen. Touch the picture at the top of the box. Get ready. (Signal.) ✓
      Listen. Touch the picture at the bottom of the box. Get ready. (Signal.) ✓
      Listen. Touch the picture in the middle of the box. Get ready. (Signal.) ✓

2. This time, you'll tell me where the pictures are. You'll tell me top, middle, or bottom.
   a. Listen. Tell me if the pencil is at the top, at the bottom, or in the middle.
      Everybody, where is the pencil? (Signal.)
      Bottom.
   b. Listen. Tell me if the car is at the top, at the bottom, or in the middle.
      Everybody, where is the car? (Signal.)
      Middle.
   c. Listen. Tell me if the tree is at the top, at the bottom, or in the middle.
      Everybody, where is the tree? (Signal.)
      Top.

3. Here's what you'll do:
   a. You'll circle the picture in the middle of the box. You'll cross out the other pictures. Listen again. Circle the picture in the middle. Cross out the other pictures.
   b. Do it. ✓

Part/Whole

Part/whole activities begin in lesson 51. In one variation, children draw lines to connect parts of objects to pictures of objects lacking these parts. Here is the student material from lesson 64.

The children identify which wagons do not have wheels. Then they draw lines from each set of wheels to a wagon that does not have wheels.

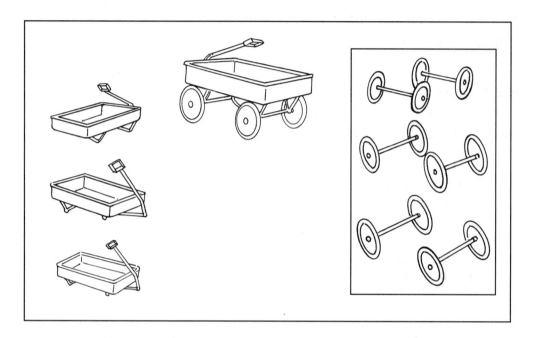

In a later variation, the children identify the missing parts of four illustrated objects. Then they draw the missing parts and color the objects. Here is the student material from lesson 140.

Shapes

Shapes are introduced in lesson 57. The schedule shows when different shapes are introduced.

Shape	Lesson
triangle	57
circle	60
rectangle	78
square	85

In addition to learning the names of shapes, the children engage in a variety of activities involving shapes. Some of these direct the children to color specific shapes; others are similar to the pair relations activities. Below is an example from lesson 69.

In some lessons the children are told that part of each triangle is missing. Before they color the triangles, they complete the missing parts. In later activities they draw shapes.

Opposites

Opposites begin in lesson 58. In the first opposite activities, the children are given coloring rules for opposites. For example, Color all of the big bikes green. Color all of the small bikes yellow. Here is the student material from lesson 58.

In later lessons the worksheet activities are similar, but the teacher directions contain the term *opposite.* For example, All of the dogs that are the opposite of wet should be brown.

Plurals

Plurals appear as worksheet activities in lesson 62. Here are the teacher directions and student material from lesson 62.

Notice that the activity involves crossing out and coloring. To do this activity, the children must listen carefully to the directions.

In a later variation, the children fix up pictures. For example, the picture shows a cup on a table. You tell the children *Some objects are missing from the table. The picture should show* cups on the table. *Fix up the picture so there are cups on the table. Then make all the cups red.*

Worksheet 62 continued

Plurals

1. Listen. One picture on your worksheet shows hands. Hands.
   a. Touch the picture that shows hands. ✓ (Hold up worksheet. Point to the picture of hands.) Here's the picture that shows hands.
   b. Listen. One picture shows a hand. Touch the picture that shows a hand. ✓ (Hold up worksheet. Point to picture of a hand.) Here's the picture that shows a hand.
   c. Listen. One picture shows cats. Touch the picture that shows cats. ✓ (Hold up worksheet. Point to the picture of cats.) Here's the picture that shows cats.

2. Here's the coloring rule for the picture that shows hands.
   Listen. The hands in that picture should be brown.
   Make a brown mark in the picture that shows hands. ✓

3. Here's the coloring rule for the picture that shows cats.
   Listen. The cats in that picture should be yellow.
   Make a yellow mark in the picture that shows cats. ✓

4. Here's the last rule.
   a. Cross out any picture that does not show cats or hands. Listen again. Cross out any picture that does not show cats or hands.
   b. Do it. ✓

5. Later you may color the pictures of hands and cats.

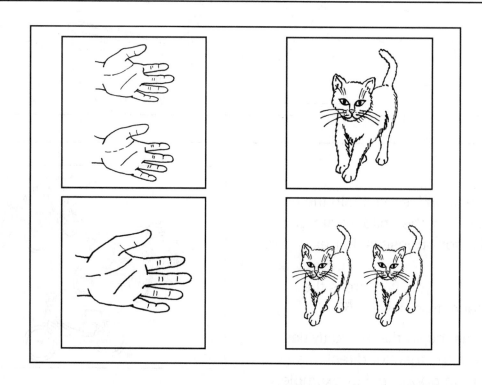

Classification

A variety of classification activities is presented in the program, starting in lesson 66. In the first variation, children mark the objects that are in a class you specify. For example, Make a line over every vehicle. In a later variation, the children draw lines from objects of a particular class to a particular location. Here are the teacher directions and student material from lesson 78.

Worksheet 78
SIDE 1

Classification

1. Find the boat. ✓
   a. Some of these objects are food. (Point to each object and ask:) Is this food? (Children are to respond *yes* or *no*.)
   b. Some of these objects are vehicles. (Point to each object and ask:) Is this a vehicle? (Children are to respond *yes* or *no*.)

2. (Point to the house.) Listen. The objects that are food should be in the house.
   a. Where should the food be? (Signal.) *In the house.*
   b. Draw a line from each object that is food to the house. ✓
      Raise your hand when you have all the food in the house. ✓

3. Listen. All the vehicles should be in the bus.
   a. Where should the vehicles be? (Signal.) *In the bus.*
   b. Draw lines from each vehicle to the bus. ✓

4. Be careful because some objects are not foods and not vehicles.

In another variation, you tell the children the coloring rules for classes. The children mark one object from each class, then they tell you the coloring rules, based on what they have marked. Here are the teacher directions and student material from lesson 107.

Classification

1. (Hold up worksheet.) Find the tree. ✓
   a. Here's one of the coloring rules for this picture: Make all the containers red. What's the rule? (Signal.) *Make all the containers red.*
      Yes, so mark one container red. ✓
   b. Here's another coloring rule for this picture: Make all the plants yellow. What's the rule? (Signal.) *Make all the plants yellow.*
      Yes, so mark one plant yellow. ✓

2. Everybody, look at your worksheet. ✓
   a. What's the rule for all the containers? (Signal.) *Make all the containers red.*
   b. What's the rule for all the plants? (Signal.) *Make all the plants yellow.*

3. Remember, the marks show you what color to make the containers and the plants. You may color the other objects any color you want.

Draw Figures

Children draw figures starting in lesson 78. The figures have dotted outlines. The children connect the dots to complete the figures. Here is the student material from lesson 82.

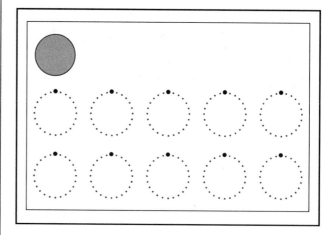

Prepositions

Preposition activities begin in lesson 96. The children follow coloring rules to identify objects that are in different places, for example, The rabbit is in the shoe. Here are the teacher directions and student material from lesson 96.

Prepositions

1. Find the dog. ✓
   a. Here's one of the coloring rules for this picture: Make the containers on the table blue.
      What's the rule? (Signal.) *Make the containers on the table blue.*
      Yes, so mark one container on the table blue. ✓
   b. Here's another coloring rule for this picture: Make the containers under the table red.
      What's the rule? (Signal.) *Make the containers under the table red.*
      Yes, so mark one container under the table red. ✓
   c. Here's another coloring rule for this picture: Make the containers next to the table yellow.
      What's the rule? (Signal.) *Make the containers next to the table yellow.*
      Yes, so mark one container next to the table yellow. ✓

2. Remember—the marks show you what color to make the containers. You may color the containers later.

Another variation requires the children to draw lines to where, for example, animals will go. Here are the teacher directions and student material from lesson 148.

Prepositions

1. (Hold up worksheet.) Find the animals. ✓
   These animals are going to move. You'll draw lines to show where each animal will go.

2. Listen. The animals that are white will go next to the boat.
   Where will they go? (Signal.) *Next to the boat.*
   Draw a line from the animals that are white to where they will go. ✓

3. Listen. The animals that are black will go in back of the boat.
   Where will the animals go that are black? (Signal.) *In back of the boat.*
   Draw a line from the animals that are black to where they will go. ✓

4. Later you will color the boat.

Locations

Locations first appear in lesson 94. The children learn a number of locations in the main part of the lesson and review them in worksheet activities. In one worksheet activity, the children show which objects do not belong in a location by crossing them out. Then they show which objects belong in the location by drawing lines from each object that belongs to the location. Here are the teacher directions and student material from lesson 94.

Locations

1. (Hold up worksheet. Point to the farm.) Everybody, what place do you see in the circle? (Touch.) *A farm.*
   Yes, a farm.

2. Some of the objects around the circle belong on a farm and some do not. (**Point to each object and ask:**) What is this? Would you find this object on a farm?
   (**Correct any wrong answers.**)

3. First you're going to cross out the objects that don't belong on a farm. The lion has already been crossed out for you. Cross out the other objects that do not belong on a farm. ✓

4. Now you're going to draw lines to show which objects belong on a farm.
   Draw the lines from the objects that belong on a farm to the picture of the farm. ✓

Same/Different

Activities involving *same* begin in lesson 102. Children follow a rule about objects that are the same. Here are the teacher directions and student material from lesson 108.

Same

1. (Hold up worksheet.) Find the nail. ✓

2. Here's a rule for this picture: The objects that are made of the same material should be connected with a blue line.
   Connect the objects that are made of the same material. ✓

3. Here is another rule: Anybody who is doing the same thing should be connected with a brown line.
   Connect anybody who is doing the same thing. ✓

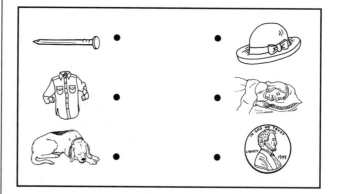

The children draw lines from objects that are made of the *same* material. Then they draw lines from characters who are doing the *same* thing.

In later variations the children engage in a number of activities involving *same.* They follow rules involving the same place, the same color, the same class, the same material, and the same actions.

Starting in lesson 122, variations appear that involve *same* and *different*. Children are given a rule about how things are the same and different. They connect the things that are the same and cross out the thing that is different. Here is the student material from lesson 122.

For the first two boxes the children draw lines to connect the two objects that are in the same class. The children then cross out the object that is not in this class. In the last box the children draw lines to connect the two animals that are doing the same thing. They cross out the animal that is not doing the same thing.

Comparatives

Activities involving comparatives begin in lesson 127. After the children have learned some comparatives, they apply what they know to follow the coloring rules. Here is the student material from lesson 127.

The children follow the two rules: Make the smaller containers yellow. Make the larger containers blue.

Some, All, None

Activities involving *some, all,* and *none* begin in lesson 127. The children follow coloring rules that involve these concepts. Here are the teacher directions and student material from lesson 127.

Some, All, None

1. Find the eggs. ✓
   You're going to color the eggs.
   a. One picture shows some of the eggs in the basket. Those eggs should be green.
   Make a green mark on the picture that shows some of the eggs in the basket. ✓
   b. Here's the rule for the picture that shows all of the eggs in the basket: Those eggs should be purple.
   Make a purple mark on the picture that shows all of the eggs in the basket. ✓
   c. Here's the rule for the picture that shows none of the eggs in the basket: Those eggs should be yellow.
   Make a yellow mark in the picture that shows none of the eggs in the basket. ✓

2. Later you'll color the pictures.

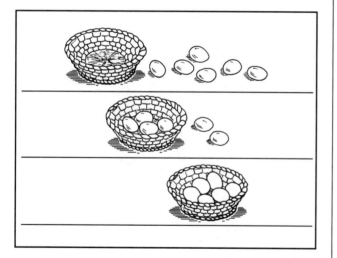

A later variation combines opposites and *some, all,* and *none.* Here are the teacher directions and student material from lesson 149.

Some, All, None

1. (Hold up worksheet.) Find the dogs. ✓
   a. Here's a rule about the animals that are not in a boat: Some of the animals that are not in a boat should be blue. Some of the animals that are not in a boat should be red.
   Make marks to show that some of the animals that are not in a boat are blue and some are red. ✓
   b. Here's a rule about the boats: Some of the boats should be black.
   Make a mark to show that some of the boats should be black. ✓
   c. Here's a rule about some of the animals that are the opposite of wet: Some of the animals that are the opposite of wet should have long whiskers.
   Make long whiskers on some of the animals that are the opposite of wet. ✓

2. Later you'll fix up this picture.

Notice that these directions require the children to use a variety of concepts that are taught in the program.

Materials

Activities that review the material the children are learning begin in lesson 131. Children apply coloring rules to identify objects made of the material they have learned. This example from lesson 131 shows a group of objects, most of which are made of glass.

The children follow the coloring rules: The things that are made of glass should be red. The things that are not made of glass should be some other color.

Stories and Poems

Twenty-three stories and six poems were written to accompany *Reading Mastery Plus*, Level K. Each story focuses on one or more of the concepts the children are learning in the daily lessons. The stories are important for a number of reasons, including the following:

1. Children are given examples of narratives that follow common story forms. For example, a character has a problem and overcomes that problem.

2. Children are familiarized with the sequence of events that occur in stories.

3. Children have to respond to questions and instructions that are presented as part of the story.

4. Children are given an opportunity to hear and practice role-playing parts of stories.

5. Teachers and children enjoy the stories.

The poems were written to be fun for the children to hear, learn, and recite.

Story or Poem	Storybook	Concepts	Lesson to Begin Reading
Polly and the Lion	1	Identity Statements	16
My Cat, My Dog, My Frog	1	(Poem)	18
Dozy, Bring a Hamburger	1	Identity Statements	21
Oscar the Worm	1	Actions	28
Painting	1	(Poem)	26
Marvin the Eagle	1	Prepositions	33
Sarah the Toymaker	1	Parts	39
In a Tree	1	(Poem)	36
Melissa Hides the Bag of Popcorn	1	Prepositions	46
Curious Carla Gets into Trouble	2	Why	51
Dozy Brings the Shovels	2	Plurals	57
What We Saw	2	(Poem)	59
Curious Carla Makes Everybody Happy	2	Why	63
What Did I Do?	2	(Poem)	66
Dozy at the Zoo	2	Prepositions	69
Melissa Will Try	2	Verb Tense	76
Dozy Gets a Vehicle	2	Classification	81
My Dream	2	(Poem)	83
Melissa on the Ranch	2	Description	86
Denise Builds a House	2	Parts of a House	92
Doris Goes to the Store	2	Or	98
The Strongest Animal in the Jungle	3	Superlatives	101
Dozy Paints the House	3	Opposites	106
Dozy Goes Fishing	3	Before/After	111
Dozy Goes on a Hike	3	Some/All	116
Denise Fixes the Inside of the House	3	Absurdities	121
Dozy Delivers the Nails	3	Location	126
The Little Blue Bug	3	Rules	131
Miss Edna Does the Same Thing	3	Same/Different	136

Stories and poems are found at the end of each presentation book in the Storybook section. Storybook 1 appears in Language Presentation Book A, Storybook 2 appears in Book B, and Storybook 3 appears in Book C. The list on page 160 gives the titles of the stories and poems, the concepts emphasized in each story, and the lesson number at which the story or poem is to be first read to the children. The schedule was designed so that the children hear a story about a set of concepts **after** they have been presented in the lessons.

Presenting Storybook Stories and Poems

The reference for which story or poem is to be read appears at the end of each lesson, starting in lesson 16. These directions indicate that you alternate among the stories, introducing new stories on some days and rereading stories on other days. Some days are "Children's Choice." The children pick the story they want to hear. The idea is that you will read the stories often enough for the children to become familiar with the story line and the vocabulary, just as children become familiar with stories read to them many times at home.

When you read a storybook story, react to it in the way you expect the children to respond. Laugh when the story is funny; sound concerned when one of the characters seems headed for trouble. Make sure that the children respond to the questions that appear in the stories. You may want to add other questions as well.

Expanded Language Activities

The expanded language activities provide you with ideas that will give your children some additional experiences with the language concepts and skills of the program. A schedule and description of the expanded language activities appear at the beginning of each teacher's presentation book. The activities give the children the opportunity to use and apply what they are learning in a variety of contexts: stories, poems, games, and art projects.

The expanded language activities include

- songs, games, and other activities to help children learn names, colors, shapes, and actions;

- drawings and other activities that support concept learning, story narratives, and other sequencing activities;

- ideas for creating puzzles, posters, murals, calendars, and a variety of scrapbooks;

- suggestions for playing finger games, circle games, word games, board games, and logic games.

The expanded language activities are a supplement to the daily lessons and can be presented at either the end of the lesson or at another time during the day. The children will be able to do some of the activities independently, whereas others must be led by an adult. If you have two groups of children at about the same lesson in the program, they can be combined for expanded language activities. If you have an aide or volunteer helping out in your classroom, the expanded language activities can be a part of their assignment.

The expanded language activities are enjoyable—your children will have fun and at the same time learn a lot as they play games, create art projects, and role-play stories and poems. You are encouraged to develop other language activities that will provide children opportunities to apply the language concepts and skills they are learning to new situations and contexts.

Literature Lessons

Nine **Responding to Literature** selections and seven **Literature Lesson** selections are designed to accompany *Reading Mastery Plus,* Level K Language component. The selections elaborate on skills children are learning in *Reading Mastery Plus,* provide them with a wider genre of literature than provided elsewhere in the program, and sharpen their understanding of story grammar, structure, and object lessons developed in *Reading Mastery Plus.*

The following two lists indicate the earliest *Reading Mastery Plus* lesson after which each selection is to be presented. Most selections have predictable text that is presented either in rhyme or in a thematic context that is familiar to the children. These stories are designed so children can recite words from the text.

Responding to Literature Selections: Lessons 1–45

Follows Lessons	Title	Genre
1–5	*Jack and Jill*	nursery rhyme
6–10	*Hickory, Dickory, Dock*	nursery rhyme
11–15	*Diddle, Diddle, Dumpling, My Son John*	nursery rhyme
16–20	*Hey, Diddle, Diddle!*	nursery rhyme
21–25	[teacher's choice]	contemporary poem
26–30	*The Three Little Kittens*	picture book
31–35	*The Tortoise and the Hare*	fable
36–40	*The Three Little Pigs*	picture book
41–45	[teacher's choice]	[teacher's choice]

Directions for presenting these **Responding to Literature** selections appear toward the end of each Language lesson, from lesson 1 through lesson 45.

You will need to obtain illustrated versions of the Responding to Literature selections before you can present them.

Literature Lesson Selections: Lessons 45–145

Follows Lessons	Title	Author
45, 50, 55	*What Are You Called?*	Honey Andersen and Bill Reinholtd
60, 65, 70	*Dog Went for a Walk*	Sally Farrell Odgers
75, 80, 85	*Goodnight*	Penelope Coad
90, 95, 100	*Farmer Schnuck*	Brenda Parkes
105, 110, 115	*This and That*	Vic Warren
120, 125, 130	*Nibbly Mouse*	David Drew
135, 140, 145	*Little Dinosaur*	Trevor Wilson

Copies of the seven trade books are included as part of the Literature Collection. Presentation questions for these seven selections are provided in the Literature Guide.

Teaching Children Whose First Language Is Not English

Reading Mastery Plus, Level K is effective with children whose first language is not English. It has been used with ESL children who are in preschool, level k, the primary grades, and with older children who know little or no English. The program is well designed for teaching English to children who do not know English.

Reading Mastery Plus, Level K provides both the instruction and the practice to accelerate the children's ability to construct new sentences that describe (a) what they want to do or have, (b) what they are doing, (c) what they were doing, (d) what and where things are. Within one school year, children who have never spoken English speak English so well that it is hard to believe they learned so much in less than a calendar year. The teaching requires no knowledge of the children's first language. It does, however, require some adaptation of the program. Here are the general guidelines for using *Reading Mastery Plus,* Level K with children whose first language is not English.

Action Exercises First (See Actions in the Language Tracks section of this guide.) Make the actions exercises the primary teaching vehicle. These exercises are labeled *Actions* or have the word *Actions* in the exercise title (for example, Actions–Prepositions, Actions–Pronouns).

Start with the actions exercises in lessons 1–10. Teach these exercises until the children's responses are firm. Do this by repeating them. But make the exercises a game, not a drill. Do the actions exercises in more than one lesson during each period.

In the first actions exercises, the children learn the instructions "stand up" and "sit down." Most of the directions in the actions exercises also include the word *everybody:* for example, Everybody, stand up and Everybody, sit down.

In teaching the actions exercises, model each action by demonstrating how to do it. For example, point to yourself and say My turn. Stand up. Then stand up. You can help the children learn the word *everybody* by saying Everybody several times as you motion to or tap each child. Then say Stand up. If the children do not stand up, motion or physically help them stand up. Then point to the children and say Stand up as they are standing. Show your approval by smiling or clapping your hands.

Repeat the same procedure for "Everybody, sit down."

The effectiveness of the exercises in the actions track is that you give the children a simple direction and the children are able to do what you say immediately—on the first day. No translation is required; no

readiness activities are necessary. The children experience success on the first day of instruction.

By lesson 3, the children are not only following directions for performing simple actions, they are telling you what they are doing. Here is the exercise from lesson 3 of the actions track.

EXERCISE 1   Actions—Following Directions

1. Get ready to do some actions. Watch my hand. Remember to wait for the signal.
   a. Everybody, stand up. (Signal. The children are to stand up.)
      Everybody, sit down. (Signal. The children are to sit down.)
   b. (Repeat step a until all children respond to your signal.)

2. Let's do those actions again.
   a. Everybody, stand up. (Signal.) What are you doing? (Signal.) *Standing up.*
   b. Everybody, sit down. (Signal.) What are you doing? (Signal.) *Sitting down.*

3. Let's do those actions some more. (Repeat part 2 until all children can perform the actions and say what they are doing.)

Note that what the children tell you is a simple transformation of what you tell them. You say, Stand up. After they stand up, you ask, What are you doing? The answer is not *Stand up* but *Standing up.* You help the children produce the response and repeat the exercise until all of the children are able to follow the routine:

Everybody, stand up. (Children respond.)

What are you doing? *Standing up.*

Everybody, sit down. (Children respond.)

What are you doing? **Sitting down.**

If the children make mistakes, stress the word *doing.* They will soon catch on that the ending they add is the same as the ending on *doing.* The children's responses must be firm. Present a lot of repetition, but make it fun and be positive.

Information Exercises (See Information and Background Knowledge in the Language tracks section of this guide.)

You may also want to teach the exercises in the information track as part of your initial lessons with the children. Here is one of these exercises.

EXERCISE 4   Information—School

1. Here are some things you should know.
   a. Listen. I'm your teacher. My name is
   _____. Everybody, what's your
   teacher's name? (Pause. Signal. The
   children respond.)
   b. (Repeat step a until all children's
   responses are firm.)
   c. Listen. You go to _____ School.
   Everybody, what's the name of the school
   you go to? (Pause. Signal. The children
   say the name of their school.)
   d. (Repeat step c until all children's
   responses are firm.)

2. Let's try those questions again.
   a. Everybody, what's your teacher's name?
   (Pause. Signal.)
   b. What's the name of the school you go to?
   (Pause. Signal.)

3. (Repeat part 2 until all children's responses
   are firm.)

Individual Turns
(Repeat the exercise, calling on different
children for each step.)

If the children have trouble answering the questions in step 2, shorten the questions: Teacher's name? Name of the school? After the children respond correctly to these abbreviated questions, return to the questions that appear in the exercise.

When the children are firm on the actions and information exercises in the first ten lessons, return to lesson 1 and present complete lessons (including the actions and information exercises). The new tracks they will work on are object identification and identity statements.

Developing Speech and Understanding (See Descriptions of Objects material in the Language tracks section of this guide.)

After completing lesson 10, continue through the language lessons, trying to complete a lesson a day. You will discover that the program develops speech and understanding together in a systematic way. For example, after the children learn to identify objects with a two-word phrase, they learn to make complete statements. Here is a part of an identity statement exercise:

What is this? *A ball.*

Say the whole thing. *This is a ball.*

If children have trouble with this exercise, change your directions to Say the whole thing about what **this is.** Now the last two words you say are the first two words the children say. Use these directions for a few days, and then return to Say the whole thing.

Children also learn to "Say the whole thing" about actions. They go through three steps:

1. Touch the floor.

2. What are you doing? *Touching the floor.*

3. Say the whole thing about what you are doing. *I am touching the floor.*

Note that the children construct the entire statement by simply saying the words *I am* before saying the words that tell what they are doing.

Therefore, for both the identity statements and actions exercises, the children learn a variation of the same pattern. They answer the question that asks what something is or what they are doing with a word or two. Then they "Say the whole thing" by saying *I am* or *This is* before the familiar words. With this knowledge, children can speak in the present tense. They know how to identify things and how to explain what they are doing.

Pronouns and Tense (See Actions in the Language tracks section of this guide.) The program adds to the children's knowledge by showing them how to construct sentences that tell what (a) *he* is doing, (b) *she* is doing, (c) *we* are doing, (d) *they* are doing. Then the children learn how to tell about past events. The children first learn to use statements that tell what they were doing (not what they did). The statements are the same as those that tell what the person **is** doing, except for the verb.

I am walking. I was walking.

I am touching my head. I was touching my head.

The pairing is obvious. The reason this approach is so effective is that it permits the children to describe events that have taken place without having to learn a host of irregular verbs to tell what happened. For example:

say—said	stand—stood
take—took	go—went
eat—ate	ride—rode
ran—run	drink—drank
sit—sat	feel—felt

The ability to generalize is very important for the emergent language learner. In *Reading Mastery Plus,* Level K the children first learn to express meanings in the present tense (I am riding a bike) but soon are able to construct past-tense statements (I was riding a bike).

More Objects and More Words (See Descriptions of Objects in the Language tracks section of this guide.) Because ESL children have more to learn than children whose first language is English, they may not be able to complete a lesson a day during the first 50 lessons of the program. Furthermore, they will probably need additional demonstrations of some of the objects that are named in the common objects track. After lesson 20, a good practice is to begin lessons with a routine in which you point to different objects in the room. For each object, you ask a series of yes/no questions: Is this a table? Is this a window? Is this a chair? If the answer is *yes,* give the children the instruction Say the whole thing. If the answer is *no,* present another or go to another object.

The value of this kind of "yes/no routine" early in the program is that although the children may not be able to produce the names of the various objects, they will recognize the name when you say it in your questions. But, after about lesson 50, you should change the routine so that the children answer the question What is this?

Note that the program does not teach all the common objects the children need to know. You can provide additional practice with other common objects that are in the classroom and that you and the children bring from home or from outside the school. A good plan is to make a list of all the common-object words the children have learned. These are words that should be reviewed. You can post the list with the words written and pictures next to the words. The list provides you with a measure of what the children have learned and provides the children with a way of reviewing what they are learning. Make sure that once you introduce a new object, you give children practice in identifying it on at least five different occasions before assuming that they have learned it. Then add the word to the list of words that should be reviewed.

After lesson 50, the children should begin to progress faster through the program. By lesson 100, they should be able to complete most lessons during a single period.

Language Games The children really like to play language games. As the children progress through the program, you can develop a number of language games based on what they are learning. For example, after the children learn new class names and opposites, you can play games that give children practice in applying this knowledge. Here are some ideas to start with:

Classification Games Announce a class that the children have learned, then point to different children. The children are to name something in that class. For example, Listen. You are going to name vehicles. Point to each child in turn. Each child names one vehicle. When the group runs out of vehicle names, challenge them with another classification term. (Possibly animals.)

Materials Games A similar game can be played with materials. For example, I am thinking of wood. Name some things that can be made of wood.

Opposites Games As children are learning opposites, you can play a variety of opposite games. You can present pairs of things or pictures of pairs of things, (for example, a tall building and a short building). Touch one member of the pair. Ask, Is this building tall or the opposite of tall? Or say, Tell me about this building. Tell me about the other building. You can collect sets of objects and pictures to use to play this game and add to your collection as the children learn more opposites.

For some opposites, you can play a kind of guessing game. For example, walk slowly. The children are to guess that you are *slow.* Ask, What is the opposite of slow? Another example: make a sad face. Children are to guess the word *sad.* Ask, What is the opposite of sad? You can use a variation of this game for quiet/noisy, old/young, awake/asleep, and other opposites.

Combination Games Another activity is a combination game in which children make statements about the color and name of an article of clothing that one child is wearing. As you point to an article of clothing that one child is wearing, the other children are to name the article of clothing and name its color. The statements should start with *He is wearing . . .* or *She is wearing . . .* and are completed with the color and name of the article. For example, *She is wearing orange socks* or *He is wearing a brown shirt.*

This game provides a lot of opportunities for the children to construct descriptive statements. Expect the children to have problems constructing statements that use plurals such as *She is wearing brown shoes.* Sometimes they leave out the verb or add an unwanted article. For example, *She is wearing a brown shoes.* Correct any mistakes by first letting the child know that the **observations** are correct. Then model a correct **statement** and have all the children in the group repeat it. For example, You are right. But listen: She is wearing brown shoes. Let's all say that.

If-Then Games An if-then game can be played when the children are learning about if-then reasoning. For example, say:

If you are wearing some blue clothing, stand up. Ask each child who stands, Why are you standing up? *I am wearing some blue clothing.*

What are you wearing that is blue? *Jeans.*

Have fun with the directions: If you have two legs, clap your hands. If you like dogs, jump up and down.

Real-Life Routines As a rule, use real-life routines for all the new concepts the children are learning. For instance, when the preposition *over* is introduced, go through this type of routine several times a day: Watch my hand. Is it over the desk? Is it on the desk? Where is my hand? Say the whole thing. When prepositions are introduced, play a variation of the same real-life routine.

Go through similar routines with other language concepts. For example, when children learn the classification term *containers,* you can point to different things in the classroom and ask about the classes the children are learning. Point to a wastebasket and ask, Is this a vehicle? Is this a container? What kind of container is it? Say the whole thing about this container. (Note that these routines are the same routines that children practice during the language lesson.)

Use the same approach for the materials the children are learning to identify. Display objects made of the different materials they are learning about, such as cloth, paper, metal, wood, glass, and plastic. Review these objects regularly by asking, What is this? and What is it made of?

With the addition of each new language concept, the children learn new statement patterns. Throughout the program, follow this general rule: Once children learn a new concept and a new statement pattern in the program, make sure that they use them in real-life situations. This will show you if the children have any problems understanding what they are learning and if they are having trouble applying the new concepts and statements in real-life situations.

The games and demonstrations described in this section are appropriate for all children. For children who do not speak English, however, the demonstrations are very important. They will help bridge the gap between simply understanding English and being able to use it as a means of communication.

The Pre-Reading Tracks

Pre-reading activities begin in lesson 41 as part of the daily language lessons. From lesson 51 through lesson 100, they continue in the Pre-Reading Presentation Book. The first two pre-reading activities, (both introduced in lesson 41) are the alphabet song and letter identification. Letter writing begins in lesson 47. Letter writing is replaced by **sound** writing after lesson 135. Most of the pre-reading activity ends around lesson 101 when the phonological skills are introduced. For example, the letter cross-out game is replaced at lesson 101 with a **sound** cross-out game.

		40	50	60	70	80	90	100	110	120	130	140	150
Alphabet	Alphabet Song	41	53										
	Letter Identification	41						100					
	Capital Identification								111-116				
Letter Writing	Regular Letters		47								135		
	(Sound Writing Starts at 136)												
	Capital Letters								111-122				
	Words from Capitals									123-130			
Oral Stories and Sequences						81			113				
	Story-Picture Book					81			112				
	Workbook					81			113				
Independent Activity	Letter Cross-Out Game						85	100					
	(Sound Cross-Out Starts at 101)												
	Picture Completion						87		116				
Materials Needed	Language Presentation A	41-50											
	Pre-Reading Presentation Book		51					100					
	Reading Presentation Book								101		135		
	Workbook A	41-50											
	Workbook B (Side 2)		51					100					
	Workbook C (Side 2)								101		135		
	Story-Picture Book					81			112				

Alphabet Track

The Alphabet Song (Lessons 41–53)

Children learn to identify letters. They also learn the alphabetical order. The work on alphabetical order familiarizes them with the letter names and sets the stage for later work that involves arranging words according to alphabetical order.

The main vehicle for the teaching of alphabetical order is the "Alphabet Song" that children learn starting with lesson 41. They work on the song for about 16 lessons. You use the "Alphabet Song" on side A of the tape (part of the presentation material) to teach the "Alphabet Song."

You will write the letters on the board and name them as part of the initial instruction. Note, however, that you should not expect children to learn the letters from this exposure. The reason is that the letters are always presented in the same order. Children who are able to recite the letter names and even point to them as they are named do not necessarily know how to identify the individual letters. They may be simply following the rule of pointing to the next letter when the next letter is named.

Think of the work with the "Alphabet Song" as a means of teaching the children alphabetical order and at the same time teaching them that the different letters have different appearances and different names. Later in the program, children will receive further work to refine their knowledge of the various letters.

Lesson 41: Alphabet Song

Below is the first "Alphabet Song" exercise.

EXERCISE 6   Alphabet Song

[**Note:** You will need "Alphabet Song" cassette and cassette player.]

a. (Write on the board:)

> **a   b   c**

You're going to learn the alphabet song. The alphabet song. Say that. (Signal.) *The alphabet song.*
The alphabet is made up of all the letters you will read. I have written the first three letters on the board.

b. (Point to **a**.) This letter is **A**.
What letter? (Signal.) *A.*
(Point to **b**.) This letter is **B**.
What letter? (Signal.) *B.*
(Point to **c**.) This letter is **C**.
What letter? (Signal.) *C.*

c. There are many more letters in the alphabet. We'll listen to the whole song. It names all the letters. (Play song.)

d. (Write to show:)

> **a   b   c   d**

Here are the first four letters. Listen. (Touch each letter as you say:) **A, B, C, D.**
Say that much with me. (Touch each letter as you and children say:) A, B, C, D.

e. Say it with me again. (Touch each letter as you and children say:) A, B, C, D.

f. (Repeat step e until firm.)

g. All by yourself. (Touch each letter as children say:) *A, B, C, D.*

h. (Repeat step g until firm.)

i. Let's listen to the whole song again. You can sing along for the first four letters. (Play song twice. Point to letters as they are named. Praise children who sing the part correctly.)

Teaching notes: You write the letters on the board in step a and step d.

You play the alphabet song in step c and in step i. Make sure that children are listening. Encourage them to clap as the letters are named. Also, if you sing along and show that you're having fun, you serve as a good model for them. In step i, praise children who sing the letter names correctly. Did you hear Mariko? She really knows the first letters.

In step d, after you play the song, you say the first four letters—**a, b, c, d.** Touch each letter as you say it. Repeat the touching and saying until the children's responses are firm. Praise children who say all four letters.

In step g, you direct the children to say the letters without your help. You may want to repeat this step several times until children's responses are firm.

When you play the song the second time in step i, you point to the letters as they are sung. Sing along with the tape and praise children who join in.

The same general procedure occurs on the following lessons. Children learn three or four more new letters at a time. New letters are introduced in every other lesson. You write letters on the board—the letters they have already learned and the letters that they are learning.

Lesson 50: Alphabet Song

Here is an alphabet exercise from lesson 50. In exercise 7, children are learning the letters **t, u, v.**

EXERCISE 7   Alphabet Song

[**Note:** You will need "Alphabet Song" cassette and cassette player.]

a. (Write on the board:)

```
a   b   c   d   e   f   g
      h   i   j   k
  l   m   n   o   p
      q   r   s
      t   u   v
```

(Point to last line.) Here are some new letters. I'll touch these new letters and say their names. (Touch each letter as you say:) **T, U, V.**
Say them with me. Get ready. (Touch each letter as you and children say:) T, U, V.
All by yourself. Say the new letters. Get ready. (Touch each letter as children say:) *T, U, V.*

b. I'll say the first parts. When I stop, you say the rest of the parts through the letter **V.** Listen: **A, B, C, D, E, F, G, H, I, J, K.** (Tap for each letter.) *L, M, N, O, P, Q, R, S, T, U, V.*

c. (Repeat step b until firm.) (Praise children who say all letters from **L** to **V.**)

d. I'll play the song. Sing along for the first parts, all the way through the letter **V.** (Play recording twice. Point to letters as they are named. Praise children who sing the part correctly.)

Teaching notes: In step d, children are expected to sing along through the letter **v.** Children should be firm on the previous parts of the song, particularly through the letter **s.** They have worked on this part for three days.

Lesson 52: Alphabet

By lesson 52, children have completed the song. They continue to sing and recite the alphabet. Here is exercise 1 from lesson 56. Children say the entire alphabet.

EXERCISE 1

ALPHABET

a. You've learned the whole alphabet.
b. Start with the letter **A** and say the whole alphabet. Get ready. (Tap for each letter.) *A, B, C, D, E, F, G, H, I, J, K, L, M, N, O, P, Q, R, S, T, U, V, W, X, Y, Z.*

Individual Turns
- (Call on individual children to say the alphabet. Praise good performers.)

Teaching note: Use the individual turns as an indicator of how firm the children's responses are. The goal is for all of them to be perfectly firm on the entire sequence of letters. If some children's responses are weak, provide more practice in saying the sequence.

Letter Identification (Lessons 41–100)

Letter identification is coordinated with the "Alphabet Song." The song first introduces the letters; the letter-identification exercises give children practice in identifying letters. The general pattern of introduction is for a new letter to be introduced about every other day. Once a letter is introduced, it is reviewed cumulatively. The chart on page 263 shows when each letter is introduced and shows the lessons in which each letter is reviewed. As the chart shows, new letters are not always introduced in every other lesson; however, they average every other lesson.

The first letter is introduced in lesson 41, the same lesson that presents the first "Alphabet Song" exercise. The letter-identification exercise occurs immediately after the alphabet exercise. Children have already seen the letters **a, b, c** on the board and have responded with the letter names.

Lesson 41: Letter Identification

Here's letter identification exercise 7, from lesson 41. Letters **a** through **d** are on the board.

EXERCISE 7   Letter Identification

a. (Underline the letter **c**. Point to **c**.) This is the letter **C**. What letter? (Signal.) *C.* I'm going to see if I can fool you. Tell me if I write the letter **C**.

b. (Write the letter **f**.) Is this the letter **C**? (Signal.) *No.* (Erase **f**.) (Write the letter **a**.) Is this the letter **C**? (Signal.) *No.* (Erase **a**.) (Write the letter **c**.) Is this the letter **C**? (Signal.) *Yes.* I wrote the letter **C**. (Erase **c**.)

Teaching notes: The reason **c** is presented as the first letter that children learn to discriminate is that it is not the first letter of the alphabet. If the first letter taught were **a,** some children would not pay attention to how it looks and would assume that the next letter they examined in isolation would be **b.**

In step a, you underline the letter **c** in the letters you have on the board (**a, b, c, d**). You identify the letter and then play a "fooler" game with the children. You write different letters on the board. Children tell you if each letter is **c.**

To correct mistakes, act amused. Tell the child who made a mistake, I fooled you. Then tell the children whether or not the letter is **c.** Do not identify the letter if it is not **c.** In step b, for instance, do not correct by telling children that the letter is **f.** Following a mistake tell children either:

This is **c.**

This is not **c.**

Do not let the exercise drag. Children have been working on letters for possibly five minutes by the time you have presented the letter-identification exercise. If children continue to make mistakes, tell them that you will come back to the exercise later. Point to the underlined **c** and remind them: This is **c.** Then go to the next exercise in the program. Return to the letter-identification exercise later, if possible.

A different type of letter-identification exercise is presented in lesson 44. This exercise relates what children are learning about letter names to the alphabetical order they are learning.

Here's exercise 7 from lesson 46. The letters **a** through **g** are already on the board.

EXERCISE 7   Letter Identification

a. (Underline **d.**)
This letter is **D.** What letter? (Signal.) *D.*

b. (Underline **a, c, f.**)
Look at the underlined letters. Tell me if I touch the letter **D.**
(Touch under **f.**) Is this **D**? (Signal.) *No.*
(Touch under **c.**) Is this **D**? (Signal.) *No.*
(Touch under **d.**) Is this **D**? (Signal.) *Yes.*
What letter is this? (Signal.) *D.*

c. I'll touch each underlined letter. You'll tell me the name.
(Touch under **d.**) What letter? (Signal.) *D.*
(Touch under **f.**) What letter? (Signal.) *F.*
(Touch under **c.**) What letter? (Signal.) *C.*
(Touch under **a.**) What letter? (Signal.) *A.*

d. (Repeat step c until firm.)

Worksheet 46

e. Find the snake. ✓
(Teacher reference:)

h	d	a	c	d	k	l	d	c

Some of the letters are **D.** Some are not **D.**

f. Touch the first letter in the row. ✓
Is that letter **D**? (Signal.) *No.*

g. Touch the next letter in the row. ✓
Is that letter **D**? (Signal.) *Yes.*

h. (Repeat step g for **a, c, d, k, l, d, c.**)

i. Listen. Circle all the **D**s. There are three **D**s.
(Observe children and give feedback.)
Everybody, what letter did you just circle? (Signal.) *D.*

j. Some of the letters that are not circled are **C.** Touch the first letter in the row. ✓
Is that letter **C**? (Signal.) *No.*

k. Touch the next letter in the row. ✓
Is that letter **C**? (Signal.) *No.*

l. (Repeat step k for **a, c, d, k, l, d, c.**)

m. Listen. Cross out all the **C**s. There are two **C**s.
(Observe children and give feedback.)
Everybody, what letter did you just cross out? (Signal.) *C.*

Teaching notes: Children have recently finished with the daily work on alphabetical order. You have written the letters **a** through **p** on the board. In step a, you underline a new letter, **d.** In step b, you underline the three letters children have learned to identify so far: **a, c, f.** In steps b and c, you refer to these letters. This work shows the relationship of the letters to their alphabetical order.

In steps f through m, you present tasks that are based on the appearance of individual letters, not on their order. The material for this part of the exercise is on worksheet 46. Steps f and g of the exercise show children a systematic way of finding letters. Children touch each letter and answer the question, Is that letter **d**?

Make sure that children are touching the letters and are not covering up the letters with their point.

If children make mistakes in step i, when they are supposed to circle all the **d**s, have them check their work by pointing to each letter and asking the question, Is that **d**?

Hold children to a high standard of performance. If they make a lot of mistakes, they are not firm in the skills that have been taught earlier in the program. You may have to do some firming before going on in the program.

This activity sets the stage for independent letter cross-out game (lessons 85–100).

Letter Writing (Lessons 47–135)

As part of the instruction in letter identification, children write letters. Letter writing starts in lesson 47 and ends in lesson 135. After lesson 135, children write **sounds.**

The letter writing chart (see Appendix G, page 264) shows the order of introduction of the letters children write and the lesson in which the letter is first written. The chart also shows how children are taught to write the letter. The steps are shown in black. Children start at the dot and complete the stroke that is shown. If there is more than one stroke, additional steps are shown.

The general scheme is for children to start out by tracing letters that are fully dotted. Children trace the letters by starting at the big dot and following the dotted line. If the letter has more than one part, children start the second part at the smaller dot and follow those dots.

Here's an exercise that shows the initial introduction of a letter.

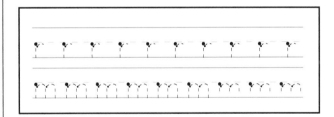

After children have completed several exercises of tracing completely dotted letters, succeeding exercises will present only the first five letters fulled dotted. The rest of the letters will be partly dotted.

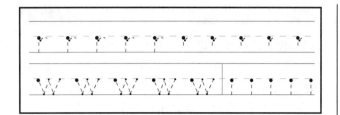

After a few more exercises, only the first three letters in a row are dotted and the rest partly dotted. The dotted prompts continue to fade until children are writing letters with minimal prompts or no prompts at all.

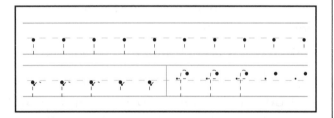

In the first letter-writing exercise (lesson 47), children write the letter **c**. In the following lesson, they write the letters **d** and **c**. They review **c** and write **d** for the first time. Here's part of the exercise from lesson 48. Children have already reviewed **c** and written a row of **c**s.

Teaching notes: Children learn that part of the letter **d** is the letter **c**. They first trace the **c,** then make a line that goes straight down.

Give students feedback when they are working. In step h, you observe children. Direct them to tell you how to make a **d.** Reinforce children who use the words, Follow the **c** around. Make a line straight down. When children verbalize that they make a **c** before they make the line straight down, they indicate a strategy that they can use later to discriminate **b** from **d.**

The same general strategies for responding to the children hold throughout the writing sequence. If children verbalize the rules you give them, they will tend to learn the letter writing tasks faster. If they receive feedback as they write, they will tend to be more careful in the way they make the letters. Initially praise children for following the dots closely. When dots are faded, praise children for making the letters without

---

EXERCISE 9 Letter Writing

a. Find the rows of dotted letters. ✓
Touch the first letter. ✓
Everybody, what letter is that? (Signal.) *C.*

b. I'll show you how to write the letter **C.**
(Hold up worksheet and pencil.)
I'll start at the big dot and trace the dotted line all the way around. Watch.
(Trace first three **C**s.)

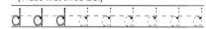

c. Everybody, touch the big dot on the first **C.** ✓
Start at the dot and trace the first **C.** Pencils down when you're finished.
(Observe children and give feedback.)

d. Complete the rest of the **C**s. Remember, start at the big dot and trace the dotted line. Pencils down when you're finished.
(Observe children and give feedback.)
Everybody, what letter did you write?
(Signal.) *C.*

e. Find the next row of dotted letters. ✓
Everybody, what letter is that? (Signal.) *D.*
D is a tall letter. Part of **D** is the letter **C.** The other part is a line that goes straight down. I'll show you how to write the letter **D.**
(Hold up worksheet and pencil.)

f. I'll start at the big dot and trace the **C** all the way around. Then I'll make the line that goes straight down. Watch.
(Trace first three **D**s.)

g. Everybody, touch the first **D.** ✓
Start at the big dot and trace the **C** all the way around. Pencils down when you've done that much. ✓
Now go to the little dot and trace the line straight down. Pencils down when you've completed the first **D.**
(Observe children and give feedback.)

h. Everybody, touch the next **D.** Start at the big dot and trace the **C** all the way around. Then go to the little dot and trace the line straight down. Pencils down when you've completed that **D.**
(Observe children and give feedback.)

i. Complete the rest of the **D**s. Pencils down when you're finished.
(Observe children and give feedback.)

dots look just like the letters that are fully dotted. Children always have a model for what they are to write. Refer to this model when telling them about their letters. Wow, you made those **m**s just like the first one in the row.

Writing a and ɑ

Children learn to write the letter a in lesson 91. The introduction shows two ways of writing the letter—**a** and ɑ. At first, children write the "curved top" **a.** In lesson 93, they do the "ball-and-stick" ɑ. In subsequent lessons, the children practice writing both styles of a.

Later in the Reading track (lessons 101–150), letters are referred to as sounds. The sound for each letter is the same sound that children use when they sound out words. The sound for the letter **a** or ɑ is **aaa** (as in **and**).

Capital Letters

Starting in lesson 111, children learn to identify capital letters and to write them. The capital letters are shown on a chart that is in the back of Workbook C.

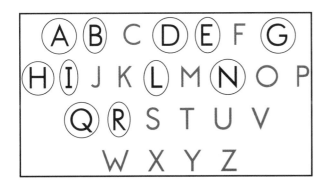

The circled letters are those that differ significantly from their lowercase counterparts. These are the first letters the children learn. The first letters introduced are **A, B, D,** and **E.** (**C** is not introduced because capital **C** is not significantly different from lowercase **C**). Children trace capitals that are next to their lowercase counterparts.

Here's part of the worksheet from lesson 111.

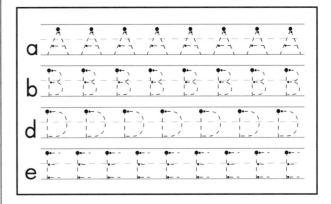

Teaching notes: When children are writing, ask them the name of the letter they are writing. The answer is not simply "A" or "D" but "Capital A" or "Capital D." If children have trouble identifying the letter, point to the lowercase letter at the left of the row and say something like, You're writing the capital for this letter. What's this letter? . . . So what's the capital you're writing?

Don't expect children to be firm on the various capitals in the first lesson in which they are introduced. Generally, you should expect them to be firm on the second day in which a particular capital has been practiced.

Starting with lesson 112, some of the letters children write are not fully dotted. Here's the letter-writing exercise from the worksheet for lesson 112.

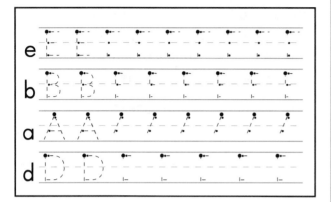

Only the first two letters in each row are fully dotted. The rest are partially dotted to prompt children with general directions to form the letter.

By lesson 117, children have completed writing the irregular capitals. They now write the lowercase version of those letters. This practice helps them identify each capital and associate it with the correct lowercase letter.

Here's the teacher presentation for lesson 117.

EXERCISE 12

Children write small letters below capital letters

a. (Hold up worksheet. Point to the row of capital letters.) Find the capital letters. ✓
b. You'll touch each letter and tell me the name.
• First capital. What letter? (Signal.) *Capital E.*
• Next capital. What letter? (Signal.) *Capital R.*

• Next capital. What letter? (Signal.) *Capital G.*
• Next capital. What letter? (Signal.) *Capital Z.*
• Next capital. What letter? (Signal.) *Capital S.*
• Next capital. What letter? (Signal.) *Capital A.*
• Next capital. What letter? (Signal.) *Capital N.*
c. Below each capital letter, you'll write the small letter. What's the first capital letter? (Signal.) *Capital E.*
• Right below the capital **E,** write a small **e.** Pencils down when you're finished. (Observe children and give feedback.)
d. (Hold up worksheet and write one **e.**)

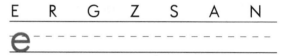

• Here's what you should have.
e. Your turn to write small letters below each of the other capital letters. (Observe children and give feedback.)

Words From Capitals

Children practice similar exercises until lesson 123, where they are presented with **words** in capital letters. They write those words in lowercase letters.

EXERCISE 10

Children write words from capitals to small letters, then read them

a. (Hold up worksheet. Point to **AM.**) Find the words and lines. ✓
These words are written with capital letters. Below each word, you'll write the same word with small letters.
b. Write the first word in small letters. Pencils down when you're finished. (Observe children and give feedback.)
• (Write on the board:)

am

- Here's what you should have.
c. Touch the next word. ✓
  Write the next word in small letters. Pencils down when you're finished. (Observe children and give feedback.)
- (Write on the board:)

me

- Here's what you should have.
d. Now you're going to read the words you wrote.
  Touch the first word. ✓
  Sound it out. Get ready. (Tap for each sound.) *Aaammm.*
  What word? (Signal.) *Am.*
  Yes, **am.**
e. Touch the next word. ✓
  Sound it out. Get ready. (Tap for each sound.) *Mmmēēē.*
  What word? (Signal.) *Me.*
  Yes, **me.**
f. Good writing and reading words.

After children have written their words, direct them to read the words. Praise children who work quickly and accurately.

Students practice exercises similar to the one above through lesson 130.

Oral Stories and Sequences (Lessons 81–113)

*R*eading Mastery Plus, Level K presents children with a series of oral stories and related sequencing tasks to introduce them to story-comprehension activities. These start as part of the daily Pre-Reading lessons at lesson 81 and continue through lesson 113. When the Reading lessons start at lesson 101, you may need to schedule the stories at another time of the day.

The only difference between the comprehension activities presented for oral stories and for stories that children read is how the children receive information about what happened. When they listen to a story read aloud, they **learn** this information.

If they were to read the same story, they would learn the information. Both oral stories and written stories present the same kind of information about what characters do and what motivates them. Both presentations present the same information about the setting, the problems confronting characters, the solution, and other details of the plot. Children show that they understand the information by answering comprehension questions.

A list of the stories and the lesson number for each appears on page 180.

Oral Stories and Sequences		
Story	Appears in Pre-Reading lessons (51–100)	Appears in Reading lessons (101–150)
Paul Paints Plums	81, 82, 85	
Paul Paints a Pot Pink	87	
Paul Paints Purple	89	
Paul Paints a Paddle	96	
Sweetie and the Birdbath	83, 84, 86, 90	
Sweetie and the Red Bow	98	101
Honey, Andrea, and Sweetie		105, 107
The Bragging Rats Race	88, 92, 95	
The Bragging Rats Have a Breathing Contest	93	
The Bragging Rats Have an Eating Contest	97	
The Bragging Rats Argue		111
Clarabelle and the Bluebirds	99, 100	102, 103
Clarabelle and the Bus		106
Roger and the Frog		108
Roger and the Bluebird at the Park		109
Rolla, the Merry-Go-Round Horse		110, 112
Story Character Preference		113

You'll read a story to the children more than one time, during more than one lesson. Some of the plots may be difficult for children at first. For these stories, you'll have to model the punch lines or the "moral" of the story and ask questions about the relevant details. After the children have listened to a story several times, they catch onto the sequence of events and they understand later stories with the same story line the first time they are read.

For example, in one story Sweetie is a nasty yellow cat who is always plotting to catch little birds or mice. In the first episode, Sweetie plans to catch birds that are in a birdbath, but he becomes completely confused about what happens. Here's the introduction of that story.

Story-Picture Book

EXERCISE 1

STORYTELLING

Sweetie and the Birdbath

a. (Hold up a story-picture book.)
- Here's your story-picture book.
b. (Open story-picture book and display story 2, page 4. Point to the large 2 at the top of the page.)
- This is the number **2.** Open your story-picture book and find the page with the big number 2. I'll help you. (Observe children and give assistance.)

c. Everybody, I'm going to tell you a new story that a lot of children really enjoy. Listen to the things that happen in the story, because you're going to have to fix up a picture that shows part of the story.

d. This is a story about a mean cat named Sweetie and the adventure he had with a birdbath. The story starts before there was a birdbath. Listen:

SWEETIE AND THE BIRDBATH

A woman named Bonnie loved birds. One day she noticed some birds cleaning themselves by splashing in a puddle. She said, "Those birds shouldn't have to splash in a puddle to get clean. They need a birdbath." That was a good idea.

- Listen: What did Bonnie see that gave her the idea that the birds needed a birdbath? (Call on a child. Idea: *Bonnie saw the birds splashing in a puddle.*)
- Everybody, look at the picture of the birds in a puddle. ✓

- Who is that person looking at the birds? (Call on a child. Idea: *Bonnie.*)
- (Hold up story-picture book. Point to thought balloon.)
- This balloon shows what Bonnie was thinking.
  Touch the balloon in your book. ✓
- What is Bonnie thinking about? (Call on a child. Idea: *Birds in a birdbath.*)
- That's the idea that Bonnie had. These birds need a birdbath.

The more Bonnie thought about getting a birdbath, the more she liked the idea. "I will get a birdbath big enough for all the birds that want to take a bath."

So Bonnie went to the pet store and looked at birdbaths. She picked out the biggest birdbath they had.

- Listen: Where did Bonnie go to get a birdbath? (Call on a child. Idea: *To the pet store.*)
- Which birdbath did she pick out? (Call on a child. Idea: *The biggest one they had.*)

The next day, a truck delivered the birdbath. Bonnie set it up in her backyard, and soon some birds saw it. They called to their friends, and, the first thing you know, all kinds of birds were splashing in the birdbath— red birds, yellow birds, spotted birds, and little brown birds.

- See if you can get a picture in your mind of that birdbath with lots of birds in it.
- What color are the birds in the birdbath? (Call on a child. Idea: *Red, yellow, brown, and spotted.*)
- What are those birds doing? (Call on a child. Idea: *Splashing in the birdbath.*)

A big yellow cat lived in the house next to Bonnie's house. That cat's name was Sweetie, but that cat was anything but sweet. Sweetie loved to chase birds. When Sweetie saw all the birds in Bonnie's birdbath, Sweetie said to himself, "Yum, yum. Look at all those little birds. I'm going to sneak over to that birdbath, jump up before they know I'm around, and grab some birds. Yum, yum."

e. Listen to Sweetie's plan again: **I'm going to sneak over to that birdbath, jump up before they know I'm around, and grab some birds. Yum, yum.**

f. Tell me the things that Sweetie plans to do. (Call on a child. Idea: *He plans to sneak over to the birdbath, jump up, and grab some birds.*)
• (Repeat until firm.)
g. Next page. Look at the picture of the cat behind the fence.
• Touch the cat. ✓

• What's the name of that cat? (Signal.) *Sweetie.*
• What's he looking at? (Call on a child. Idea: *The birds.*)
• What does he plan to do? (Call on a child. Idea: *Sneak over to the birdbath, jump up, and grab some birds.*)

So Sweetie crouched down and went through a hole in the fence. Then Sweetie snuck through some bushes that were near the birdbath—closer, closer, and closer until he was almost underneath the birdbath.

• Listen: How did Sweetie get into Bonnie's yard? (Call on a child. Idea: *He went through a hole in the fence.*)
• After Sweetie snuck through the hole in the fence, what did Sweetie do? (Call on a child. Idea: *He snuck through the bushes.*)
• Why didn't Sweetie just walk right up to the birdbath? (Call on a child. Ideas: *He didn't want the birds to see him; the birds would have flown away.*)
• So Sweetie snuck through the bushes until he was almost underneath the birdbath.
• Touch the picture that shows Sweetie in the bushes that are close to the birdbath. (Observe children and give feedback.)

Sweetie heard some chirping and fluttering, so he crouched down and waited—very still, without moving anything but the tip of his tail, which moved back and forth.

• Listen: What made Sweetie crouch down and become very still? (Call on a child. Idea: *He heard chirping and fluttering.*)
• I bet you wonder why those birds started fluttering and chirping. You're going to find out.

Well, Sweetie couldn't see what was happening in the birdbath, because Sweetie was in the bushes. But all that fluttering and chirping came about because a huge eagle decided to take a bath in the birdbath. So the eagle swooped down. And as soon as the other birds saw this huge eagle, with its great beak and its huge claws, they took off—fluttering and chirping.

• Listen: What made all the fluttering and chirping? (Call on a child. Idea: *The little birds started fluttering and chirping when the big eagle swooped down.*)
• Everybody, did Sweetie see the eagle? (Signal.) *No.*
• Why not? (Call on a child. Idea: *Because he was hiding in the bushes.*)
• Look at the picture that shows Sweetie in the bushes again. ✓
• Everybody, touch the eagle in that picture. That's the great big bird. (Observe children and give feedback.)
• Can Sweetie see that eagle? (Signal.) *No.*

- Why not? (Call on a child. Idea: *He's in the bushes.*)

> **Sweetie didn't know it, but there wasn't a group of little birds in that birdbath anymore. There was one huge bird—about three times as big as Sweetie.**

- Listen: What did Sweetie **think** was in the birdbath? (Call on a child. Idea: *Little birds.*)
- Everybody, what was **really** in the birdbath? (Signal.) *The eagle.*
- I think Sweetie is in for a big surprise.

> **Things were quiet now, so Sweetie got ready to leap up to the edge of the birdbath and grab some tiny birds. Sweetie crouched down and, with a great leap, shot out of the bushes and landed on the edge of the birdbath. He landed with his claws out, grabbing at the first thing he saw. He grabbed the eagle, and before Sweetie knew what was happening, that eagle grabbed him. The eagle picked Sweetie up and slammed him down into the middle of the birdbath. Splash!**

- Listen: Sweetie jumped out of the bushes and landed on the edge of the birdbath. What did Sweetie do next? (Call on a child. Idea: *He grabbed the eagle.*)
- What did the eagle do to Sweetie? (Call on a child. Idea: *Slammed Sweetie into the birdbath.*)
- I'll bet Sweetie was surprised to find himself slammed into the water.
- Turn the page. ✓
- Look at the picture of Sweetie leaping into the birdbath. ✓

- Does Sweetie know that he's grabbing an eagle? (Call on a child. *No.*)
- What's that eagle going to do to Sweetie? (Call on a child. Idea: *Slam him into the birdbath.*)

> **Sweetie hated water, and he was all wet. He put his ears back, and shot out of that birdbath so fast he looked like a wet yellow streak. He darted across the yard and through the hole in the fence. Then he just sat there with his mouth open and his eyes very wide.**

- Everybody, when Sweetie went back to his yard, did he sneak through the bushes? (Signal.) *No.*
- What did he do? (Call on a child. Idea: *He ran across the yard and through the hole in the fence.*)

> **"What happened?" Sweetie said to himself. One second he was grabbing at something, and the next second he was getting slammed into the birdbath.**
> **While Sweetie was trying to figure out what happened, he wasn't looking at the birdbath. He didn't see the eagle. That eagle finished bathing and took off. As soon as the eagle left, all the little birds returned to the birdbath.**
> **So when Sweetie finally peeked through the hole in the fence, he didn't see the eagle. He saw a bunch of little birds, twittering and splashing around in the water.**

- Everybody, **before** Sweetie snuck over to the birdbath, what did he see in the birdbath? (Signal.) *Little birds.*
- Now, when he was all wet, what did he see in the birdbath? (Signal.) *Little birds.*
- So he never saw the eagle when he looked through the hole in the fence.

Sweetie looked and looked at those birds for a long time. Then he said to himself, "From here those birds look pretty small and helpless. But when you get close to them, they are really big and strong. I don't think I'll go near that birdbath again."

- Poor Sweetie has the wrong idea about what happened.
- Listen once more to what Sweetie said to himself: **From here those birds look pretty small and helpless. But when you get close to them, they are really big and strong. I don't think I'll go near that birdbath again.**
- What kind of bird did he **think** threw him into the birdbath? (Call on a child. Idea: *A little bird.*)
- Those are the only birds Sweetie ever saw from his side of the fence—those little birds. And he's afraid to go near them because he thinks they're big and strong.
- Look at the picture of Sweetie all wet. ✓

- Why is Sweetie all wet? (Call on a child. Idea: *Because the eagle slammed him into the birdbath.*)
- Is he in Bonnie's yard now? (Call on a child. *No.*)
- Where is he? (Call on a child. Idea: *In his yard.*)
- The balloon above him shows what he is thinking. Touch that balloon. ✓
- The balloon shows how he thinks those little birds look if you get close to them. What kind of birds are those? (Call on a child. Idea: *Big and strong.*)
- Poor Sweetie got the wrong idea.

So now Bonnie is happy because her birdbath always has a lot of birds in it. The birds are happy because they can meet all their friends and have a nice bath whenever they want. Sweetie is the only one who is not all that happy. He looks at the birds in Bonnie's yard a lot, but he never goes over there, and he spends a lot of time trying to figure out how those birds could look so small but be so big and strong.

Worksheet 83

SIDE 2

EXERCISE 2
STORY EXTENSION

Note: Each child needs crayons.

a. (Hold up worksheet.) Everybody, find the picture of Sweetie. ✓
Here's a picture of something that happened in the story.

- What's Sweetie doing in this picture? (Call on a child. Idea: *Grabbing the eagle.*)
- Everybody, is Sweetie all wet yet? (Signal.) *No.*
- There are birds in the trees. See if you can find all of them and color them the right colors. Who remembers what colors they are? (Call on a child. Idea: *Red, yellow, brown, and spotted.*)
b. You'll color the birds. Then you'll color the rest of the picture.
- Everybody, what color is Sweetie? (Signal.) *Yellow.*
- That eagle is brown and white.

Teaching notes: You ask comprehension questions about the text you have read. The story has several pictures that show parts of the text. You refer to the pictures, ask questions about details, and relate the picture to the story students have just heard. A picture that shows part of the story is never presented until after the relevant part of the story has been read.

If children have trouble answering any questions, reread the part of the text that answers the question and repeat the question.

If children have persistent problems with a question, make sure that you tell them the answer and that they learn the answer; then plan to ask them the question again after you've completed the story.

Remember, if children perform well on the oral story questions that you present, they will have a far better understanding of stories that they read themselves and of the kind of story lines they will encounter in their reading.

Worksheet Activities

Following some of the oral stories are related worksheet activities. Later when children read stories, they will also complete worksheet activities that are related to the story.

Following the oral presentation of the Sweetie story, you introduce a worksheet activity.

The worksheet activity is signaled by the heading:

The heading indicates that children need worksheet 83 for this activity. You'll direct them to find the picture of Sweetie.

Here's the worksheet activity from lesson 83.

Teaching notes: If children are not reliable at remembering directions like color the little birds red, yellow, brown, and spotted, tell them to mark at least one bird red, one yellow, and one brown. When they color the worksheet picture later, the marks will serve as a reminder for the colors of the birds. They can do the same thing by marking the brown part of the eagle.

You'll reread "Sweetie and the Birdbath" in later lessons. These rereadings will make the details of the story memorable for the children. After they have listened to this story several times, you'll present other Sweetie stories. The children will be able to anticipate what will happen because they will have learned the basic theme: Sweetie doesn't actually see something that happens, and he draws the wrong conclusion about who did it or what actually happened.

Sequencing Exercises

Some of the sequencing exercises that children do are extensions of the basic stories that they hear. These exercises are presented after the children have listened to the story. The sequencing activity has an illustration of a character doing an action similar to one described in the story. There are letters on the pictures to indicate the sequence of actions the character will perform after completing the illustration action. The children retell the sequence of actions by referring to the letters.

The sequencing activities have several important purposes: (a) They sharpen retelling skills; (b) They reinforce the children's knowledge of story lines, and (c) They reinforce alphabetizing skills (when children order the events shown in the pictures, the letter A cues the first thing that happens, B the next, and so forth).

For example, in one story, Paul is a character who paints things either pink or purple. (Paul's preferred words start with the letter **p**.) He also uses a strange strategy when some paint drips onto an object that he is not painting. He "fixes" the mess by painting the entire object. For example, if he paints a paddle and some paint plops on a purse, he paints the entire purse. After children listen to different Paul stories, they do sequencing activities.

Here's a sequencing activity from lesson 96.

Story-Picture Book

EXERCISE 1

SEQUENCE STORY
Paul Paints a Paddle
a. (Open a story-picture book and display story 7.) This is the number 7.
• Open your book to the page with the big number 7. ✓
   (Observe children and give feedback.)

- Here's a new picture that shows the things that Paul painted pink. You can see that can of paint. It says, "Peony Pink" on it. That's the color of the paint that Paul is using—Peony Pink. A peony is a big flower. Some of them are a pretty pink. I'll bet Paul would like those flowers.

b. Everybody, touch letter **a.** ✓
- Touch **b.** ✓
- Touch **c.** ✓
- (Repeat step b until firm.)

c. Touch **a** again. ✓
The letter **a** shows what Paul painted first.
- Everybody, what is that? (Signal.)
A paddle.
- Yes, Paul was painting the paddle pink because he wanted a pink paddle for paddling with his pals down at Poplar Pond.

d. Touch letter **b.** ✓
The letter **b** shows what he painted next.
- Everybody, what is that? (Signal.)
A purse.
- Why do you think Paul painted the purse pink? (Call on a child. *Ideas: He got some pink paint on it while he was painting the paddle.*)

e. Touch letter **c.** ✓
That's what he painted next.
- Everybody, what is that? (Signal.)
A plate.
Yes, that's a plate.

- Why do you think he painted the plate pink? (Call on a child. Idea: *He got some pink paint on it while he was painting the purse.*)

f. Look at the letters and say the story to yourself. Then I'll call on several children to see if they can say the whole story to the rest of us. Raise your hand when you're ready to tell the story. ✓

g. (Call on a child:) You tell the story. A really good story would start out by telling that Paul wanted to paddle with his pals at Poplar Pond. Then tell the color he was painting. Then tell what happened at each letter, but don't say the letters. Everybody else, follow along and see if (child's name) tells what happened for each letter.
(Praise child for a story that tells the sequence of things that were painted.)

h. (Repeat step g, calling on a different child.)

Teaching notes: The letters show the order of things that were splattered with paint that is peony pink.

In steps f and g, you call on different children to tell the story. For each letter, children are to tell what Paul was painting, what happened while he was painting, and what he did next.

If children have trouble telling the story and keeping track of which letter they are telling about, model how to tell the story. Children are to touch the objects you tell about. Don't say the letters. As soon as you start talking about the purse, however, children should touch B. You can ask them what letter they are touching. For each object, keep your storytelling brief. Identify what Paul was painting, what got splattered or dripped on, and what Paul did.

When children try to tell what happened at the various letters, they tend to make two types of mistakes:

1. They tell what Paul paints, but they don't tell why.

2. They tell why Paul paints the various objects, but they don't tell what he did next.

Here's an example of each type of mistake and the correction.

1. "Paul painted the paddle with peony pink paint. Then he painted the purse. Then he painted . . ."

Stop. Why did he paint the purse? You have to tell that before you tell that he painted the purse. Listen. Paul was painting the paddle when some paint dropped on the purse. So Paul painted the whole purse.

Your turn. Remember to tell what he painted and then tell what happened to make him paint the next object.

2. "Paul painted the paddle with peony pink paint. Some paint fell on the purse. Then some paint spilled on the plate . . ."

Stop. You're not telling about what Paul did when the paint fell on something. What did he do when paint fell on the purse?

Listen. Paul was painting the paddle when some paint fell on the purse. So Paul painted the whole purse pink . . .

Your turn. Remember to tell what he painted and then tell what happened to make him paint the next object.

Remember the steps in the basic correction.

1. Tell the child about the mistake. Ask a "why" question or a question about what the character did.

2. Model an acceptable telling.

3. Finally, direct the child to retell the sequence.

The program has another variation of sequencing activities. For this variation, the students write letters to show a sequence of events. Here is an example.

Worksheet 89

SIDE 2

EXERCISE 2

SEQUENCE STORY

Paul Paints a Parrot

a. Everybody, find the picture of Paul painting. ✓

- I'll tell you a story about Paul two times. The first time I tell it, you'll touch the things that Paul paints. The second time I tell it, you'll write letters in the circles.
b. The picture shows where Paul was at the beginning of the story. Where is Paul? (Call on a child. Idea: *At his desk in his room.*)
- Here's the story:

PAUL PAINTS A PARROT

Paul was in his room painting a picture of a purple parrot.

- Everybody, touch the circle on the picture of the parrot. ✓

Paul painted every part of the parrot purple, but just when he finished, some purple paint plopped onto his pencil.

- Everybody, touch the circle on the pencil. ✓

Paul looked at the part of his pencil that was purple and said, "I'll fix up that pencil." So he did.

- What do you think he did? (Call on a child. Idea: *Painted his whole pencil purple.*)

He painted the whole pencil purple, but just as he was finishing up, he noticed purple paint on his pajama pants.

- Everybody, touch the circle on Paul's pajama pants. ✓

Paul said, "Oh, pooh. The purple part of these pajamas looks poor. But I can fix up these pajama pants." So he did just that.

- What did he do? (Call on a child. Idea: *Painted his pajama pants purple.*)

And just as he was almost finished painting his pajama pants purple, he noticed some purple paint in the palm of his hand.

- Listen: The palm of your hand is the inside, not the back, of your hand. Everybody, touch the palm of your hand. ✓
- Everybody, touch the circle on Paul's palm. ✓

Paul said, "Part of my palm is purple. I can fix that." So he did.

- What do you think he did? (Call on a child. Idea: *Painted his palm purple.*)
c. That's the story about Paul. I'll tell the story one more time, and you'll write letters in the circles. (Write on the board:)

a b c d

- You'll write **a, b, c,** and **d** to show which things were painted first and next.
- Listen: What was the first thing Paul painted in this story? (Call on a child. Idea: *A picture of a parrot.*)
- Everybody, touch the circle on the picture of the parrot. ✓
- Write a letter **a** in that circle. Raise your hand when you're finished. (Observe children and give feedback.)
d. Listen:

When Paul was just finishing painting the parrot purple, some purple paint plopped onto his pencil.

- Everybody, touch the circle on the pencil. ✓
- You already used the letter **a.** So what letter goes in this circle? (Signal.) *B.*
- Write a letter **b** in the circle. Raise your hand when you're finished. (Observe children and give feedback.)
e. Listen:

Paul painted the whole pencil purple. Just as he was finishing up, he noticed purple paint on his pajama pants.

- Everybody, touch the circle on Paul's pajama pants. ✓
- Think big. You already used the letters **a** and **b.** So what letter goes in this circle? (Signal.) *C.*

- Write a letter **c** in that circle. Raise your hand when you're finished.
  (Observe children and give feedback.)
  f. Listen:

> **Paul painted his pajama pants purple. But just when he was almost done, he noticed some purple paint in the palm of his hand.**

- Everybody, touch the circle on Paul's palm. ✓
- Think big. Everybody, what letter goes in that circle? (Signal.) *D.*
- Write a letter **d** in that circle. Raise your hand when you're finished.
  (Observe children and give feedback.)

g. Now you have letters that tell about the things that Paul did in this story. Who can tell the whole story? Remember, you have to tell where Paul was at the beginning and what he did for each letter. Don't say the letters. Just tell what he did first, what he did next, and so on.

h. (Call on a child:) You tell the story. Everybody else, follow along and see if (child's name) tells what happened for each letter.
  (Praise child for a story that tells the sequence of things that were painted.)
  (To correct omissions, say:)
  a. You missed something. Who knows what was missed?
  b. (Call on another child.)

i. (Repeat step h, calling on a different child.)

j. Later you can color all the things that Paul painted purple in this story. You can color the things he didn't paint any color you wish.

This sequence follows a Paul story (*Painting a Purple Parrot*). During the first telling of the story, children touch the circles that show where the paint dripped first, next, and so forth. Then children write the appropriate letters in the circles. Children retell the story and then color all the things Paul painted purple.

Story Character Preferences

The last structured activity relating to the Story-Picture Book gives the children the opportunity to pick their two favorite characters from the stories they have listened to since lesson 81. The children then determine which two characters are the most popular for their class.

Pre-Reading Independent Activity (Lessons 85–116)

The worksheet activities for the pre-reading phase include letter writing, letter cross-out games and picture completion.

Generally, a structured presentation introduces each independent activity. Following several structured lessons, children are able to perform independently.

Children's independent work should be checked daily. The answer key shows what children are to do for each part of the worksheet. Here are guidelines for checking independent work.

1. Check it either while children are doing their independent activity or at the end of the independent activity period.

2. Give children feedback on parts they did well and on any problems they had. Oral feedback while children work is very effective: Nice job, Milton. You're really writing your letters carefully.

3. Require children to fix up any errors and show you the corrected paper.

4. Encourage children to take their worksheets home and share them with their parents. A possible plan is to send the pages home weekly, perhaps every Wednesday, accompanied by a sign-off sheet. The parent signs the sheet and the child returns it to receive a home-connection bonus—possibly 3 points.

If the home connection is handled on a weekly basis, children are more likely to take care of the material, and parents are more likely to respond.

Managing Independent Activity

The simplest plan is to have a point or reinforcement system. For example, children may receive 2 points for making no more than 2 errors on the worksheet. Children who make no errors may receive 3 points. The points are awarded only after children make corrections on the worksheet. (Children who made more than 2 errors receive one point for fixing up the worksheet so it has no errors.)

A class chart for progress in independent activities is a good device for keeping a record of the children's performance and for motivating the group to get perfect papers.

Progress Chart

Names	Worksheet Errors	Corrections Made	Points
Kristine	2	✔	2
Jamal	0		3
Terry	4	✔	1
Svetlana	1	✔	2
Enrique	3	✔	1

Letter Cross-Out Games (Lessons 85–100)

Cross-out games give children practice in scanning for specified symbols. The early games show a boxed symbol that is crossed out. Children are to cross out every appearance of that symbol. Here's the cross-out game from lesson 85.

Children cross-out all the **as**. **Note:** All the letters presented in this exercise were reviewed earlier in the lesson. Children refer to the symbols by their letter names.

Later appearances of the cross-out game present a larger number of letters and letters that are more highly similar to each other.

After lesson 100, the letter cross-out games are replaced by **sound** cross-out games in which the symbols are referred to by the sound.

Picture completion requires children to follow and connect the dots. After children complete a picture, they color it. The tracing and coloring reinforce skills that children use when they copy and write. Here's the picture completion for lesson 90.

The Reading Tracks Lessons 101–150

Introduction

Reading sounds starts at lesson 101. At lesson 124 the children begin to read words. Lessons 101 to 123 are designed to set the stage for the word reading. The activities presented in this part of the Reading Component are possibly the most important in the entire program. If children master these activities, they typically have little trouble with the next instructional steps. However, if children are not taught these important sound-reading skills, they will probably have serious trouble throughout the Reading Component.

During these beginning reading lessons, children learn to identify symbols as "sounds"; they practice sequencing events—*first* and *next* events; they firm their oral-blending skills by saying words slowly and saying them fast; and they learn to rhyme. Rhyming provides a basis for seeing how words may be divided into families based on their ending sounds.

General Teaching Strategies

To teach reading successfully, you must be able to communicate clearly with the children and receive clear information on what they understand or the specific problems they are experiencing. Success in communicating implies that you give the group clear signals about when to respond; that you present the formats or activities in the program so they are well paced; that you respond quickly to mistakes by presenting the appropriate correction procedure; and that you present individual turns so that you can carefully evaluate the performance of each child.

The following section of this guide is designed to help you practice the specific skills that you will use when working with children. This section explains the purpose of each track in the reading section. It presents some of the key formats or exercises within the track. It also indicates how to correct some of the more common mistakes the children will make.

The best way to learn the skills that are required is to practice, and the best way to practice is with a partner. During the initial practice sessions, you and your partner should take turns playing the roles of teacher and child. The "child" should respond correctly to all tasks and should give the "teacher" feedback about how the teacher executed the different parts of the format.

Using the Reading Presentation Book

The Reading Presentation Book provides you with directions for presenting each exercise and also provides display material for the children. For example, some of the exercises involve identifying symbols. The symbols the children respond to are included in the Reading Presentation Book.

In each lesson, the track headings (such as Sounds–Say It Fast) are printed in boldface capitals. If a Reading track has not been presented before, its title is preceded by an **asterisk.** The track titles will tell you at a glance the skill to be developed in the exercises that follow. The Reading exercise number is followed by a brief description of that exercise's objective.

While the children are working from examples in the Reading Presentation Book, be sure to hold it so that every child in the group can see it. When pointing to or touching examples in the book, do not cover anything with your hand or arm that the children need to see.

As you progress through the lessons, you will notice that some of the exercise titles have lines above and below them. The lines signal the introduction of a new format. Since the tracks are all very tightly sequenced, there may be minor changes in a format that are not signaled by using lines; be alert for such changes and implement them in your presentation. When you see the lines, however, you will be alerted to a major change in the method of presenting the task. Be careful not to continue the pattern of the old format.

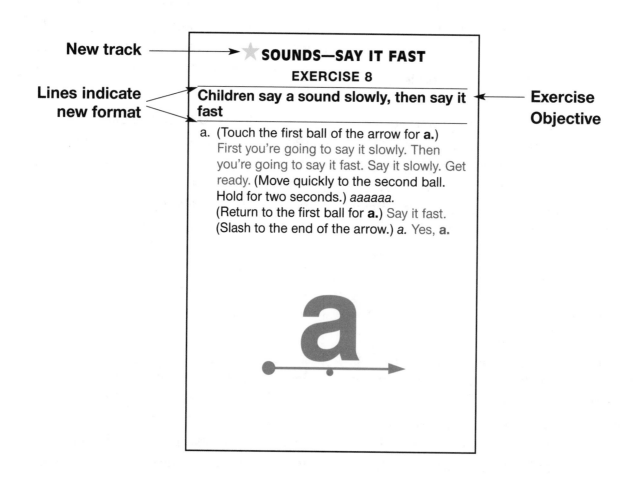

New track

Lines indicate new format

★ **SOUNDS—SAY IT FAST**

EXERCISE 8

Children say a sound slowly, then say it fast

Exercise Objective

a. (Touch the first ball of the arrow for **a.**) First you're going to say it slowly. Then you're going to say it fast. Say it slowly. Get ready. (Move quickly to the second ball. Hold for two seconds.) *aaaaaa.*
(Return to the first ball for **a.**) Say it fast. (Slash to the end of the arrow.) *a.* Yes, **a.**

Mastering Signals used in the Reading Track

Signals show each child when to respond, so that each will originate an independent response and yet all children will respond together. The signal or signals used in each reading track are described before specific formats are discussed, and should be learned through practice before you review the formats. If you learn these signals well, you will be prepared to execute the motor behaviors for any of the formats.

Here are a few suggestions for studying and practicing the reading formats.

- Learn to execute the signal or signals smoothly and automatically.

- Read the format. Remember, new reading tracks are indicated with a star. Reading exercises with new format wording are indicated with two lines.

- Review the teaching techniques.

- Rehearse the pacing of the key statements you are to make.

- Combine the script of the format with the signals.

- Practice the entire format, repeating it several times.

- Practice the format again, until you can perform it confidently.

- Practice pronouncing the 13 sounds that appear on the pronunciation chart (Appendix H).

After you are able to run the format smoothly, practice the format with corrections. Practice correcting mistakes the children are most likely to make. Anticipate that you will have to use each of these corrections. Facility in executing the corrections will make a great deal of difference in the performance of the children, especially those in your lowest-performing group.

Memorize the steps in the corrections. Continue to practice the corrections until you can respond automatically to any mistake with the appropriate correction. As soon as the error is made, go immediately into the correction, then return quickly to the appropriate step in the format.

Reading Skills

Sounds (Lessons 101–150)

In *Reading Mastery Plus,* Level K students are initially taught to decode words by sounding them out. To sound out a word successfully students must be firm in sounds identification. Sounds activities, therefore, appear in every lesson in the reading component. The two primary formats in the Sounds track are a *sound introduction* format, used to introduce and reinforce each new sound, and a *sound firming* format, in which several sounds are reviewed and firmed up. Other formats include game formats such as a cross-out game, a child-plays-teacher game, and a sounds game.

Beginning at lesson 101, letters are referred to by their *sounds* as well as by their alphabet names.

Throughout most of the reading tracks, each symbol stands for a single sound. The symbol **a** stands for the sound *aaa* (as in *and*). It does not stand for **a** as in **ate,** in **all,** or in **father.**

To allow the children to read more words as "regular words" five conventions are followed in the program:

1. The sound **ththth** is represented by joined letters:

th

2. Macrons (long lines over vowels) differentiate long vowels from short vowels:

ē makes the long vowel sound in **ēₐt**

a makes the short vowed sound in **and**

i makes the short vowel sound in **if**

o makes the short vowel sound in **ox**

3. Some symbols are altered to reduce some of the confusion children typically have between pairs of letters that appear very much alike in traditional orthography. For example:

b d   f t

4. Small symbols represent silent sounds. For example:

ēₐt   rocₖ

5. Only lowercase letters are taught as sounds in *Reading Mastery Plus*, Level K and Level 1, so that the children will not have to use two symbols for each sound.

This special orthography is continued in Level 1. By lesson 20 of *Reading Mastery Plus*, Level 2, all letters are printed in traditional orthography.

The children are taught thirteen sounds. Only one value is taught for each sound. New sounds are introduced about every three to four lessons. Here is a list of the lessons in

which new sounds are introduced. The complete pronunciation chart can be found in Appendix H.

Symbol	Pronounced	As in	Voiced or Unvoiced	Introduced in Lesson
a	aaa	<u>a</u>nd	v	101
m	mmm	ra<u>m</u>	v	104
s	sss	bu<u>s</u>	uv	109
ē	ēēē	<u>e</u>at	v	115
r	rrr	ba<u>r</u>	v	119
d	d	ma<u>d</u>	v	123
f	fff	stu<u>ff</u>	uv	127
i	iii	<u>i</u>f	v	130
th	ththth	<u>th</u>is and ba<u>th</u>e (not thing)	v	134
t	t	ca<u>t</u>	uv	137
n	nnn	pa<u>n</u>	v	140
c	c	ta<u>ck</u>	uv	144
o	ooo	<u>o</u>x	v	147

Note that children start to read words at lesson 124, after six sounds have been introduced.

The first five sounds are *a, m, s, ē,* and *r.* Before teaching lesson 101, practice pronouncing the 13 sounds. The cassette that accompanies this program models the correct pronunciation of all 13 sounds.

Note that some sounds are continuous sounds and some are stop sounds. Continuous sounds can be held until you run out of breath. Continuous sounds include all vowels and such consonants and digraphs as **s, m, r, f, th,** and **n.** Stop sounds are sounds that must be produced very quickly, like **d, b, c, g, h, p, t.**

The first sounds in the program are continuous sounds because they are easier for the children to pronounce.

Continuous Sound Signal

All signals follow the same basic rules:

- You talk first, then signal.

- You never signal when talking.

- You always pause the same length of time between the **end** of your talking and the signal for the children to respond, about one second.

Remember, talk first, then signal, and keep the timing the same for every signal.

You use signals to permit a group of children to respond together with every child in the group initiating the response, not merely imitating what others in the group do. Therefore, your signal must be very clear and easy to follow. Think of a signal as something like a dance step. If it's done right, and in time, your partner can follow. If the timing is off, somebody's going to stumble.

To signal children to respond to a continuous sound, follow these steps:

- Touch the first ball of the arrow.

- Keep your finger on that ball as you say Get ready.

- Pause for one second. Then move quickly to the ball under **a** and hold on that ball for two seconds. As soon as you touch that ball, **all** the children are to respond.

Practice touching the first ball, saying Get ready, pausing one second, then moving quickly to the second ball and holding your finger there for two seconds.

Continuous Sounds Teaching Techniques

Practice steps e through l in the following sounds-introduction format. Be very consistent with your signal. Note that the last thing you say before this signal is always Get ready. Timing is the same as it is for the simple signal that you practiced. Pause after saying Get ready and move quickly to the second ball. Hold at the second ball as either you or the children respond. The letters **aaa** in the teacher's script remind you to hold the sound.

- Steps e through g model the behavior so the children know what they should respond and how they should respond in steps h and i.

- Step h is the first time the students are to respond.

- Following step h is a correction to be used if the children respond incorrectly. Present the correction **as soon as** you hear or see any child responding incorrectly. The correction steps have been labeled to help you see the model-lead-test procedure.

- Step j directs you to repeat step i until firm. "Firm" means that all children are responding clearly as soon as you touch under the sound and that all children are saying the sound as long as you touch under it.

- At step k you call on different children to identify the sound. Remember to include lower-performing children in your individual turns. If a child makes a mistake on step k, **present the correction to the group,** then repeat steps i through k.

Lesson 101

LETTER SOUNDS
EXERCISE 2
Introducing the sound aaa as in and

a. (Touch the first ball of the arrow.) Everybody, what letter is this? (Signal.) *A*.
- That letter makes the sound you hear at the beginning of some words.
b. Listen: **am.** What word? (Signal.) *Am*.
- The first sound in **am** is **aaa.** What sound? (Signal.) *aaa*.
c. (Repeat b until firm.)
d. The letter **A** makes that sound.
e. When I move under the letter, I'll say the sound. I'll keep on saying it as long as I touch under it. Watch. (Quickly move to the second ball. Hold for two seconds.) *aaa*.
f. (Touch the first ball of the arrow.) My turn again. Get ready. (Move quickly to the second ball of the arrow. Hold for two seconds.) *aaa*.
g. (Touch the first ball of the arrow.) My turn again. Get ready. (Move quickly to the second ball of the arrow. Hold for two seconds.) *aaa*.
h. (Touch the first ball of the arrow.) Your turn. When I move under the sound, you say it. Keep on saying it as long as I touch under it. Get ready. (Move quickly to the second ball of the arrow. Hold for two seconds.) *aaa.* Yes, **aaa.**

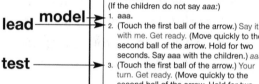

To correct
(If the children do not say *aaa:*)
1. **aaa.**
2. (Touch the first ball of the arrow.) Say it with me. Get ready. (Move quickly to the second ball of the arrow. Hold for two seconds. Say aaa with the children.) *aaa.*
3. (Touch the first ball of the arrow.) Your turn. Get ready. (Move quickly to the second ball of the arrow. Hold for two seconds.) *aaa.*

i. (Touch the first ball of the arrow.) Again. Get ready. (Move quickly to the second ball of the arrow. Hold for two seconds.) *aaa.* Yes, **aaa.**
j. (Repeat i until firm.)
k. (Call on different children to do h.)
l. Good saying **aaa.**

Stop Sound Signal

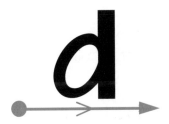

The sound *d* above is a stop sound, a sound that cannot be held for more than an instant without distorting it.

The following procedures are used to signal for stop sounds:

- Touch the first ball of the arrow.

- Say Say it fast.

- Pause for one second.

- Quickly move your finger to the end of the arrow. As you pass under the arrowhead that is directly under the **d,** the children are to say the sound, *d* (not *duh* or *dih,* simply *d*).

Note that the signal for the stop sound involves the same timing as the signal for the continuous sound. The only difference is that you don't stop under the sound; you just keep moving to the end of the arrow.

If you have trouble pronouncing a stop sound, say a word that ends in the sound. Say the sound in an exaggerated manner. That is the way you would pronounce it when teaching children to identify the symbol. For instance, say the word **sad,** exaggerating the **d.** Be careful not to say *saduh.*

Stop Sounds Teaching Techniques

In the teacher's script and on the pronunciation guide, stop sounds are represented by a single letter such as **d, t,** or **c,** to help you remember to say the sound fast. This compares with the three letters **(aaa)** used to remind you to hold continuous sounds. After practicing the basic signal for stop sounds, practice the following sounds-introduction format.

Lesson 123

LETTER SOUNDS
EXERCISE 2

Introducing the new sound d as in dad

a. (Touch the ball of the arrow for **d.**) Everybody, what letter is this? (Signal.) *D.* Listen: We always have to say the sound for this letter fast. The little arrow under the sound tells me that I can't stop under this sound. My turn to say it fast. (Slash to the end of the arrow as you say **d.** Return to the ball.) My turn to say it fast again. (Slash to the end of the arrow as you say **d.**)

b. (Touch the ball of the arrow.) Your turn. Say it fast. (Slash to the end of the arrow.) *d.* Yes, **d.**

c. (Repeat *b* until firm.)

d. (Call on different children to do *b.*)

d

In step *b,* pause after you say Your turn, and before you say Say it fast, to give the children a moment to think.

Corrections

If students mispronounce the sound at step *b,* correct as follows:

model → 1. (Say:) d.

test ⟶ 2. (Touch the ball of the arrow. Say:) Your turn. Say it fast. (Slash to the end of the arrow. Children say:) *d.*

Sounds Firm-up Teaching Techniques

In sounds firm-up exercises children review and practice the sounds they have learned. Sounds firm-up exercises appear in every lesson starting with lesson 104. Firm-up exercises are the most important source of feedback about how well children have learned sounds. There are no new signals in the exercise. Use the signals for a continuous sound and for a stop sound that you have already practiced.

Lesson 123

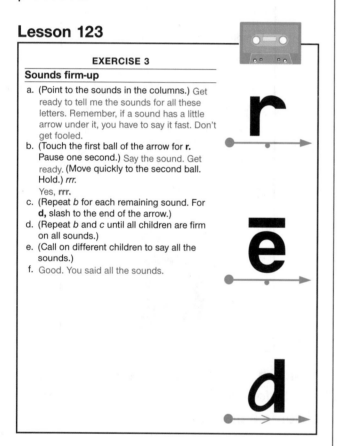

EXERCISE 3

Sounds firm-up

a. (Point to the sounds in the columns.) Get ready to tell me the sounds for all these letters. Remember, if a sound has a little arrow under it, you have to say it fast. Don't get fooled.

b. (Touch the first ball of the arrow for **r.** Pause one second.) Say the sound. Get ready. (Move quickly to the second ball. Hold.) *rrr.*
Yes, **rrr.**

c. (Repeat b for each remaining sound. For **d,** slash to the end of the arrow.)

d. (Repeat b and c until all children are firm on all sounds.)

e. (Call on different children to say all the sounds.)

f. Good. You said all the sounds.

Step *e* of the format calls for individual children to say all the sounds in the column. The individual test is very important. You will receive feedback about how well each child has learned the sounds. Make sure that you give turns to the lower-performing children.

Corrections

No correction box is in the exercise. If any child in the group misidentifies the sound at step *b*, correct as follows:

model → 1. (Say:) rrr.

test → 2. (Touch the first ball of the arrow for **r.** Pause one second. Say:) **Everybody, get ready.** (Move to the second ball. Hold. Children say:) *rrr.*

The following dialogue illustrates how to handle mistakes on individual turns. The teacher presents an individual turn to Lucy, who makes a mistake at step *d*. The teacher corrects **the group,** then returns to Lucy. This procedure is important. If an individual child makes a mistake, assume that others in the group would make the same mistake. By first correcting the group, you save time, because you won't have to present the same correction to other members of the group.

Read the dialogue out loud. Make sure that you understand why the teacher takes each of the steps that appears in the script.

Script For Step e

1. <u>Teacher:</u> (Touch the first ball of the arrow for **r.**) Lucy, your turn to say all the sounds in this column. (Pause one second.) Get ready. (Move quickly to the second ball. Hold.)

2. <u>Lucy:</u> *rrr.*

3. <u>Teacher:</u> Yes, **rrr.** (Touch the first ball of the arrow for **ē.** Pause one second.) Get ready. (Move quickly to the second ball. Hold.)

4. Lucy: *aaa.*

5. Teacher: ē̄ē̄ē̄. (Return to the first ball of the arrow for ē̄. Pause one second.) Everybody, get ready. (Move quickly to the second ball. Hold.)

6. Group: ē̄ē̄ē̄.

7. Teacher: Yes, ē̄ē̄ē̄. (Return to the first ball of the arrow for ē̄. Pause one second.) Lucy, get ready. (Move quickly to the second ball. Hold.)

8. Lucy: ē̄ē̄ē̄.

9. Teacher: Yes, ē̄ē̄ē̄. (Return to the top of the column. Touch the first ball of the arrow for **r.**) Starting over. (Pause one second.) Lucy, get ready. (Move quickly to the second ball. Hold.)

10. Lucy: *rrr.*

11. Teacher: Yes, **rrr.** (Touch the first ball of the arrow for ē̄. Pause one second.) Get ready. (Move quickly to the second ball. Hold.)

12. Lucy: ē̄ē̄ē̄.

13. Teacher: Yes, ē̄ē̄ē̄. (Touch the ball of the arrow for **d.** Pause one second.) Get ready. (Slash to the end of the arrow.)

14. Lucy: *d.*

15. Teacher: Yes, **d.** Good. You said all the sounds in the column.

Saying the Sounds (Lessons 101–144)

Purpose of the Track

This track provides practice in pronouncing sounds. All Saying the Sounds exercises are oral. The children practice saying a sound before they identify the written symbol for that sound.

The sounds that are practiced include those that may be difficult to pronounce. Pronunciation exercises precede Sounds exercises, and always include any new sounds that will be introduced in that lesson.

Pronunciation Signal

To signal a sound response, hold up one finger. This signal will be used in several other tracks, including those oral tracks in which students say words or word parts slowly.

Lesson 111

SAYING SOUNDS

EXERCISE 1

Children say the sounds

a. You're going to say some sounds. When I hold up my finger, say (pause) **sss.** Get ready. (Hold up one finger.) *sss.*

b. Next sound. Say (pause) **t.** Get ready. (Hold up one finger.) *t.*

c. Next sound. Say (pause) **ăăă.** Get ready. (Hold up one finger.) *ăăă.*

d. (Repeat c for sounds **sss, t,** and **ăăă.**)

e. (Call on different children to do *a, b,* or *c.*)

f. Good saying the sounds.

Note that only in this oral task are short vowels written as ăăă (or ŏŏŏ or ĭĭĭ).

Pronunciation Teaching Techniques

- Signal so that continuous sounds like *aaa* or *sss* are held for about two seconds, and stop sounds such as *t* are said fast.

- Make sure that children are pronouncing sounds correctly.

- When presenting a sound, remember to pause when saying "Say (pause) **ăăă.**"

- Remember to present step *c* for each sound.

Corrections

Correct mistakes by presenting a lead, then a test.

lead ⟶ 1. (Say:) Say it with me. Get ready. (Hold up one finger.) *aaa.* **Again. Get ready.** (Hold up one finger.) *aaa.*

test ⟶ 2. Your turn. Get ready. (Hold up one finger. The students say:) *aaa.*

Symbol Action (Lessons 101–115)

The symbol action sequencing games give the children practice in using the same "code" for sequencing events that they use in reading words. Written words contain letters that stand for sounds. The sounds are to be produced in order, from left to right.

The sequencing games present the same left-to-right code. The difference is that the events to be sequenced are not letters or sounds, but actions that are pictured on an arrow.

The sequencing games teach students to respond to the words *first* and *next.* These words will be used on work-sheet activities, in sequencing word parts, in sounding-out, in word-reading, and in sentence-reading.

The sequencing games are highly reinforcing to the children and easy for you to correct. They use the same starting ball, balls under the pictures, and arrows that will later appear when word reading is introduced.

Before lesson 111, the children practice performing the one or two actions pictured on the arrow. In the next several lessons they perform the actions you refer to as *first* and *next.*

Children must remember what to do *first* and *next* before they do it. They then perform the actions without looking at the pictures.

Lesson 111

SYMBOL ACTION
EXERCISE 3

Children do first and next

a. (Touch the first ball of the arrow.) First you'll do what it shows on the arrow. Then we'll see if you can do it without looking at the picture. My turn. Watch. (Move quickly to the second ball and stop.) This is what you do **first.** (Open your mouth.) Show me what you do **first.** (Tap the second ball.) *Children open their mouth.*
Watch. (Move quickly to the third ball and stop.) This is what you do **next.** (Raise your hand.) Show me what you do **next.** (Tap the third ball.) *Children raise their hand.*

b. (Touch the first ball of the arrow.) Let's do it again. Show me what you're going to do **first.** (Move quickly to the second ball and stop.) *Children open their mouth.*
Show me what you're going to do **next.** (Move quickly to the third ball and stop.) *Children raise their hand.*

c. (Repeat *b* until firm.)

d. (Do not show the pictures.) Let's see if you remember what you did **first** and what you did **next.** Show me what you did **first.** Get ready. (Signal.) *Children open their mouth.*
Show me what you did **next.** Get ready. (Signal.) *Children raise their hand.*

e. (Repeat *d* until firm.)

f. (Call on different children to do *d*.)

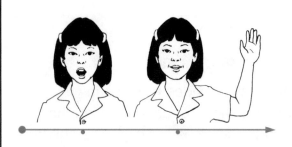

- Practice step *a* several times. You will need to coordinate saying your lines with the various motor activities called for. Place the book on a table or use the teacher box as an easel. This makes it possible for you to use both hands.

- At step *b,* tap the ball under the picture to signal the children to respond.

- At steps *d* and *f,* turn the book so that the children can not see the page. To signal, hold up a finger or use a hand-drop signal. (See page 204.)

Corrections

If children make a mistake at step *a,* model. (Touch under the appropriate ball of the arrow.) This is what you do **first.** Open your mouth. Show me what you do **first.** (Tap the ball.) Or, This is what you do **next.** (Raise you hand.) Show me what you do **next.** (Tap the ball.)

Children should not have difficulties at steps *d* and *f* if you repeat step *b* until they are firm.

When symbol action becomes a worksheet activity (lessons 113–115) you have to use audible signals, such as taps or claps or snaps.

The worksheet symbol action exercises require children to follow the arrow on their worksheet and do what the pictures show.

The exercises in lessons 113 and 114 involve two pictures.

In lesson 115, children work with three-action sequences. During individual turns, children also perform the actions shown in the sequence without touching the marks.

When the children finish the symbol-action track, they are acquainted with the words *first, next,* and *last;* with the behaviors of touching the ball and moving along the arrow to the marks; and with the general format of processing one event at a time. These are important components of what they will do when they decode their first words.

Blending (101–150)

Children start to read words such as **mē** and **am** in lesson 124. The initial strategy the children are taught is to first sound out the word, then say it fast. This operation involves many skills. Children must be able to identify the symbols in the word. Children must understand that the written word presents a left-to-right code for sequencing the sounds. Finally, children must be able to say the sounds of the word slowly and then say the sounds fast. These skills—saying words slowly and saying them fast—are blending skills. When we remove them from the context of word reading, they are oral activities.

Oral-blending activities begin in lesson 101 and continue through the reading lessons. The first blending activity is Say It Fast, which is followed by activities in which children say words slowly.

Say It Fast (Lesson 101–120)

To introduce the children to blending in easy stages, you start by presenting long words broken into two parts—words like **motor** (pause) **boat** and **ham** (pause) **burger.** In later lessons, you say the sounds of one-syllable words without pausing between the sounds: *aaammm* and *sssēēē.* Many of the short words that the children say fast are words that they will read in the early Reading Vocabulary lessons. This initial oral practice allows them to concentrate on listening to the sounds and saying the word without interference from written symbols. Frequently, pictures will be shown to the children after they have responded successfully. The pictures relate to the word and serve as reinforcers for saying the word fast.

Hand-drop Signal

Say It Fast Signal

The key words in the Say It Fast signal are "Hold out your hand" and "Drop your hand."

- Hold out your hand as if you were stopping traffic.

- Keep it perfectly still.

- After saying Say it fast, wait one second, then pull your hand up slightly and drop it quickly.

- The interval between Say it fast and the hand drop must be one second.

Say It Fast Teaching Techniques

Following is the basic Say It Fast format. It is simple and easy to learn after you have mastered the signal.

- In step *b,* hold your hand steady until after you have said, Say it fast.

- Say the word slowly in a monotone, without inflection.

- The children should respond as soon as your hand drops.

- Always repeat the word (Yes, **me.**) to reinforce the correct response.

- Reinforce the children after they have responded correctly by saying Good. You said it fast.

Lesson 101

EXERCISE 6
Children say it fast

a. Let's play Say It Fast.
b. (Hold out your hand.) Listen. **Peanut** (pause) **butter.** (Pause.) Say it fast! (Drop your hand.) *Peanutbutter.* Yes, **peanutbutter.**

> **To correct**
> 1. You didn't say it fast.
> 2. (Point to a child who said it fast.) [Child's name] can say it fast.
> 3. (Present *b* to that child.)
> 4. (Say to the child who made the mistake:) Your turn. (Repeat *b*.)
> 5. (If the child answers correctly; say:) Now you said it fast.

c. (Repeat *b* until firm.)
d. (Call on different children to do *b*.)

Corrections

If a child does not say the word fast, follow the correction in the format. Typically, the lower-performing children will not say the word fast at first. The correction is to tell the child what he or she did wrong, have another child model the correct response to the signal, and then test the child who made the mistake to see whether the child can respond correctly.

If a child says the wrong word the fast way, correct by saying, You said the wrong word. Let's try it again. Hold out your hand and repeat the correct word slowly.

Other Say It Fast Formats

Although there is only one basic Say It Fast format, your technique is somewhat different when you teach one-syllable words. When saying **ran** or **me,** say each sound slowly, without pausing between the sounds. You will need to practice this technique. A good way to tell whether you are saying the sounds without stopping between them is to say the word *man* very slowly with your hand on your throat. If you are saying the sounds without stopping, you will feel a constant vibration of your throat as you say the word.

Lesson 105

SAY IT FAST

EXERCISE 10

Children say the words fast

a. Let's play Say It Fast.
b. (Hold out your hand.) Listen. **Rrraaannn.** Say it fast. (Drop your hand.) *Ran.* Yes, **ran.**
c. New word. (Hold out your hand.) Listen. **Mmmēēē.** Say it fast. (Drop your hand.) *Me.* Yes, **me.**
d. (Repeat *b* and *c* until firm.)
e. (Call on different children to do *b* or *c.*)

Activities in this track provide practice in **oral** sounding out. Children do not say the words fast.

Say the Sounds Signal

The signal for any sound said slowly is the same as you practiced in the Pronunciation track. You hold up one finger for the **m** in *mmmēēē,* and a second finger for the **ē** in mmmēēē. Practice saying *mmmēēē,* holding up a finger for each sound.

To help you hold each continuous sound for two seconds, you may want to tap your foot two beats for each sound.

The activity on page 206 is from the first Say the Sounds format in the program.

- Before practicing step *a,* say the sounds *mmmēēē* without stopping between the sounds. Be sure that your voice is firm and that you hold each sound for two seconds.

- Now say the sounds *rrraaannn* and *nnnōōō.* Make sure that you are not pausing between the sounds. To test for a pause, hold your hand against your throat as you say *mmmēēē.* You should feel constant vibration in the throat. If the vibrations stop between the sounds *mmm* and *ēēē,* you paused. Practice until you can consistently say the words without pausing.

Lesson 105

⭐ SAY THE SOUNDS

This is an oral exercise.

EXERCISE 11

Children say the words slowly

a. I'm going to say some words slowly, without stopping. Then you'll say them with me. First I'll say (pause) **me** slowly. Listen. (Hold up a finger for each sound. Do not stop between sounds.) **Mmmēēē.**
Now I'll say (pause) **ran** slowly. Listen. (Hold up a finger for each sound.) **Rrraaannn.**
Now I'll say (pause) **no** slowly. Listen. (Hold up a finger for each sound.) **Nnnōōō.**

b. Now it's your turn to say the words slowly with me. Take a deep breath and we'll say (pause) **mmmēēē.** Get ready. (Hold up a finger for each sound. Do not stop between the sounds. Say **mmmēēē** with the children.) *Mmmēēē.*

> **To correct**
> (If a child stops between the sounds, says the wrong sounds, or says the word fast:)
> **model** → 1. Listen. (Hold up a finger for each sound. Do not stop between the sounds.) **Mmmēēē.**
> **model** → 2. Listen again. (Hold up a finger for each sound.) **Mmmēēē.**
> **lead** → 3. Say it with me. Get ready. (Hold up a finger for each sound. Say **mmmēēē** with the children.) *Mmmēēē.*
> **test** → 4. All by yourselves. Get ready. (Hold up a finger for each sound.) *Mmmēēē.*
> **test** → 5. (Repeat *4* until firm.)
> **lead** → 6. (Repeat *b.*)

Now we'll say (pause) **rrraaannn.** Get ready. (Hold up a finger for each sound. Say **rrraaannn** with the children.) *Rrraaannn.*
Now we'll say (pause) **nnnōōō.** Get ready. (Hold up a finger for each sound. Say **nnnōōō** with the children.) *Nnnōōō.*

c. Your turn to say the words slowly by yourselves. Say (pause) **mmmēēē.** Get ready. (Hold up a finger for each sound.) *Mmmēēē.*

d. Again. Get ready. (Hold up a finger for each sound.) *Mmmēēē.*

e. (Repeat *d* until firm.)

f. Say (pause) **rrraaannn.** Get ready. (Hold up a finger for each sound.) *Rrraaannn.*

g. Again. Get ready. (Hold up a finger for each sound.) *Rrraaannn.*

h. (Repeat *g* until firm.)

i. Say (pause) **nnnōōō.** Get ready. (Hold up a finger for each sound.) *Nnnōōō.*

j. Again. Get ready. (Hold up a finger for each sound.) *Nnnōōō.*

k. (Repeat *j* until firm.)

l. (Repeat *c* through *k* until firm.)

m. (Call on different children. Each child does one word from *c, f,* or *i*.)

n. Good saying the words slowly.

Corrections

The correction steps have been labeled to help you see the **model-lead-test** procedure.

Practice steps *a* and *b* with an adult partner. At step *b,* check to see if your partner makes any of the following errors: stops between the sounds (*mmm . . . ēēē*), says the wrong sounds (*nnnēēē*), or says the word fast *(mē)*. Correct your partner using steps 1 through 6 of the correction. Note that step 5 tells you to repeat step 4—the test—until the "child" is firm. Step 6 sends you back to step *b* in the exercise.

Practice the correction with your partner making each of the mistakes listed above. Practice the correction until you feel firm.

Some children need considerable practice before they are able to say words slowly without stopping between the sounds. The program provides this practice, so don't be overly concerned if a child needs several lessons to master this skill. Correct the group and give the child several turns each day. Praise the child for trying hard.

Some children pronounce sounds inarticulately. Their pronunciation will improve, but the improvement is gradual. Praise a child whose pronunciation is improving. You are really learning to say those sounds. I like it when you watch my mouth.

Say The Sounds—Say It Fast (Lessons 108–136)

This track consolidates the skills of saying words fast (taught in the Say It Fast track) and saying words slowly (taught in the Say the Sounds track).

Say the Sounds—Say It Fast Signals

Use the two signals that you have already practiced—holding up one finger for each sound then dropping your hand to signal say it fast.

Practice steps *a* through *f* with another adult making no mistakes.

Lesson 108

 SAY THE SOUNDS—SAY IT FAST

This is an oral exercise.

EXERCISE 11

Children say the word slowly, then say it fast

a. First you're going to say a word slowly without stopping between the sounds. Then you're going to say the word fast.
b. Listen. (Hold up a finger for each sound.) Say (pause) **mmmēēē.** Get ready. (Hold up a finger for each sound.) *Mmmēēē.* Again. Get ready. (Hold up a finger for each sound.) *Mmmēēē.* Say it fast. (Signal.) *Me.* Yes, **me.**
c. Listen. (Hold up a finger for each sound.) Say (pause) **rrraaannn.** Get ready. (Hold up a finger for each sound.) *Rrraaannn.* Again. Get ready. (Hold up a finger for each sound.) *Rrraaannn.* Say it fast. (Signal.) *Ran.* Yes, **ran.**
d. Listen. (Hold up a finger for each sound.) Say (pause) **ooonnn.** Get ready. (Hold up a finger for each sound.) *Ooonnn.* Again. Get ready. (Hold up a finger for each sound.) *Ooonnn.* Say it fast. (Signal.) *On.* Yes, **on.**
e. (Repeat *b* through *d* until firm.)
f. (Call on different children to do *b, c,* or *d.*)

Correction

Use the same correction as you practiced in the Say the Sounds exercises—model, lead, and test. See page 206.

Sounds—Say It Fast (Lessons 111–122)

When children sound out words, they first say the parts slowly, then say them fast. A simple variation of this procedure is to say a single sound slowly and then say it fast. For the exercises in this track, children respond to written symbols.

Sounds—Say It Fast Signals

In the Sounds track you practiced two signals, one signal for saying a sound slowly *(mmm* or *aaa)* and one signal for saying a sound fast *(d)*. (See pages 195–199). You will use both these signals in steps *a* and *b* of this format as you model how to say a sound slowly, then say it fast.

Sounds—Say It Fast Teaching Techniques

Practice steps *a* and *c*. Remember to return to the ball for the sound before you slash along the arrow to say it fast.

Steps *c* through *e* are tests in which the children first say a sound slowly, then say the same sound fast.

Practice steps *a* through *e* with your partner making no mistakes.

Lesson 111

⭐ **SOUNDS—SAY IT FAST**
EXERCISE 8

Children say a sound slowly, then say it fast

a. (Touch the first ball of the arrow for **a.**) First you're going to say it slowly. Then you're going to say it fast. Say it slowly. Get ready. (Move quickly to the second ball. Hold for two seconds.) *aaaaaa.* (Return to the first ball for **a.**) Say it fast. (Slash to the end of the arrow.) *a.* Yes, a.
b. (Repeat *a* until firm.)
c. (Touch the first ball of the arrow for **m.**) Say it slowly. Get ready. (Move quickly to the second ball. Hold for two seconds.) *mmmmmm.* (Return to the first ball for **m.**) Say it fast. (Slash to the end of the arrow.) *m.* Yes, m.
d. (Repeat *c* until firm.)
e. (Call on different children to do *a* or *c*.)

Correction

If a child makes a mistake, present a model (step *a* or *c*) to the group, then test the group or child.

Rhyming (Lessons 112–134)

There are two rhyming tracks. The first, called Say It Fast—Rhyming, contains activities that are verbal (with no written symbols). The second, called Rhyming, contains activities that involve written symbols. The activities in both tracks are similar. The children are either told or shown a beginning sound. They are also told the ending sound (or the "word" they're to rhyme with). The children then combine the sounds to create a word that they pronounce slowly *(mmmȳ).* Then they say it fast *(My).*

The verbal exercises appear first in the Reading tracks (lessons 112 to 121). The exercises that involve symbols appear later (lessons 122–134).

At lesson 112, the children are first shown how to say a word slowly.

Lesson 112

★ SAY IT FAST–RHYMING

These are oral exercises.

EXERCISE 9
Children say word parts slowly

a. My turn to say a word slowly. First I'll say (pause) **mmm.** Then I'll say (pause) **at.**
Listen again. First I'll say (pause) **mmm.** Then I'll say (pause) **at.**
Here I go. (Hold up one finger.) **mmm.** (Hold up second finger.) **(mmm)at.**

b. Do it with me. (Hold up one finger.) First you'll say (pause) **mmm.** (Hold up second finger.) Then you'll say (pause) **at.**
Get ready. (Say mmmat with the children as you hold up a finger for each part.)

c. Again. (Hold up one finger.) First you'll say (pause) **mmm.** (Hold up second finger.) Then you'll say (pause) **at.**
Get ready. (Say mmmat with the children as you hold up a finger for each part.)

d. (Repeat c until firm.)

e. All by yourself. (Hold up one finger.) First you'll say (pause) **mmm.** (Hold up second finger.) Then you'll say (pause) **at.** Get ready. (Hold up one finger, then second finger as the children say mmmat.)

f. Again. (Repeat e until firm.)

After three words have been presented, following the procedure specified in the format, a less structured presentation is introduced. Notice that the children first indicate both "parts" they are to combine, and then they combine them. This process is very important because it demonstrates how isolated parts are combined to form "words."

Say It Fast—Rhyming Signal

For this exercise, hold up one finger for the first sound and a second finger for the word ending.

Say It Fast—Rhyming Teaching Techniques

- Establish a good rhythm in step *a* and use the same rhythm in steps *b* and *c*. Make sure that the children are responding with you in steps *b* and *c*. They should not lag behind.

- Make sure that you thoroughly firm exercise 9. Children must be able to perform on this exercise perfectly if they are to perform well on later activities.

Rhyming Signals

Beginning at lesson 122, the children are introduced to a variation of the verbal activity that is similar to exercise 9. The children identify the beginning sound, identify the ending, combine the sounds to create a word pronounced slowly, and then say it fast.

This lesson also introduces the first rhyming task that involves written symbols. The children combine the letter in the Presentation Book with the ending the teacher stipulates. The children say the word slowly, and then say it fast. Notice that the first word is "led" by the teacher. The children are not led on the second word.

When presenting Rhyming formats, you use two signals that you have already practiced. You touch the first ball on an arrow and move under the sound, as you do in the Sounds track. And you slash to signal say it fast as you do in the Sounds—Say It Fast track.

Below is the first Rhyming format, introduced in lesson 122.

Lesson 122

> ### ★ RHYMING
> #### EXERCISE 7
> **Children identify sounds, then rhyme**
>
> a. (Touch the first ball of the arrow for **m.**) My turn. (Move quickly to the second ball.) First I'll say this sound. Then I'll say (pause) ē.
> Listen again. First I'll say this sound. Then I'll say (pause) ē.
> b. (Return to the first ball of the arrow for **m.**) What is this sound? (Signal.) *mmm.* So first I'll say *mmm.* Then what will I say? (Signal.) *ēēē.*
> c. (Repeat *b* until firm.)
> d. (Tap the first ball of the **m** arrow.) Here I go. (Move quickly to the second ball and say *mmm.* Slash to the end of the arrow and say *(mmm)ē.*)
> e. (Return to the first ball of the arrow for **m.**) Do it with me. First you'll say this sound. (Quickly move to the second ball.) Then you'll say (pause) ē. (Slash to the end of the arrow.)
> (Return to the first ball for **m.**) Get ready. (Move quickly to the second ball.) *mmm.* (Slash to the end of the arrow.) *(mmm)ē.*
> f. (Repeat *e* until firm.)
> g. (Return to the first ball for **m.**) Say it fast. (Slash.) *Me.*
> Yes, **me.** Good saying it fast.
> h. (Touch the first ball of the arrow for **r.**) Here's a different sound. (Move quickly to the second ball.) First you'll say this sound. Then you'll say (pause) un.
> Listen again. First you'll say this sound. Then you'll say (pause) un.
> i. (Return to the first ball of the arrow for **r.**) What is this sound? (Signal.) *rrr.* So first I'll say *rrr.* Then what will I say? (Signal.) un.
> j. (Repeat *i* until firm.)
> k. (Tap the first ball of the **r** arrow.) What sound are you going to say first? (Move quickly to the second ball.) *rrr.* Then what will you say? (Slash to the end of the arrow.) un.
> l. (Return to the first ball of the arrow for **r.**) Yes, first you'll say this sound. Then you'll say (pause) un.
> Get ready. (Move quickly to the second ball.) *rrr.* (Slash to the end of the arrow.) *(rrr)un.*
> m. (Return to the first ball for **r.**) Again. Get ready. (Move quickly to the second ball.) *rrr.* (Slash to the end of the arrow.) *(rrr)un.*
> n. (Repeat *m* until firm.)
> o. (Return to the first ball.) Say it fast. (Slash.) *Run.*
> Yes, **run.** Good saying it fast.
> p. (Call on different children to do *m* and *o.*)

Other Rhyming Formats

Later formats provide children with practice in rhyming with all the endings they will encounter in beginning reading (**ēēd, an, at, im,** and so forth) The final format in the rhyming sequence (in lesson 132) shows children how to "blend" words that begin with stop sounds. Combining a stop-sound beginning like *d* with an ending like *im* is difficult because of the slight change that occurs in the pronunciation of the *d* sound when it is followed by the vowel sound, *iii.* The format uses the same ending *(im)* for two beginnings—first a continuous-sound beginning, then a stop-sound beginning.

Lesson 132

> ### RHYMING
> #### EXERCISE 3
> **Children rhyme with im**
>
> a. (Touch the first ball of the arrow for **r.** Move quickly to the second ball.) You're going to start with this sound and rhyme with (pause) **im.**
> b. (Return to the first ball of the arrow.) Tell me the sound you're going to say first. (Move quickly to the second ball.) *rrr.* Then what will you say? (Slash to the end of the arrow.) *im.*
> c. (Return to the first ball of the arrow.) Again. Tell me the sound you're going to say first. (Move quickly to the second ball.) *rrr.* Then what will you say? (Slash to the end of the arrow.) *im.*
> d. (Repeat *c* until firm.)
> e. (Return to the first ball of the arrow.) Get ready. (Move to the second ball.) *rrr.* (Then slash to the end of the arrow.) *(rrr)im.*
> f. (Return to the first ball of the arrow.) Again. Get ready. (Move quickly to the second ball.) *rrr.* (Then slash to the end of the arrow.) *(rrr)im.*
> g. (Return to the first ball.) Say it fast. (Slash.) *Rim.*
> Yes, **rim.** You rhymed with (pause) **im.**
> h. (Call on different children to do *f* and *g.*)
> i. (Touch the ball of the arrow for **d.**) You're going to start with this sound and rhyme with (pause) **im.**
> j. First you'll say this sound. (Slash to the > under **d.**) Then you'll say (pause) **im.** (Slash to the end of the arrow.)
> k. (Return to the first ball of the arrow.) Tell me the sound you're going to say first. (Slash to the > under **d.**) *d.* Then what will you say? (Slash to the end of the arrow.) *im.*
> l. (Return to the first ball of the arrow.) Again. Tell me the sound you're going to say first. (Slash to the > under **d.**) *d.* Then what will you say? (Slash to the end of the arrow.) *im.*
> m. (Repeat *l* until firm.)
> n. (Return to the ball of the arrow.) Get ready. (Slash to the end of the arrow.) *dim.*
> o. (Return to the ball of the arrow.) Again. Get ready. (Slash to the end of the arrow.) *dim.*
> p. (Return to the ball of the arrow.) Say it fast. (Slash.) *Dim.*
> Yes, **dim.** You rhymed with (pause) **im.**
> q. (Call on different children to do *l* through *p.*)

Rhyming Teaching Techniques

Unless this format is paced rapidly, the children won't see the relationship between **rim** and **dim.** Therefore, correct mistakes and return to the beginning of the format. Also, make liberal use of the individual test at the end of the format (step *q*).

Sound Out (Lessons 114–129)

The final prereading track is Sound Out. The activities in this track are similar to those in the Say the Sounds track with one difference. In Say the Sounds, the children repeat the sounds that the teacher says *(aaammm).* In this track, the children must **read** the sounds. In both Say the Sounds (lessons 106–109) and Sound Out, the children say sounds and do **not** say it fast.

The sounding-out skill is very important for initial word reading. And the most important part of this skill is saying the sounds of the word *without pausing* or stopping between the sounds. The reason for this is that it is much easier to identify the word if the sounded-out word sounds like the word that is said at a normal speaking rate. The sounded-out word will sound most like the word that is said fast if the sounds are linked together, without pauses between them.

Because appropriate sounding out is so important, the first sounding-out format models the procedure.

Sound Out Signal

The illustration below shows you how to move on the arrow.

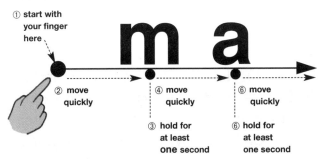

Lesson 114

★ **SOUND OUT**

EXERCISE 6

Children say the sounds without stopping

a. (Touch the first ball of the arrow for **ma.**) My turn. I'll show you how to say these sounds without stopping between the sounds.
(Move under each sound. Hold. Say **mmmaaa.**)

b. (Return to the first ball of the arrow for **ma.**) Your turn. Say the sounds as I touch under the letters. Don't stop between the sounds.
Get ready. (Move under each sound. Hold.) *Mmmaaa.*
(Return to the first ball of the arrow.) Again. Get ready. (Move under each sound. Hold.) *Mmmaaa.*
Good saying **mmmaaa.**

c. (Touch the first ball of the arrow for **am.**) My turn. I'll show you how to say these sounds without stopping between the sounds.
(Move under each sound. Hold. Say **aaammm.**)

d. (Return to the first ball of the arrow for **am.**) Your turn. Say the sounds as I touch under the letters. Don't stop between the sounds.
Get ready. (Move under each sound. Hold.) *Aaammm.*
(Return to the first ball of the arrow.) Again. Get ready. (Move under each sound. Hold.) *Aaammm.*
Good saying **aaammm.**

e. (Call on different children to do *b* or *d.*)

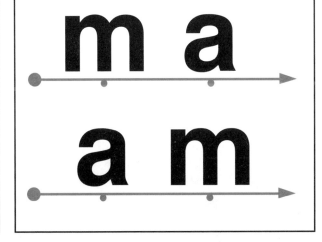

Practice the signal for step *a* without saying your lines. Become firm on the motor behaviors before you present the task to your partner. Start on the first ball of the arrow. Move quickly along the arrow, stopping for at least one second at each ball. After you have stopped at the last ball, you may either lift your finger from the page or move quickly to the end of the arrow.

Sound Out Teaching Techniques

- Practice presenting step *a* to your partner. In step *a,* you say **mmmaaa.** Do not pause between the sounds when you move from ball to ball. Remember to say **aaa** (not **ah** or **āāā.**)

- Present step *b* to your partner, who will not make any mistakes. Reinforce the sounding out at step *b* by saying, "Good saying **mmmaaa**."

- Practice steps *c* and *d.* Reinforce at step *d* by saying, "Good saying **aaammm**."

Corrections

If children stop between the sounds at step *b* or *d,* or say the incorrect sounds, stop them immediately. Tell the children what they did, and then repeat step *a* (model) and return to step *b* (test), or repeat *c* and return to *d.*

Reading Skills Worksheet Activities (Lessons 101–135)

The reading skills activities you have been practicing are presented through the teacher-presentation material. Other reading skills activities are included as part of the daily Worksheet activities presented at the end of each lesson. These reading skills activities prepare the children for Worksheet 123, which is the first worksheet to present word writing and reading exercises.

To prepare for these word-reading tasks, children practice moving their finger under a single sound and saying it, beginning with lesson 101.

Starting in lesson 113, children touch under symbol action pictures. In lesson 115, they touch under the sounds of a "word" like **am,** as they say the sounds.

In worksheet 130, the children touch under the sounds of a word as they say the sounds without stopping between them. Then the children say the word fast.

Worksheet Signal

Because many worksheet activities require the children to look at symbols on their worksheets, you have to use audible signals to direct them. The simplest signals are taps, or snaps. The timing for these signals is exactly the same as it is for the other signals you have practiced.

Sound Out Teaching Techniques ($\frac{s}{\bar{e}}$)

Part of a worksheet is reproduced on page 213. Note that each sound (**s** and **ē**) is on a ball and arrow. At step *a* children put their finger on the first ball of the first arrow. Children have learned the wording *first* and *next* in the Symbol Action sequencing games.

Practice exercise 10 with your partner. Be sure that your partner is touching the correct starting ball. If not, move your partner's finger, and then repeat the step.

Lesson 115

EXERCISE 10

Children move their finger under s or ē and say it

a. Everybody, finger on the first ball of the first arrow ✓
When I tap, quickly move your finger under the sound and say it. (Pause.) Get ready. (Tap. Children move their finger under **s** and say *sss.*)
Yes, **sss.**

b. Again. Finger on the first ball of the first arrow. ✓
Get ready. (Tap. Children move their finger under **s** and say *sss.*)
Yes, **sss.**

c. (Repeat *b* until firm.)

d. Everybody, finger on the first ball of the next arrow. ✓
When I tap, quickly move your finger under the sound and say it. (Pause.) Get ready. (Tap. Children move their finger under **ē** and say *ēēē.*)
Yes, **ēēē.**

e. Again. Finger on the first ball of the arrow. ✓
Get ready. (Tap. Children move their finger under **ē** and say *ēēē.*)
Yes, **ēēē.**

f. (Repeat *e* until firm.)

EXERCISE 11

Individual test

a. (Call on a child. Show the child which ball to touch.) Get ready. (Tap.) *Child moves finger under the sound and says it.*

b. (Call on different children to do *a.*)

c. Good. You really know how to move your finger under the sound and say it.

Worksheet 115

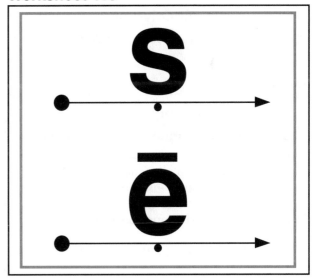

The timing of the tap signal is very important. If the timing is questionable, children will glance up at you. They will be able to respond together and on signal if the time between Get ready and the tap is always the same, always predictable. If you have trouble maintaining a precise time interval, try softly tapping your foot, as if in time with a march. Time your Get ready . . . Tap so that it is in time with the foot tapping or use a metronome or practice in time with a recording of a march.

Sound Out Teaching Techniques ( )

In Sound Out exercise 10, the children moved under two sounds on separate arrows as they said the sounds.

In the Sound Out exercise below, the children move under two sounds on the same arrow as they say the sounds.

Lesson 115

EXERCISE 12

Children touch under the sounds and sound out

a. (Hold up worksheet. Touch the first ball of the arrow for **am.**) Put your finger on the first ball of this arrow.
b. What's the first sound you'll say? (Signal.) *aaa.*
   What's the next sound you'll say? (Signal.) *mmm.*
c. Everybody, put your finger on the first ball of the arrow. ✓
   When I tap, you're going to quickly move your finger under each sound and say (pause) **aaammm.**
   Sound it out. Get ready. (Tap for each sound, pausing about 2 seconds between taps. Check that children are moving their finger under each sound as they say *aaammm.*)
d. Again. Finger on the first ball of the arrow. Get ready. (Tap for each sound, pausing about two seconds between taps. Check that the children are moving their finger under each sound as they say *aaammm.*)
e. (Repeat *d* until firm.)

EXERCISE 13

Individual test

a. (Call on a child.) Finger on the first ball of the arrow. ✓
   Quickly move your finger under each sound as you say it. Get ready. (Tap for each sound, pausing about two seconds between taps.)
b. (Call on different children to do *a.*)
c. Good moving your finger under each letter and saying each sound.

Worksheet 115

The most important teaching technique is the timing of the exercise. Use the same timing for Get ready . . . aaammm as you used for the preceding format (Get ready . . . Tap).

Corrections

If children do not move under the appropriate sound as soon as you start to say it, guide their finger as you repeat step *c* of the format. After children can perform with no prompting (such as guiding their finger), repeat step *c* at least two or three more times, until the children are quite firm in their response.

If children have trouble when you call on them for individual turns, repeat step *c* with the group.

Reading Vocabulary (Lessons 124–150)

Overview

1. The first word-reading (reading vocabulary) formats are introduced in lesson 124. In lessons 130 to 135, the children read words on their worksheets. Beginning at lesson 136, the children read stories composed of words that have been introduced earlier.

2. The first reading-vocabulary words begin with continuous sounds like **a, m, s,** or **th.** Some words may end with a stop sound like **d, t,** or **c,** but none begin with stop sounds. The reason is that sounding out a word that begins with a stop sound is much more

difficult than sounding out a word that begins with a continuous sound. Words beginning with stop sounds are introduced at lesson 139, after the children have been reading simple, regular words for fifteen lessons.

3. In lesson 138, the first "slightly irregular" word is taught. The word is **is.** It is irregular because it is sounded out as **iiiss** (which rhymes with **miss**) but is pronounced **iz.** The teacher directs the children to sound out the word **is,** and then "translates" by saying, Yes, **iz.** We say **iz.** She **is** happy.

The purpose of introducing words that are slightly irregular is to make the children aware that not everything they read is perfectly regular. By introducing some words that are not perfectly regular early in the reading program, you alert the children to what will come. Note that children still sound out all words—regular or irregular—but they learn to discriminate between how the irregular word is sounded out and how it is pronounced.

4. Other slightly irregular words (such as **a, has**) and highly irregular words (such as **was, said**) are introduced in the next level after children have mastered slightly irregular words.

A variety of word-attack skills is taught. The same word may appear in a rhyming format or a sound-out format.

The reading-vocabulary portion of the lesson should take no more than ten minutes. The exercises in this guide will help you teach economically.

Although the emphasis of the reading-vocabulary activities is on decoding, we want to make sure the children understand that they are reading real words. Therefore, the program specifies "meaning" sentences to be presented after children read certain words. For instance, after they read the word **meat** in lesson 142; you are instructed to say, A hamburger is made of (pause) **meat.** Meaning sentences are not specified for all words. If you feel that a sentence would help the children understand a particular word that may not be well understood in isolation, put it in a sentence. But **don't** use the meaning sentence as a substitute for decoding. Children do not become facile at decoding words by understanding the words. They become facile at decoding by practicing decoding.

Regular Words (Lessons 124–150)

Regular words, such as **can, man, sit, if,** and **not,** are easy to read. Each word can be sounded out and said fast without mispronouncing the word. But the number of simple, regular words is very limited. To increase the number of regular words (words that children can pronounce the way they are sounded out), *Reading Mastery Plus* uses a modified orthography, or print, which is faded out in level 2 of the program.

The modified orthography presents three conventions:

1. *Diacritical marks.* Long lines appear over the symbols for the vowels that sound like their letter names (ā, ē, ī, ō, ū). The symbol **e** signals the sound in **end,** while **ē** signals the sound in **me.**

2. *Small letters.* Small letters appear in some words. Children are taught to sound out only full-size letters, not small ones. The small letters permit many words with silent letters to be spelled correctly. As the children progress through the program, the small letters are increased in size. The examples below illustrate the long lines and small letters:

roc_k   ē_at

3. *Joined letters.* If two or more letters function as a single sound, they are joined. The joined letters allow many additional words to become regular words.

Level K examples:

this   thē   that

Level 1 examples:

shop   her

teacher   slīding

Children Say the Sounds, Then Sound Out the Word (Lessons 124–130)

The first reading-vocabulary format requires a simple extension of the behaviors that have been taught in the say it fast—rhyming, the rhyming, and the sound-out formats. Note that the children read words that are presented on an arrow with a ball beneath each sound. At lesson 150, the arrow is retained, but the balls are removed.

★ **READING VOCABULARY**
EXERCISE 6

Children say the sounds, then sound out the word

a. (Point to the first ball of the arrow for **am.**) This is the word (pause) **am.** What word? (Touch the first ball.) *Am.*
Yes, **am.**

b. (Point to the ball for **a.**) When you sound out (pause) **am,** what sound do you say first? (Touch the ball for **a.**) *aaa.* Yes, **aaa.** (Point to the ball for **m.**) What sound do you say next? (Touch the ball for **m.**) *mmm.*
Yes, **mmm.**

c. (Repeat *b* until firm.)

d. (Return to the first ball.) You're going to sound it out, then say it fast. Everybody, sound it out. Get ready. (Move under each sound. Hold under each sound for two seconds.) *Aaammm.*

e. (Return to the first ball.) Again. Sound it out. Get ready. (Move under each sound. Hold under each sound for two seconds.) *Aaammm.*

f. (Repeat *e* until firm.)

g. (Return to the first ball.) Say it fast. (Slash to the end of the arrow.) *Am.*
Yes, **am.** You read the word (pause) **am.**
I (pause) **am** (pause) happy.

h. (Call on different children to do *e* and *g*.)

Point and Touch Signal

The signal in steps *a* through *c* is different from those you practiced earlier. In step *a*, you point to the starting ball for the word without touching the ball. Then you touch it. Your touch is the signal for the children to respond.

In steps *b* and *c,* you point to the ball for a sound. Then you touch the ball. The children respond when you touch. Be sure you lift your finger when you move along the arrow so you can point to the next sound without touching it.

Practice pointing and touching in steps *a* through *c.* When you point, be careful not to hold your finger so you hide part of the sound from the children's view. Point from below, and use the same timing that you use for all other signals.

Sound It Out—Say It Fast Signal

The signal you will use to direct the children to sound out words in steps *d* through *g* of this format (and in all sound-out formats through lesson 150) is exactly the same as you practiced in Sound Out (page 211). After the children sound out the word, you direct them to say it fast.

The illustration below demonstrates the correct procedures for presenting the word **meat** from lesson 142. Practice this procedure.

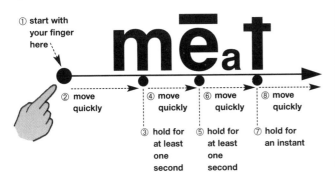

① start with your finger here

② move quickly

③ hold for at least one second

④ move quickly

⑤ hold for at least one second

⑥ move quickly

⑦ hold for an instant

⑧ move quickly

- Hold under the **m** for at least one second; hold under the **ē** for at least one second; move past the **a** (it has no ball under it); hold under the **t for only an instant;** and then move quickly to the end of the arrow. The children respond, *mmmēēēt.*

- After you reach the end of the arrow, return to the first ball of the arrow. Say, Say it fast. Pause one second. Then slash from the first ball to the end of the arrow. The children respond, *meat.* Remember, first you talk—then you signal. Practice this timing. Start with your finger on the first ball. Keep your finger on the ball as you say, Say it fast . . . and pause one second. Signal by slashing along the arrow.

Practice exercise 6, page 216, from the beginning, with your partner making no mistakes.

Corrections

1. If the children don't respond firmly for each sound, say, Starting over . . . and repeat step *b* until the children reliably say both sounds. Present a delayed test by repeating steps *a* through *c.*

2. Use the correction below for steps *d* through *h* if a child breaks between the sounds *(aaa . . . mmm)* or is unable to say the word fast after sounding it out *(aaammm).* Your correction will show the children how word reading relates to the oral blending tasks they have already learned.

1. **Teacher:** Everybody, say (pause) **aaammm.** Get ready. (Hold up a finger for each sound.)

2. **Group:** *aaammm.*

3. **Teacher:** Say it fast. (Drop your hand.)

4. **Group:** *am.*

5. **Teacher:** (Quickly touch the first ball for **am.**) Now do it here. Sound it out. Get ready. (Move quickly under each sound. Hold under each sound for two seconds.)

6. **Group:** *aaammm.*

7. **Teacher:** (Return to the first ball.) Say it fast. (Slash to the end of the arrow.)

8. **Group:** *am.*

9. **Teacher:** You did it.

If the mistake occurred on an individual turn, after correcting the group with steps 1 to 8 above, present steps *e* and *g* to the child who made the mistake.

Children Think about the Sounds, Then Sound Out the Word (Lessons 131–137)

During this lesson range, increasing demands are placed on the children through a series of small changes in the directions they are given. The first change involves identifying individual sounds before sounding out a word. In earlier formats, you directed the identification of each sound before directing the children to sound out the word. At lesson 136, you simply direct the children to think about the sounds, without saying them out loud.

Lesson 136

READING VOCABULARY
EXERCISE 5

Children think about the sounds, then sound out the word

a. (Touch the first ball of the arrow for **this**.) I'll move down the arrow and stop under the sounds. But don't say the sounds out loud. Just figure out what you're going to say. (Move quickly under each sound.) *Children do not respond.*

b. (Return to the first ball. Pause for three seconds.) Sound it out. Get ready. (Move quickly under each sound.) *Thhththtiiisss.*

c. (Return to the first ball.) Again, sound it out. Get ready. (Move quickly under each sound.) *Thhththiiisss.*

d. (Repeat *c* until firm.)

e. (Return to the first ball.) Say it fast. (Slash.) *This.*
Yes, what word? (Signal.) *This.*
I like (pause) **this** (pause) book.

f. (Call on different children to do *c* and *e*.)

- *Step a.* Watch the children's eyes as they sound out the word to themselves. Tell them to sound out silently or whisper Come on. Figure out what you're going to say. If the children produce no mouth movements, or if they have trouble in step *b,* tell them, Whisper the sounds to yourselves. Just don't say them out loud. Repeat step *a.*

- *Step b.* Remember to pause for three seconds before telling the children to sound it out. This thinking time is very important. To help you pace the three-second pause, tap your foot softly three beats.

Children Sound Out the Word and Say It Fast (Lessons 136–150)

During these lessons, the children read a group of words on a page. A performance criterion is specified. The group must read all the words on the page in order without making a mistake before you present the next page. The children will make some mistakes. When they make a mistake on a word, you correct the mistake and go to the next word. When you finish the last word, you tell the children, That was pretty good. Let's read the words again. See if you can read them without making a mistake. Return to the first word on the page and present all the words in order until the children meet the page criterion.

Note: The word **is** is slightly irregular. It is sounded out as **iiisss,** but it is pronounced **iz,** not **iss.** When this word was first introduced in lesson 138, the children sounded it out and said it fast, **iss,** after which you said, Yes, **iz.** We say **iz.** She (pause) **is** happy. By lesson 143, the children continue to sound out the word as *iiisss,* but they are familiar enough with the word to pronounce it correctly when you tell them to say it fast.

Lesson 142

READING VOCABULARY
Do not touch any small letters

As soon as you read all the words on this page without making a mistake, we'll go on to the next page.

EXERCISE 6
Children sound out the word and say it fast

a. (Touch the first ball of the arrow for **sad.**) Sound it out. Get ready. (Move quickly under each sound.) Sssaaad.
b. (Return to the first ball.) Again, sound it out. Get ready. (Move quickly under each sound.) Sssaaad.
c. (Repeat b until firm.)
d. (Return to the first ball.) Say it fast. (Slash.) Sad. Yes, what word? (Signal.) Sad.

EXERCISE 7
Children sound out the word and say it fast

a. (Touch the first ball of the arrow for **ēat.**) Sound it out. Get ready. (Move quickly under each sound.) Eēēt.
b. (Return to the first ball.) Again, sound it out. Get ready. (Move quickly under each sound.) Eēēt.
c. (Repeat b until firm.)
d. (Return to the first ball.) Say it fast. (Slash.) Eat. Yes, what word? (Signal.) Eat. She likes to (pause) eat.

EXERCISE 8
Children sound out the word and say it fast

a. (Touch the first ball of the arrow for **sat.**) Sound it out. Get ready. (Move quickly under each sound.) Sssaaat.
b. (Return to the first ball.) Again, sound it out. Get ready. (Move quickly under each sound.) Sssaaat.
c. (Repeat b until firm.)
d. (Return to the first ball.) Say it fast. (Slash.) Sat. Yes, what word? (Signal.) Sat.

EXERCISE 9
Children sound out the word and say it fast

a. (Touch the first ball of the arrow for **mēat.**) Sound it out. Get ready. (Move quickly under each sound.) Mmmēēt.
b. (Return to the first ball.) Again, sound it out. Get ready. (Move quickly under each sound.) Mmmēēt.
c. (Repeat b until firm.)
d. (Return to the first ball.) Say it fast. (Slash.) Meat. Yes, what word? (Signal.) Meat. A hamburger is made of (pause) meat.

EXERCISE 10
Children sound out the word and say it fast

a. (Touch the first ball of the arrow for **is.**) Sound it out. Get ready. (Move quickly under each sound.) iiisss. (Children should not say iiizzz.)
b. (Return to the first ball.) Again, sound it out. Get ready. (Move quickly under each sound.) iiisss.
c. (Repeat b until firm.)
d. (Return to the first ball.) Say it fast. (Slash.) Is. Yes, iz. We say, **iz. Is** (pause) it raining today?

Criterion
(If the children read the words in exercises 6, 7, 8, 9, and 10 without making any mistakes, present individual turns.)
(If the children made mistakes, say:) That was pretty good. Let's read the words again. See if you can read them without making a mistake.

EXERCISE 11
Individual test
(Call on different children. Each child is to do exercise 6, 7, 8, 9, or 10.)

Rhyming Words (Lessons 133–150)

Beginning at lesson 133, the children read some words as rhyming words by applying the rhyming skills practiced in the oral-rhyming tracks.

The rhyming skill allows the children to read many new words by blending different initial sounds with word endings. A child with good rhyming skills can see that words that rhyme have ending parts that sound alike and look alike.

In rhyming formats from lessons 133 to 150, two or more words in a series are presented. The rhyming part of each word is in red type. The beginning sounds are in black type. Children sound out and then identify the ending part. Then they identify the beginning sound and blend it with the ending part. Their behavior is very similar to that called for in the oral-rhyming formats.

Rhyming—Words That Begin with Continuous Sounds (Lesson 136)

- *Steps b to d.* Use the same signal as you practiced in the sound it out—say it fast formats on page 217.

- *Step e.* Keep your finger on the first ball of the arrow for **sēēd** as you ask, So what does this word rhyme with? Tap the ball. The children respond ēēd. Keep touching the first ball until after you say, Rhyme with (pause) ēēd. Get ready . . . Move quickly to the second ball and hold. The children respond sss. When you slash, they complete the unblended word—sssēēd. Return to the first ball. Keep touching the ball as you ask, What word? Pause one second. Slash. The children should say, sēēd.

Lesson 136

READING VOCABULARY—RHYMING
EXERCISE 8

Children rhyme with ēēd

a. (Point to **ēēd, sēēd,** and **fēēd.**) These words rhyme.

b. (Touch the first ball of the arrow for **ēēd.** Pause.) Sound it out. Get ready. (Move quickly under each sound.) *Eēēd.*

c. (Return to the first ball.) Again, sound it out. Get ready. (Move quickly under each sound.) *Eēēd.*

d. (Return to the first ball.) Say it fast. (Slash.) *Eēēd.* Yes, **ēēd.**

e. (Touch the first ball of the arrow for **sēēd.**) The red part of this word is (pause) **ēēd.** So what does this word rhyme with? (Tap the ball.) *Eēēd.* Yes, **ēēd.**
Rhyme with (pause) **ēēd.** Get ready. (Move quickly to the second ball. Hold.) *sss.* (Slash.) *Sssēēd.*
(Return to the first ball.) What word? (Slash.) *Seed.* Yes, **seed.**

f. (Touch the first ball of the arrow to **fēēd.**) The red part of this word is (pause) **ēēd.** So what does this word rhyme with? (Tap the ball.) *Eēēd.* Yes, **ēēd.**
Rhyme with (pause) **ēēd.** Get ready. (Move quickly to the second ball. Hold.) *fff.* (Slash.) *Fffēēd.*
(Return to the first ball.) What word? (Slash.) *Feed.* Yes, **feed.**

g. (Call on different children to do e or f.)

Corrections—Step e

1. When you tap the first ball of the arrow, the children may respond by saying *sss* because they are not attending to your question. If they say *sss,* correct by saying ēēd. It rhymes with ēēd. Listen again. Repeat step *e* from the beginning.

2. When you hold your finger under the **s,** the children are supposed to hold the **sss** until you slash. If a child says *sssēēd* before you slash, tell the group, I'm still touching under the **sss.** Repeat step *e* from "Rhyme with (pause) **ēēd.** Get ready," until the children are firm at holding the **sss.**

Rhyming—Words That Begin with Stop Sounds (Lesson 144)

Words that begin with stop sounds, such as **c, d,** or **t,** are hard for children to sound out because the sound cannot be held for more than an instant. If the sound is held longer, it becomes distorted with an inappropriate vowel sound—**duuuuuu.** A variation of the word-rhyming format teaches children to process words that begin with stop sounds (lessons 139 to 150).

Lesson 144

EXERCISE 15

Children rhyme with an

a. (Point to **an** and **dan.**) These words rhyme.
b. (Touch the first ball of the arrow for **an.** Pause.) Sound it out. Get ready. (Move quickly under each sound.) *Aaannn.*
c. (Return to the first ball.) Again, sound it out. Get ready. (Move quickly under each sound.) *Aaannn.*
d. (Return to the first ball.) Say it fast. (Slash.) *An.* Yes, **an.**
e. (Touch the first ball of the arrow for **dan.**) This word rhymes with (pause) **an.** Say it fast and rhyme with (pause) **an.** (Pause.) Get ready. (Slash.) *Dan.* Yes, **dan.**
f. (Return to the first ball for **dan.**) Again, rhyme with (pause) **an.** Get ready. (Slash.) *Dan.* Yes, **dan.**
g. (Repeat *f* until firm.)
h. (Call on different children to do *f.*)

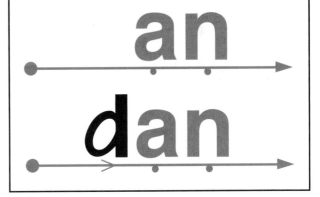

The arrowhead prompts children to say the sound fast and to blend the sound with the ending part of the word. If the stop sound appears at the end of a word, it has a ball under it rather than an arrowhead because the children stop at the end of a word.

Story Reading (Lessons 136–150)

Story Reading starts with one-word stories at lesson 136. The stories increase to two and three words by the end of the program. The words used in the stories are coordinated with the words introduced in the reading-vocabulary presentations. The stories and art are designed to be interesting, amusing, and appealing to the children. The children's stories are in Workbook C.

All story-reading exercises are part of the structured lesson. They follow the sounds and reading-vocabulary exercises. The allotted lesson time permits the group to read each story more than one time. In Level K, the stories are not the major part of the reading lesson.

Overview

The major topics in the story track (Sounding Out Words and Comprehension) are outlined in the scope and sequence chart on pages 240–241. In this story section of the guide, each topic is described and teaching techniques and corrections are provided.

Sounding Out Story Words (Lessons 124–150)

Starting at lesson 124, children sound out each word and then say it fast. Sounding out begins in reading vocabulary at lesson 124. The children sound out one word on their worksheets in lessons 130 to 143. Three-word stories start on worksheet 144.

You model how to read the fast way after the children sound out the story words in lessons 136 to 149. In lesson 150, the children practice the skills they need to make the transition from sounding out to reading the fast way.

Story Picture Comprehension (Lessons 136–150)

Comprehension of reading-vocabulary words begins in lesson 124 with the introduction of "meaning" sentences. Starting at lesson 136, comprehension skills are taught within the story track through the oral questions you present and through discussion of the pictures for the stories.

Pictures. In lessons 136 to 150, the children first read the words; **then** they look at the picture. They do not use "picture cues" to help them figure out words because pictures do not imply specific words.

How to Conduct Group Story Activities

1. Seat children so that all are close to you and all can see the Presentation Book. Sit so that you can observe whether each child's finger is pointing to the words and can see whether each child's mouth is forming the words.

2. Seat the higher-performing children on the ends of the group. Place the lower-performing children in the middle of the group.

3. Give all children lap boards or large books on which to place their worksheet.

4. Do not allow the children to look at the picture until you tell them to.

5. Each time you give an instruction to point, quickly check to see that each child is pointing appropriately.

6. During reading, make sure that the children look at the words, not at you.

7. Use an audible signal to elicit their responses.

8. Make sure you listen most frequently to the lowest-performing children in the group.

Sounding Out Story Words
(Lessons 136–150)

Children Sound Out the Word and Say It Fast

During lessons 136 to 143, the children do not read actual stories; they read an isolated story word on their worksheets. The illustration below presents the story word **am.** The children sound out the story word and then say the word fast. Then individual children read the word. You model reading the word the fast way. The children use the word as a basis for discussing what they will see in the story picture. The children look at the picture and answer some questions that relate to it.

Lesson 139

EXERCISE 13
Children sound out the story word and say it fast

a. (Hold up worksheet. Point to **am.**) You're going to read this word. After you read this word, we'll talk about the picture.
b. Everybody, touch the first ball for the word. ✓
   Look at the sounds in the word and figure out what you're going to say. (Pause three seconds.)
c. Sound it out. Get ready. (Tap for each sound, pausing about two seconds between taps. Children move their finger under each sound as they say *aaammm*.)
d. Again, finger on the first ball. ✓
   Sound it out. Get ready. (Tap for each sound, pausing about two seconds between taps.) *Aaammm.*
e. (Repeat *d* until firm.)
f. Everybody, say it fast. (Signal.) *Am.* What word? (Signal.) *Am.* Yes, **am.**
g. (Repeat *d* and *f* until firm.)

EXERCISE 14
Individual test

a. Everybody, follow along with your finger as I call on different children to read the word.
b. Everybody, touch the first ball for the word. ✓
   (Call on a child.) Sound it out. Get ready. (Tap for each sound, pausing about two seconds between taps.) *Aaammm.* Say it fast. (Signal.) *Am.* Yes, **am.**
c. (Call on different children to do *b*.)

EXERCISE 15
Teacher reads the fast way

a. (Hold up worksheet.)
b. (Touch the first ball of the arrow for **am.**) Everybody, I'm going to read this word the fast way. (Slash as you say:) **am.** I read it the fast way.
c. (Touch the first ball of the arrow for **am.**) I'll read it again. (Slash as you say:) **am.**

COMPREHENSION
EXERCISE 16
Picture comprehension

a. You've read the word (pause) **am.** The picture shows who I really . . . . (Signal.) *Am.* Yes, **am.**
b. Everybody, look at the picture. ✓
c. (Ask these questions:)
   1. Is that who I really am? (Signal.) *No.* No, that's not who I am.
   2. Who is that in the picture? (Call on a child.) *A tiger.* Yes, a big, mean tiger.
   3. Am I really a big, mean tiger? (Signal.) *No.*
   4. What would you do if you had that big, mean tiger? (Call on a child. Accept reasonable responses.)

Worksheet 139, Side 2

Exercise 13 Teaching Techniques

- *Step a.* Do not let the children look at the picture until exercise 16. You want them to read the word before they relate it to the picture. Enforce this rule.

- *Step b.* Be sure that the children figure out the sounds in the word **am** before sounding it out. If the children are not obviously attending to the sounds, tell them to move under each sound and say it to themselves. Pause at least three seconds before beginning the sounding out. This pause is critical to give the children time to look at the sounds.

- *Step c.* Pause about two seconds between taps. Check to see that the children are touching under each sound as you tap. (They practiced this behavior on worksheets 115 to 129.) The children are not to stop between the sounds when they say them.

- *Step f.* Give an audible signal—a tap or a snap—for the children to say the word fast. They must be looking at their papers, not at you.

Exercises 14–16 Teaching Techniques

- *Exercise 14.* Check to see that all the children are following along with their fingers as different children read the word. You may have to move some children's fingers.

- *Exercise 15.* Be sure the children are looking at your worksheet as you model how to read the word the fast way.

- *Exercise 16, step a.* Be sure the children are looking at you.

- *Exercise 16, step c.* The children should be looking at the picture. Do not signal. Let different children respond. But do not let the discussion continue for more than about ten seconds.

Corrections

Correct sound misidentification by telling (modeling) the correct sound and repeating the step in which the mistake occurred.

Correct touching errors by physically moving the children's fingers and repeating the step. If children stop between the sounds, present a model by calling on an individual to sound out the word.

If children cannot say a word fast, correct as you did in reading vocabulary (page 217) by changing the exercise into an oral task. Then direct the children to sound out and identify the word on their worksheet.

Remember to follow each correction with a repetition of the step that was missed.

On pages 226–227, there is a series of correction procedures for word-identification errors on group reading or on individual tests. If you compare the procedures, you'll see that they are similar to each other, with only slight variations. For group reading, the last step in the correction in lessons 136 to 143 involves repeating the **word** that was missed. In lessons 144 to 150, it involves repeating the **sentence** that was missed.

Similarly, for an individual test, in lessons 136 to 150, the last step in the correction involves repeating the **word** that was missed.

Group Reading, Lessons 136–143
Correction for Word-Identification Errors

Worksheet 139, Side 2

The correction involves the following steps:

1. Identifying the word

2. Directing the group to sound out and identify the word

3. Repeating the steps for sounding out the word

The group is reading the word **am** (see page 224, steps *d* to *f*). Jim and Ed make mistakes at step 4.

1. <u>Teacher:</u> Again, finger on the first ball. ✓
   Sound it out. Get ready. (Tap for each sound, pausing about two seconds between taps.)

2. <u>Group:</u> *Aaammm.*

3. <u>Teacher:</u> Everybody, say it fast. (Signal.)

4. <u>Jim:</u> *Aaa.*
   <u>Terry:</u> *Am*
   <u>Ed:</u> *It.*

5. <u>Teacher:</u> That word is am. Everybody, finger on the ball. ✓
   Sound it out. Get ready. (Tap for each sound, pausing about two seconds between taps.)

6. <u>Group:</u> *Aaammm.*

7. <u>Teacher:</u> Everybody, say it fast. (Signal.)

8. <u>Group:</u> *Am*

9. <u>Teacher:</u> What word? (Signal)

10. <u>Group:</u> *Am.*

11. <u>Teacher:</u> Yes, am. Good. You said it fast. Starting over. (Return to step *d* and present steps *d* through *f*.)

Group Reading, Lessons 144–150
Correction for Word-Identification errors

Worksheet 144

The correction involves returning to the beginning of the sentence and rereading the sentence. Here are the steps:

1. Identify the word. That word is. . . .

2. Direct the group to sound out and identify the word. Everybody, sound it out. Get ready . . . What word?

3. Direct the group to return to the first word of the sentence and read the entire sentence. Starting over or Back to the first word (of the sentence.)

Teacher and Children Read the Fast Way (Lesson 150)

In lessons 136 to 149, you modeled how to read the fast way after the children sounded out the words in the story. In lesson 150, you and the children read part of the story the fast way. You provide a strong model of inflection and whole-word reading. The lower-performing children, especially, need this strong model; so be sure to teach this exercise to criterion.

Lesson 150

EXERCISE 15

Teacher and children read the fast way

a. (Hold up worksheet. Point to the words on the arrow. Touch under **mē**.) Everybody, this word is (pause) **me**. What word? (Signal.) *Me.*
Yes, **me**. Remember that.

b. We're going to read this story the fast way.

c. (Point to **mad at**.) I'll read these words the fast way.

d. (Point to **mē**.) When I touch this word, you're going to say . . . . (Signal.) *Me.*
Yes, **me**.

e. (Repeat *d* until firm.)

f. (Touch the first ball of the arrow.) Reading the fast way. (Pause three seconds. Touch under **mad** and say:) **mad**. (Touch under **at** and say:) **at**.

g. (Then touch under **mē**.) *Me.*

h. (Repeat *f* and *g* until firm.)

i. Yes, **mad at me**.

Worksheet 150, Side 2

```
.mad at mē␤
 •  •   •  •   •  •
```

- *Step a.* After you ask, What word? move to the end of the arrow. The children should respond *me*.

- *Step d.* Signal the children to complete the sentence. Watch your voice cue and your timing. Say, When I touch this word, you're going to saaaaaay. . . . and move to the end of the arrow.

- *Step f.* After you say, Reading the fast way, be sure to pause for three seconds. Move quickly to **mad** and say mad. (If you move slowly, the children may try to respond with you.) Then move quickly to **at** and say at.

- *Step g.* Move more slowly to **me**. Children are to respond the instant you stop under the word, not before.

- Repeat steps *f* and *g* until the children are firm. Then say, Yes. Mad at me.

Correction

Use this correction procedure for step *g* if the children begin to sound out the word instead of saying it fast.

model ⟶ 1. Immediately say the word **me**.

lead ⟶ 2. Repeat steps *f* and *g*, responding with the children at step *g*. Repeat the lead.

test ⟶ 3. Repeat step *f*. Then present step *g*. Do not respond with the children.

delayed test ⟶ 4. Say, Let's do it again. Return to step a and present the format. Do not lead the children at step *g*.

Worksheets (Lessons 101–150)

Overview

The worksheets for lessons 101–150 support many skills that are taught in the Pre-Reading and Reading tracks. Worksheet activities shape the children's ability to work independently. Each Reading Worksheet (Side 2) presents four or more different activities and will usually occupy the children in independent work for ten to twenty minutes. The worksheets also contain the story words that the children read from lessons 130 to 150.

Taking home their worksheets serves an important function when the children begin to read. It allows children to relate what goes on in school to what goes on at home. It provides parents with a potential basis for praising their child's performance in school. Equally important, it shows parents on a day-to-day basis what is happening in school and what their child is being taught. The worksheets extend and reinforce the teacher-directed activities.

As with earlier worksheets, when new worksheet activities are introduced, they are teacher-directed. After two or three days of such direction, the children work on the activities independently. When the children work independently, they should work with as little help from you as possible. Some children may need help with writing early in the program. Work with these children and praise them for progress in working independently.

The Work Check

Check the children's worksheets each day. Mark errors in pencil or in some way that your marks can be erased so the parent or guardian will see a corrected paper. Set up a simple rule that children must have everything corrected on their worksheets before they take them home. Pay close attention to the worksheets. The children's performance on their worksheets reflects how well they have learned a particular skill. If you see a pattern of errors, reteach that skill.

For additional information on managing the independent activities and motivating the children, see pages 190–191 of this guide.

Summary of Independent Activity

After the children have learned how to do a particular kind of exercise, it becomes part of their independent activity. At the end of each lesson you indicate to the children which worksheet exercises they will complete independently. These activities are specified for you in the Summary of Independent Work exercise for each lesson.

Worksheet Track Development

Each of the worksheet activities shown on the scope and sequence chart on pages 240–241 is developed in a sequence of increasing complexity. The exact steps for teaching these activities are detailed in exercises that appear at the end of each lesson in the Reading Presentation Book.

The exercises from the Reading Presentation Book are self-explanatory, carefully detailed, and easy to follow. You should become familiar with them before teaching the worksheet activities. The first time a new format appears in the Presentation Book, its title has lines above and below it. Follow the directions carefully during the days you present the exercise to the children. Your careful, exact presentation will pay off in fewer errors when the children begin doing the exercises independently.

The following worksheet activities will be discussed in this guide: sound writing, sounds cross-out game, story copying, and pair relations.

Sound Writing (Lessons 136–150)

The children write letters from lesson 47 through 135. Starting at lesson 136, they write **sounds.** They practice the sounds they have already learned. Symbols in the sound writing track have a different appearance from the symbols in the letter writing track.

Worksheet 136

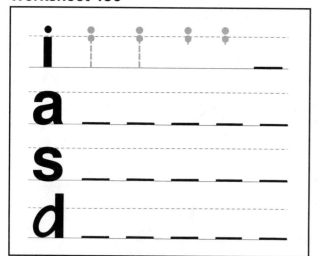

At lesson 136, the children will be making several different symbols freehand on the same sheet.

Sounds Cross-out Game (Lessons 101–150)

The children cross out symbols from lesson 85 through 150. Starting at lesson 101, the symbols children cross out are no longer identified by their letter name, but by their sound. Starting at lesson 138, children cross out one symbol and circle another.

Worksheet 138

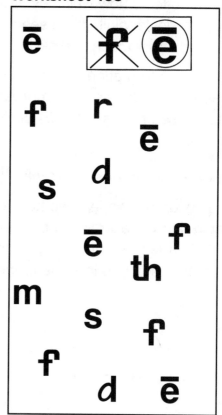

Note that children identify and circle the sound ē, but they never write the symbol ē or **th.** They only write real letters.

Story Word Copying and Sentence Copying (Lessons 136–150)

These worksheet exercises teach the children to copy an entire story sentence. In the first exercise, at lesson 136, the children copy directly beneath the story.

They trace the letters by following dots on the first line. In lessons 144–150, blocks appear between the words and there are macrons over the long vowels. All the letters in the words the children write are full-size. Blocks are printed to show the children where they are to write each word.

Worksheet 144

Watch the children carefully to be sure they are writing the letters small enough to fit into the available space. Be sure that they complete one word at a time. The children may try copying a whole row of the first letter, then a row of the next letter, and so on. This defeats the purpose of the exercise—to practice writing whole words.

After children copy their story, they can color the story picture.

The writing exercises reinforce the sounds and words being taught. They are not intended to be a handwriting program.

Children who complete the pair-relations exercises are in a good position to understand the kind of workbook activities they will encounter in a variety of school subjects and on standardized tests. For all pair relations, symbols must be paired with the appropriate object or an illustration paired with the appropriate sentence. The example below shows the first pair-relations exercise in the program. Children complete the pairs.

Worksheet 117

The purpose of this exercise is to show the children that pairs such as airplane/m can be repeated. Each time the pair appears, it must say airplane/m.

Literature Component

Literature Guide

Reading Mastery Plus, Level K has a literature component that consists of the Literature Guide and seven trade books that are used in the literature lessons. Presentation questions for the seven selections are provided in the Literature Guide. The Literature Guide also contains a Bibliography of Trade Literature that is correlated to the oral stories and sequences in Reading lessons 81–112.

Literature Lessons

Time Requirements

Literature Lessons begin after lesson 45. Ideally, the literature lessons should not be presented as part of the regular reading or language lessons. Allow about 15–20 minutes for each literature lesson.

Schedule

The schedule on page 233 shows that each book should be read to the children at least three times. For some of the selections, the questions are different for the first and second presentations. As a general rule, present the first reading of the story as soon as the children complete the specified lesson indicated for the story introduction. For instance, present *What Are You Called?* after the children complete *Reading Mastery Plus* lesson 45, but before you present lesson 51.

Schedule the second reading of the story about five lessons later and the third reading of the story about ten lessons later. The following chart shows a schedule for three readings for each book. This schedule provides for literature selections every fifth lesson (or every fifth day).

Following *Reading Mastery Plus* Lesson	45	50	55	60	65	70	75	80	85	90	95	100	105	110	115	120	125	130	135	140	145	150
Title																						
What Are You Called?	•	•	•																			
Dog Went for a Walk				•	•	•																
Goodnight							•	•	•													
Farmer Schnuck										•	•	•										
This and That													•	•	•							
Nibbly Mouse																•	•	•				
Little Dinosaur																			•	•	•	

Presenting the Literature Lessons

The literature selections may be presented to the entire class; however, it may be difficult for all of the children to see the illustrations. A workable plan is to present the lesson to the entire class and then arrange a schedule for circulating the books to the children. For lower-level performers, small groups are preferable so you can verify that the children understand the text and the illustrations.

Literature Collection Story Summaries

What Are You Called? presents information about names of baby animals (pup, foal, calf, cub, kid). The text follows a repetitive format: A baby _____ is called a _____, but so is a baby . . . (Children indicate the other animal that has the same baby name.)

Dog Went for a Walk has repetitive text that relates who walked the dog and what the dog did. (Dog went for a walk with Jenny. Dog got hungry.) The structure of the story permits interesting rereading of the text. Children indicate what the dog will do after each walk. They also answer questions about the person associated with each outcome.

Goodnight is a predictable text that has rhyming words. (This little fish sleeps in the sea. This little bird sleeps in the tree.) The structure permits engagement of children when the story is reread. (This little fish sleeps in . . . This little bird sleeps in . . .)

Farmer Schnuck uses a format of repeated expressions to introduce new characters. Rereading of this story permits children to complete expressions and indicate what will happen next in the story.

This and That introduces different compound words and shows pictures of the component words. (Take some **butter.** Add a **fly.** Now you have a . . . **butterfly.**) Like most of the other books, *This and That* promotes participation of children when they put the component words together and take the compound words apart. (What words did you put together to make **butterfly**?) Also, like the other stories in the first set, *This and That* works on skills that are important for the beginning reader.

Nibbly Mouse is about a mouse that eats holes in the pages of the book. The holes reveal parts of pictures, while the text gives sound clues about the objects. For example, "Nibbly Mouse ate a hole in my apple. Then what did she see? It starts with *b.*" Through the hole we see a pattern, but we don't know until we turn the page that the object is a **b**lanket.

Little Dinosaur is the most sophisticated story in the Level K collection. The little dinosaur is frustrated because he is so small compared to the brontosaurus, pteranodon, and diplodocus. In the end, he discovers that he is very large compared to a teeny, weeny dinosaur. The story presents possible object lessons: Size is relative; the way people feel about themselves has a lot to do with how others respond to them.

Placement

Placement Test Procedures

The placement test on page 236 is to be administered individually to each child before instruction begins. All testing should be completed during the first week. The placement test, a sample scoring sheet, and directions for giving and scoring the test appear on the next few pages.

Before Giving the Test

The testing material consists of a test and a score sheet. You will need a score sheet for each child in your class. (See page 237 for the score sheet that can be duplicated for each child.)

Familiarize yourself with the instructions and the score sheet before testing. Practice presenting the test items and using the score sheet.

A child's test score is based on the number of errors made.

How to Give the Test

1. Allow 3 to 5 minutes per child for administering the placement test.

2. Sit at a low table with a child, preferably in a quiet corner of the room.

3. Score the child's response on his or her scoring sheet as you present the test. Circle 0 to indicate a correct response to a test item. Circle 1 to indicate an incorrect response.

4. Accept all reasonable answers, using the suggested answers as guidelines.

5. On statement repetition items (9, 11, and 13 for example) circle a 1 each time you have to repeat the statement until the student produces a correct response. Repeat the statement no more than four times. (If the student repeats the statement the first time you say it, circle the zero.)

6. At the end of the test, total the 1s you have circled. Write the number of these incorrect responses in the box.

Determining the Starting Lesson

The directions at the bottom of the scoring sheet of the placement test indicate the lesson at which each child should be placed in the program.

- Children who score six or more errors begin at lesson 1.

- Children who score four or five errors begin at lesson 11.

- Children who score less than four errors begin at lesson 21.

PLACEMENT TEST

1. Show me your nose.
   (The child must point to his/her nose.)

2. Show me your head.
   (The child may point anywhere on his/her head.)

3. Show me your ear.
   (The child may point to one or both ears.)

4. Show me your hand.
   (The child may hold up one hand or both hands.)

5. Show me your chin.
   (The child must point to his/her chin.)

6. Show me your cheek.
   (The child may touch one cheek or both cheeks.)

7. Show me your shoulder.
   (The child may point to one shoulder or both shoulders.)

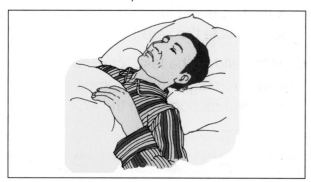

8. (Point to the man.)
   What is this man doing?
   (Accept *Sleeping, going to sleep,* or *lying down.* Don't accept *Sleep, eyes shut,* or *got to sleep.*)

9. My turn to say the whole thing.
   This man is sleeping. Say that.
   This (or *that*) *man is sleeping.*

10. (Point to the girl.)
    What is this girl doing?
    (Accept *Eating, eating a hamburger,* or an entire correct sentence. Don't accept *Eat* or *eat a hamburger.*)

11. My turn to say the whole thing.
    This girl is eating. Say that.
    This girl is eating or
    This girl is eating a hamburger.

12. (Point to the cat.)
    What is this cat doing?
    (Accept *Climbing the tree, going up the tree, climbing on a tree, climbing up there,* or *climbing.*)

13. My turn to say the whole thing.
    This cat is climbing the tree. Say that.
    This cat is climbing the tree.

14. What's your whole name?
    (The child must give first and last name; middle name is optional.)

15. What's your first name?
    (The child must give first name only.)

PLACEMENT SCORING SHEET

Student's Name _____ Date _____

Items	Correct Responses	Incorrect Responses
1	0	1
2	0	1
3	0	1
4	0	1
5	0	1
6	0	1
7	0	1
8	0	1
9	0	1 1 1 1
10	0	1
11	0	1 1 1 1
12	0	1
13	0	1 1 1 1
14	0	1
15	0	1

Total of All Incorrect Responses

☐ **Score**

Student's Score	Starts at Lesson
6 or more	1
4 or 5	11
less than 4	21

(Circle the lesson)

APPENDIX A   Language Scope and Sequence

10 20 30 40 50 60 70 80 90 100 110 120 130 140 150

Actions
Beginning Actions
Parts of the Body
Pronouns
Pictures—Actions
Actions—Tense
Tense—Pictures
Actions—Review

Descriptions of Objects
Object Identification
Identity Statements
Common Objects
Missing Objects
Plurals
Opposites
Comparatives

Information and Background Knowledge
Names
School Information
Days of the Week
Months of the Year
Seasons
Part/Whole Relationships
Materials
Common Information
Locations
Signs

Instructional Words and Problem-Solving Concepts
Spatial and Temporal Relations
Before/After
Prepositions
And
Same/Different
Some, All, None
Or
Where, Who, When, What
If-Then Rules

Classification
Classification

Rhyming
Rhyming

Problem-Solving Strategies and Applications
Review
Concept Applications
Absurdities
Inquiry

APPENDIX A
Language Worksheet Scope and Sequence

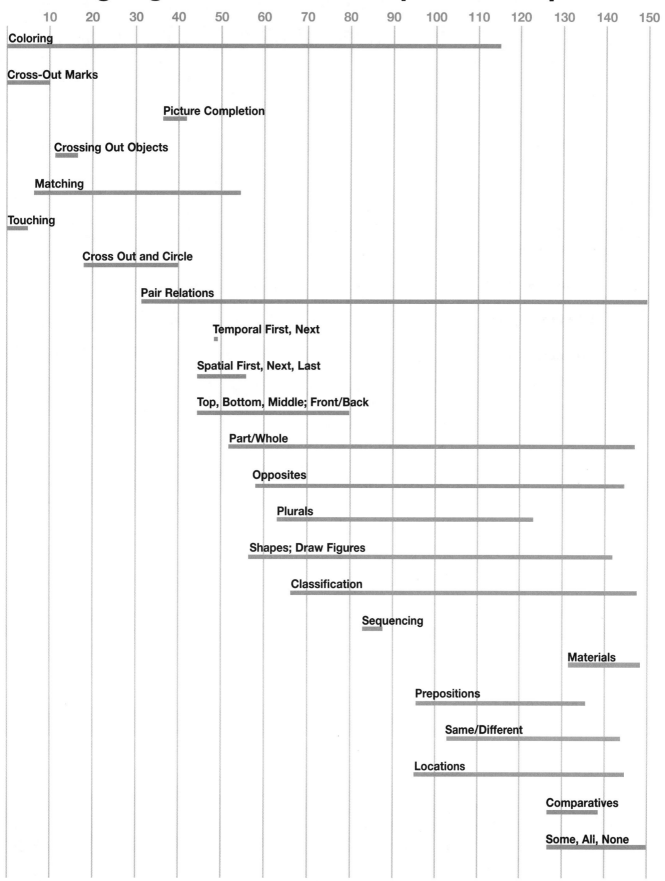

Reading Scope and Sequence

of skills presented in *Reading Mastery Plus* Kindergarten

Alphabet Song

Letter Identification
- Lowercase
- Capitals

Oral Stories & Sequences
(Story Picture Book)

Letter Sounds

Saying Sounds

Symbol Action

Blending
- Say it Fast
- Say the Sounds
- Say the Sounds—Say It Fast
- Sounds—Say It Fast
- Say It Fast—Rhyming
- Rhyming
- Sound Out

Reading Vocabulary
- Sounding Out Words
- Rhyming Words

Story Reading
- Sounding Out Words
- Picture Comprehension Questions

Worksheet Activity
- Say It Fast Picture
- Sound Out
- Reading Vocabulary
- Symbol Action

Independent Activity
- Regular Letters
- Capital Letters
- Words from Capitals
- Sound Writing
- Letter Cross-Out Game
- Sound Cross-Out Game
- Picture Completion
- Pair Relations
- Matching
- Word and Story Copying

Lessons 51–100	Lessons 101–150
Pre-Reading Presentation Book	**Reading Presentaton Book**

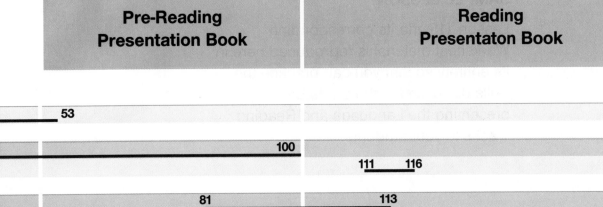

41   53

41   100

111   116

81   113

101   150

101   144

119   150

101   113

101   120

106 109

108   136

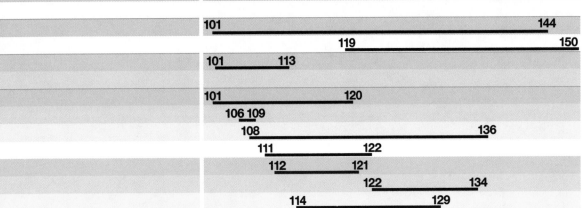

111   122

112   121

122   134

114   129

124   150

133   150

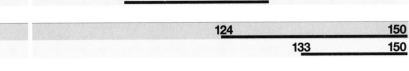

136   150

136   150

101   109

115   129

130 135

113 115

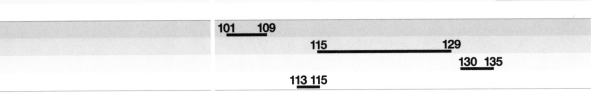

47   135

111   116

123   130

136   150

85   100

101   150

87   116

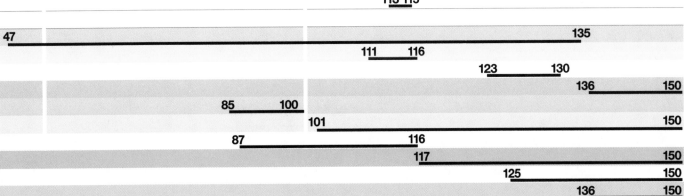

117   150

125   150

136   150

APPENDIX B

SAMPLE LESSON

Lesson 115 and its corresponding Worksheet material is reproduced here in its entirety so that you can practice the skills discussed in the guide before presenting the Language and Reading Tracks to your students.

Lesson 115

EXERCISE 1   Actions—Review

1. Here's our first action game.

a. Watch me. (Touch your knees. Keep touching them.)
What am I doing? (Signal.) *Touching your knees.*

b. (Stop touching your knees. Touch your ears and keep touching them.) What am I doing now? (Signal.) *Touching your ears.*

c. What did I do **before** I touched my ears? (Signal.) *Touched your knees.*
Yes, I touched my knees.
(Repeat until all children's responses are firm.)

d. Say the whole thing about what I did before I touched my ears. (Signal.) *You touched your knees before you touched your ears.*
(Repeat until all children's responses are firm.)

e. What am I doing now? (Signal.) *Touching your ears.*
Say the whole thing about what I am doing. (Signal.) *You are touching your ears.*

2. Here's our last action game.

a. Watch me. (Point to the ceiling. Keep pointing.)
What am I doing? (Signal.) *Pointing to the ceiling.*

b. (Stop pointing to the ceiling. Point to the wall and keep pointing to it.) What am I doing now? (Signal.) *Pointing to the wall.*

c. What did I do **before** I pointed to the wall? (Signal.) *Pointed to the ceiling.*
Yes, I pointed to the ceiling.
(Repeat until all children's responses are firm.)

d. Say the whole thing about what I did before I pointed to the wall. (Signal.) *You pointed to the ceiling before you pointed to the wall.*
(Repeat until all children's responses are firm.)

e. What am I doing now? (Signal.) *Pointing to the wall.*
Say the whole thing about what I am doing. (Signal.) *You are pointing to the wall.*
(Repeat until all children's responses are firm.)

82

83

EXERCISE 2 Same

1. We're going to tell why things are the same. Listen.
a. A saw and an axe. Think of them. Why are they the same? (Call on different children. Accept reasonable responses such as *They cut things; they are tools; they have handles.*)
b. Listen. A saw and an axe are the same because they both cut things. Everybody, why are they the same? (Signal.) *They both cut things.* (Repeat until all the children's responses are firm.)

2. Listen.
a. A broom and a toothbrush. Think of them. Why are they the same? (Call on different children. Accept reasonable responses such as *They both have bristles; they clean things.*)
b. Listen. A broom and a toothbrush are the same because they both clean things. Everybody, why are they the same? (Signal.) *They both clean things.* (Repeat until all the children's responses are firm.)

3. Listen.
a. A ladder and stairs. Think of them. Why are they the same? (Call on different children. Accept reasonable responses such as *You can walk on them; you climb them.*)
b. Listen. A ladder and stairs are the same because you can climb them. Everybody, why are they the same? (Signal.) *Because you can climb them.* (Repeat until all the children's responses are firm.)

4. Now let's see if you can answer these questions. (Call on different children.)
a. Why are a saw and an axe the same? (Accept reasonable responses.)
b. Why are a ladder and stairs the same? (Accept reasonable responses.)
c. Why are a broom and a toothbrush the same? (Accept reasonable responses.)

EXERCISE 3 Opposites

1. We're going to play a word game.
a. Listen. I'm thinking about an alligator that is the opposite of young. So what do you know about it? (Pause. Signal.) *It's old.*
b. Listen. I'm thinking about umbrellas that are the opposite of dry. So what do you know about them? (Pause. Signal.) *They're wet.*
c. Listen. I'm thinking about a tree that is the opposite of tall. So what do you know about it? (Pause. Signal.) *It's short.*

2. (Repeat part 1 until all children's responses are firm.)

EXERCISE 4 Common Information

1. Let's see how much information you remember.
a. What do we call a person who drives a vehicle? (Signal.) *A driver.*
Say the whole thing about a driver. (Signal.) *A driver is a person who drives a vehicle.*
b. What do we call a forest in a hot place? (Signal.) *A jungle.*
Say the whole thing about a jungle. (Signal.) *A jungle is a forest in a hot place.*
c. What do we call a person who rides in a vehicle? (Signal.) *A passenger.*
Say the whole thing about a passenger. (Signal.) *A passenger is a person who rides in a vehicle.*
d. What do we call a person who puts out fires? (Signal.) *A firefighter.*
Say the whole thing about a firefighter. (Signal.) *A firefighter is a person who puts out fires.*
e. What do we call a person who helps keep people safe? (Signal.) *A police officer.*
Say the whole thing about a police officer. (Signal.) *A police officer is a person who helps keep people safe.*

2. (Repeat part 1 until all children can make the statements.)

3. Get ready for some new information.
a. Listen. A beach is a sandy place next to water. What do we call a sandy place next to water? (Signal.) *A beach.*
Say the whole thing about a beach. (Signal.) *A beach is a sandy place next to water.*
b. What do we call a person who puts out fires? (Signal.) *A firefighter.*
Say the whole thing about a firefighter. (Signal.) *A firefighter is a person who puts out fires.*
c. What do we call a sandy place next to water? (Signal.) *A beach.*
Say the whole thing about a beach. (Signal.) *A beach is a sandy place next to water.*

4. (Repeat part 3 until all children can make the statements.)

5. I'll turn the page and we'll see a picture of a beach.
(Turn the page quickly.)

Lesson 115

EXERCISE 4 Common Information (cont.)

6. (Show the picture to the children.)
   What place do you see in this picture?
   (Call on different children.)
   Point to the girl who is making a building.
   Point to the containers.
   Point to the vehicles.
   Point to some food.
   (Praise good responses.)

84

Worksheet 115

SIDE 1

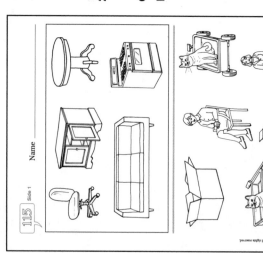

[115] Side 1

Name

© SRA/McGraw-Hill. All rights reserved.

Color

1. (Hold up worksheet.) Find the chair. ✓
   (Point to each object and ask:) What is this?
   (The children are to respond *a chair,*
   a cabinet, a table, a couch, a stove.)

   a. Everybody, you are going to color the
   table brown, so put a brown mark on
   the table. ✓
   What color is that mark? (Signal.) *Brown.*

   b. Everybody, you are going to color the
   couch purple, so put a purple mark on the
   couch. ✓
   What color is that mark? (Signal.) *Purple.*

   c. Everybody, you are going to color the
   chair yellow, so put a yellow mark on
   the chair. ✓
   What color is that mark? (Signal.) *Yellow.*

2. Later you are going to color all the objects.

Opposites

Find the box. ✓

a. Listen. Here's the rule for the woman who
is not sitting: The woman who is not sitting
should be wearing a red coat.
Put a red mark on the coat of the woman
who is not sitting. ✓

b. Here's another rule: The big box should
have a cross-out mark on the side.
What should that box have? (Signal.)
A cross-out mark on the side.
Draw a cross-out mark on the side of the
box that is big. ✓

c. Here's the last rule: The cat that is not next
to the wagon should be wearing earmuffs.
Put a mark on the cat that is not next to the
wagon. ✓
Later you may fix up the cat.

[Note: Before presenting lesson 116, present
Reading lesson 115.]

85

Lesson 115

SAYING SOUNDS
EXERCISE 1

Children say the sounds

a. You're going to say some sounds. When I hold up my finger, say (pause) ēēē. Get ready. (Hold up one finger.) ēēē.

b. Next sound. Say (pause) rrr. Get ready. (Hold up one finger.) rrr.

c. Next sound. Say (pause) nnn. Get ready. (Hold up one finger.) nnn.

d. (Repeat c for sounds ēēē, rrr, and nnn.)

e. (Call on different children to do a, b, or c.)

f. Good saying the sounds.

LETTER SOUNDS
EXERCISE 2

Sounds firm-up

a. (Point to the column of sounds.) See if you can say the sounds for all these letters without making a mistake. (Touch the first ball of the arrow for **a**. Pause one second.) Say the sound. Get ready. (Move quickly to the second ball. Hold.) aaa. Yes, aaa.

b. (Touch the first ball of the arrow for **s**. Pause one second.) Get ready. (Move quickly to the second ball. Hold.) sss. Yes, **sss**.

c. (Repeat b for each remaining sound in the column.)

d. (Repeat the column until all children are firm on all sounds.)

e. (Call on different children to say all the sounds in the column.)

f. Good. You said all the sounds in the column.

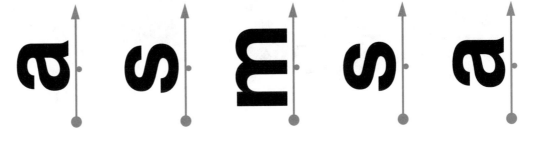

SAY THE SOUNDS—SAY IT FAST
EXERCISE 3

Children say a word or sound slowly, then say it fast

a. I'm going to say some words and some sounds. First you're going to say them slowly. Then you're going to say them fast.

b. Listen. (Hold up a finger for each sound.) Say (pause) **rrraaat**. Get ready. (Hold up a finger for each sound.) *Rrraaat.* Again. Get ready. (Hold up a finger for each sound.) *Rrraaat.* Say it fast. (Signal.) *Rat.* Yes, **rat**.

c. Listen. (Hold up one finger.) Say (pause) **ĭĭĭ**. Get ready. (Hold up one finger.) *ĭĭĭ.* Again. Get ready. (Hold up one finger.) *ĭĭĭ.* Say it fast. (Signal.) *ĭ.* Yes, **ĭ**.

d. Listen. (Hold up a finger for each sound.) Say (pause) **zzzooooo**. Get ready. (Hold up a finger for each sound.) *Zzzooooo.* Again. Get ready. (Hold up a finger for each sound.) *Zzzooooo.* Say it fast. (Signal.) *Zoo.* Yes, **zoo**.

e. (Repeat b through d until firm.)

f. (Call on different children to do b, c, or d.)

111   Lesson 115

Do not show the picture until step *g*, exercise 4.

SAY IT FAST
EXERCISE 4

Children say it fast, then see a picture

a. (Do not show the picture until step *g*.)
b. Say it fast and I'll show you a picture.
c. Listen. **Piiicnic.** (Pause.) Say it fast!
   (Signal.) *Picnic.*
   What word? (Signal.) *Picnic.*
d. Yes, what is the picture going to show?
   (Signal.) *Picnic.* Yes, **picnic.**
e. In the picture you will see a family in the
   park having a . . . . (Pause.) **Piiicnic.**
   (Pause.) Say it fast! (Signal.) *Picnic.*
f. (Repeat *e* until firm.)
g. Here's the picture. (Show the picture.)

112   Lesson 115

SOUNDS—SAY IT FAST
EXERCISE 5

Children say a sound slowly, then say it fast

a. (Touch the first ball of the arrow for **s.**) First you're going to say it slowly. Then you're going to say it fast. Say it slowly. Get ready. (Move quickly under each sound. Hold under each sound for one second.) sssssss.
(Return to the first ball for **s.**) Say it fast. (Slash.) s. Yes, s.

b. (Repeat a until firm.)

c. (Touch the first ball of the arrow for **a.**) Say it slowly. Get ready. (Move quickly to the second ball. Hold.) aaa.
(Return to the first ball for **a.**) Say it fast. (Slash.) a. Yes, a.

d. (Repeat c until firm.)

e. (Call on different children to do a or c.)

LETTER SOUNDS
EXERCISE 6

Introducing the new sound ēēē as in ēat; children discriminate e—ē

a. (Point to **e.**) Everybody, what letter is this? (Signal.) *E.*

b. (Point to **ē.**) This is also the letter **e** with a line over it.

• (Point to **ē.**) Here's the rule about this **e:** It always makes the sound ēēē. Everybody, what sound does this **e** make? (Signal.) *ēēē.*

c. (Point to **e.**) This **e** does not always make the sound ēēē.

d. I'll point to each letter. You tell me if it always makes the sound ēēē.

• (Point to **e.**) Does this letter always make the sound ēēē? (Signal.) *No.*

• (Point to **ē.**) Does this letter always make the sound ēēē? (Signal.) *Yes.*

e. (Repeat d until firm.)

SOUND OUT
EXERCISE 7

Children say the sounds without stopping

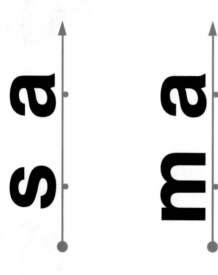

a. (Touch the first ball of the arrow for **sa.**) My turn. I'll show you how to say these sounds without stopping between the sounds. (Move under each sound. Hold. Say sssaaa.)

b. (Return to the first ball of the arrow for **sa.**) Your turn. Say the sounds as I touch under them. Don't stop between the sounds. Get ready. (Move under each sound. Hold.) *Sssaaa.*
(Return to the first ball of the arrow.) Again. Get ready. (Move under each sound. Hold.) *Sssaaaa.*

Good saying **sssaaa.**

c. (Touch the first ball of the arrow for **ma.**) My turn. I'll show you how to say these sounds without stopping between the sounds. (Move under each sound. Hold. Say mmmaaa.)

d. (Return to the first ball of the arrow for **ma.**) Your turn. Say the sounds as I touch under them. Don't stop between the sounds. Get ready. (Move under each sound. Hold.) *Mmmaaa.*
(Return to the first ball of the arrow.) Again. Get ready. (Move under each sound. Hold.) *Mmmaaa.*

Good saying **mmmaaa.**

e. (Call on different children to do *b* or *d*.)

114   Lesson 115

LETTER SOUNDS
EXERCISE 8

Sounds firm-up

a. (Point to **ē**.) Remember, this new sound is (pause) ēēē.

b. (Point to the column of sounds.) See if you can say the sounds for all these letters without making a mistake. (Touch the first ball of the arrow for **m**. Pause one second.) Say the sound. Get ready. (Move quickly to the second ball. Hold.) *mmm*. Yes, **mmm**.

c. (Touch the first ball of the arrow for **ē**. Pause one second.) Get ready. (Move quickly to the second ball. Hold.) ēēē. Yes, ēēē.

d. (Repeat c for each remaining sound in the column.)

e. (Repeat the column until all children are firm on all sounds.)

f. (Call on different children to say all the sounds in the column.)

g. Good. You said all the sounds in the column.

115   Lesson 115

SAY IT FAST—RHYMING

This is an oral exercise.

EXERCISE 9

Children say word parts slowly, then say them fast

a. Let's do the hard Say It Fast. Listen. (Hold up one finger.) First you'll say (pause) **mmm.** (Hold up second finger.) Then you'll say (pause) **at.**

b. My turn: **mmmat.** Listen again. (Hold up one finger.) First you'll say (pause) **mmm.** (Hold up second finger.) Then you'll say (pause) **at.**
Your turn. Say it slowly. Get ready. (Hold up one finger.) *mmm.* (Hold up second finger.) *(mmm)at.*
Again. Get ready. (Hold up one finger.) *mmm.* (Hold up second finger.) *(mmm)at.*
Say it fast. (Signal.) *Mat.* Yes, **mat.**

c. (Repeat b until firm.)

d. Here's a new word. Listen. (Hold up one finger.) First you'll say (pause) **fff.** (Hold up second finger.) Then you'll say (pause) **un.**

e. My turn: **fffun.** Listen again. (Hold up one finger.) First you'll say (pause) **fff.** (Hold up second finger.) Then you'll say **un.**
Say it slowly. Get ready. (Hold up one finger.) *fff.* (Hold up second finger.) *(fff)un.*
Again. Get ready. (Hold up one finger.) *fff.* (Hold up one finger.) *fff.* (Hold up second finger.) *(fff)un.*
Say it fast. (Signal.) *Fun.* Yes, **fun.**

f. (Repeat e until firm.)

g. Here's a new word. Listen. (Hold up one finger.) First you'll say (pause) **zzz.** (Hold up second finger.) Then you'll say (pause) **oo.**

h. My turn: **zzzoo.** Listen again. (Hold up one finger.) First you'll say (pause) **zzz.** (Hold up second finger.) Then you'll say (pause) **oo.**
Say it slowly. Get ready. (Hold up one finger.) *zzz.* (Hold up second finger.) *(zzz)oo.*
Again. Get ready. (Hold up one finger.) *zzz.* (Hold up second finger.) *(zzz)oo.*
Say it fast. (Signal.) Zoo. Yes, **zoo.**

i. (Repeat h until firm.)

j. (Call on different children to do b, e, or h.)

SOUND OUT

EXERCISE 10

Children move their finger under s or ē and say it

a. Everybody, finger on the first ball of the first arrow in the box. ✓
When I tap, quickly move your finger under the sound and say it. (Pause.) Get ready. (Tap. Children move their finger under **s** and say sss.)
Yes, **sss.**

b. Again. Finger on the first ball of the first arrow. ✓
Get ready. (Tap. Children move their finger under **s** and say sss.)
Yes, **sss.**

c. (Repeat b until firm.)

d. Everybody, finger on the first ball of the next arrow. ✓
When I tap, quickly move your finger under the sound and say it. (Pause.) Get ready. (Tap. Children move their finger under **ē** and say ēēē.)
Yes, **ēēē.**

e. Again. Finger on the first ball of the arrow. ✓
Get ready. (Tap. Children move their finger under **ē** and say ēēē.)
Yes, **ēēē.**

f. (Repeat e until firm.)

EXERCISE 11

Individual test

a. (Call on a child. Show the child which ball to touch.) Get ready. (Tap.) *Child moves finger under the sound and says it.*

b. (Call on different children to do a.)

c. Good. You really know how to move your finger under the sound and say it.

EXERCISE 12

Children touch under the sounds and sound out

a. (Hold up worksheet. Touch the first ball of the arrow for **am.**) Put your finger on the first ball of this arrow.

b. What's the first sound you'll say?
(Signal.) *aaa.*
What's the next sound you'll say?
(Signal.) *mmm.*

c. Everybody, put your finger on the first ball of the arrow. ✓
When I tap, you're going to quickly move your finger under each sound and say (pause) **aaammm.**
Sound it out. Get ready. (Tap for each sound, pausing about 2 seconds between taps. Check that children are moving their finger under each sound as they say **aaammm.**)

d. Again. Finger on the first ball of the arrow. Get ready. (Tap for each sound, pausing about two seconds between taps. Check that the children are moving their finger under each sound as they say **aaammm.**)

e. (Repeat d until firm.)

EXERCISE 13

Individual test

a. (Call on a child.) Finger on the first ball of the arrow. ✓
Quickly move your finger under each sound as you say it. Get ready. (Tap for each sound, pausing about two seconds between taps.)

b. (Call on different children to do a.)

c. Good moving your finger under each letter and saying each sound.

SYMBOL ACTION

EXERCISE 14

Children move their finger under first, next, last and do it

a. Touch the ball of the arrow that's under the pictures. ✓
• There are three pictures. When I tap, you'll touch under each picture. Then I'll tell you to do what the picture shows you to do.

b. Touch the **first** mark. Get ready. (Tap.) ✓ *Do what the picture shows.* (Tap.) *Children touch their knee.*

c. Touch the **next** mark. Get ready. (Tap.) ✓ *Do what the picture shows.* (Tap.) *Children touch their nose.*

d. Touch the **last** mark. Get ready. (Tap.) ✓ *Do what the picture shows.* (Tap.) *Children touch their chin.*

e. (Repeat b through d until firm.)
• Let's see who can do the three things, one right after the other.
• (Call on different children.) Do all three things.

LETTER IDENTIFICATION
EXERCISE 15

Children identify capital letters

a. (Point to the capital letters.)
• There are three circled capital letters you have not learned.

b. (Point to **N**.) This is capital **N**. What letter? (Touch.) *Capital N.*
• (Point to **Q**.) This is capital **Q**. What letter? (Touch.) *Capital Q.*
• (Point to **R**.) This is capital **R**. What letter? (Touch.) *Capital R.*

c. Find the capital letter chart in the back of your workbook. ✓
• Let's see if you can find the capital letters I name.

d. When I signal, touch capital **N** and keep touching it. Get ready. (Signal.) ✓
• (Point to **N**.) Here's the letter you should be touching. Everybody, what letter? (Touch.) *Capital N.*

e. Fingers up. When I signal, touch capital **R** and keep touching it. Get ready. (Signal.) ✓
• (Point to **R**.) Here's the letter you should be touching. Everybody, what letter? (Touch.) *Capital R.*

f. Fingers up. When I signal, touch capital **Q** and keep touching it. Get ready. (Signal.) ✓
• (Point to **Q**.) Here's the letter you should be touching. Everybody, what letter? (Touch.) *Capital Q.*

g. Tell me the names of these capital letters.

h. (Point to **R**.) What letter? (Touch.) *Capital R.*
• (Point to **Q**.) What letter? (Touch.) *Capital Q.*
• (Point to **N**.) What letter? (Touch.) *Capital N.*

i. (Repeat *h* until firm.)

LETTER WRITING
EXERCISE 16

Children write capital letters

a. (Hold up worksheet 115.) Find the dotted letters. ✓
• Next to each small letter you'll write the capital. I'll show you how to make each capital.
• (Hold up worksheet and pencil.) Watch. (Trace one **N**, **R**, and one **Q**.)

b. Your turn. Trace the lines for the capital letters. (Observe children and give feedback.)

Note: Before presenting lesson 116, present Language lesson 115.

A B C D E F G
H I J K L M N O P
Q R S T U V
W X Y Z

n N
r R
q Q

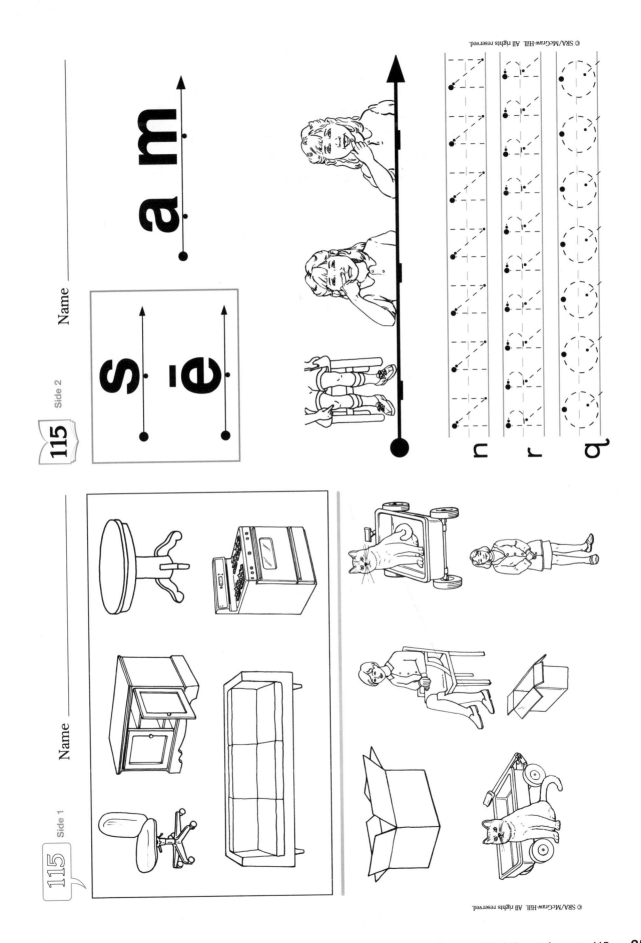

Name

Side 2

115

Name

Side 1

115

Appendix C

Appendix C contains two blackline
masters of family letters. Letter 1 is to be
sent home at the beginning of the school
year and Letter 2 at the end of the school
year.

To the family of _____

    This school year your child is enrolled in the *Reading Mastery Plus* program. *Reading Mastery Plus,* Level K will help your child learn beginning reading skills such as learning the sounds of the letters and later how to put the sounds together to read words. Your child will also learn the speaking and thinking skills needed to do well in school. Your child will learn how to listen carefully, say things well, and follow directions. Your child will learn how to remember information that is important and how to use that information to answer questions. And best of all, your child will find that learning is enjoyable.

    You can help by looking over the workbook pages your child brings home during the year. Ask questions about them. Praise your child for good answers.

    The best thing you can do this year is to let your child know that the work done in *Reading Mastery Plus,* Level K is very important. The skills your child learns this year will be needed every year in school and beyond.

    If you want more suggestions about how to help your child this year or if you have any questions about what your child is learning, please call me at the school. I'll be happy to talk with you.

Thank you,

_____

Para la familia de _____

Este año escolar su hijo está inscrito en el programa *Reading Mastery Plus. Reading Mastery Plus,* Level K ayudará a su hijo a aprender las primeras destrezas de lectura tales como los sonidos de las letras y después cómo poner los sonidos juntos para leer palabras. Su hijo también aprenderá las destrezas para hablar y pensar necesarias para triunfar en la escuela. Aprenderá a escuchar cuidadosamente, a decir las cosas bien y a seguir instrucciones. También aprenderá a recordar información que es importante y cómo usarla para responder preguntas. Y lo mejor de todo es que su hijo descubrirá que leer es divertido.

Usted puede ayudar revisando las páginas del cuaderno de trabajo que su hijo traiga a casa durante el año. Hágale preguntas acerca de ellas. Elogie a su hijo por las respuestas acertadas.

Lo mejor que usted puede hacer este año es dejar que su hijo sepa que el trabajo que hace en *Reading Mastery Plus,* Level K es muy importante. Las destrezas que su hijo aprenderá este año se necesitarán cada año en la escuela y más allá.

Si quiere sugerencias acerca de cómo ayudar a su hijo este año o si tiene alguna pregunta acerca de lo que su hijo está aprendiendo, por favor llámeme a la escuela. Me encantará hablar con usted.

Gracias,

_____

To the family of _____

    Your child has completed _____ lessons of *Reading Mastery Plus,* Level K. Every day your child has worked on reading, listening, and speaking skills. Your child has mastered the basics of reading—learning the sounds of the letters and how to put the sounds together to read words. Your child has also learned important language skills such as classification, how to sequence events in time, what occurs in different locations, and identifying how things are the same and how they are different. These skills will help your child succeed in Grade 1 and all the school years ahead.

    During this break in the school year, encourage your child to practice reading and writing letters and words. When your child colors a picture or writes something, ask your child to tell you about what has been colored or written. Tell your child you are proud of the progress he or she is making.

    If you have any questions or want more ideas about how to help your child during this break in the school year, please call me at the school. I'll be happy to talk with you.

Thank you,

_____

Para la familia de _____

   Su hijo ha terminado _____ lecciones de *Reading Mastery Plus,* Level K. Cada día su hijo ha trabajado en las destrezas para leer, escuchar y hablar. Su hijo ha dominado las básicas de la lectura y el aprendizaje de los sonidos de las letras y cómo ponerlos juntos para leer palabras. También ha aprendido destrezas de lenguaje importantes tales como clasificación, cómo ordenar acontecimientos cronológicamente, qué ocurre en diferentes lugares y a identificar las similitudes y las diferencias de las cosas. Estas destrezas lo ayudarán a triunfar en el Grado 1 y en todos los años escolares siguientes.

   Durante este receso del año escolar, anime a su hijo a practicar la lectura y escritura de letras y palabras. Cuando su hijo coloree un dibujo e escriba algo, pídale que le hable acerca de lo que coloreó o escribió. Dígale que usted está orgulloso de su progreso.

   Si usted tiene preguntas o quiere más ideas acerca de cómo ayudar a su hijo con la lectura durante este receso del año escolar, por favor llámeme a la escuela. Me encantará hablar con usted.

Gracias,

_____

Appendix D

it is fat.

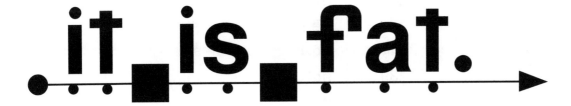

thē sad man

mad at mē

Appendix E

The number following a word is the lesson in which the word is introduced.

Word	Lesson	Word	Lesson
ad_d	137	miss	133
am	124	nē_ar	142
an	144	nē_at	149
at	139	not	148
can	147	rac_k	145
cat	146	ram	127
dan	144	ran	144
dē_ar	140	rat	147
dim	139	rē_ad	132
ē_ar	128	roc_k	147
ē_at	142	sac_k	148
fan	146	sad	126
fat	146	sam	133
fē_ar	138	sat	142
fēēd	130	sēē	125
fin	143	sēēd	129
if	133	sēēm	131
in	143	sit	139
is	138	tan	145
it	140	tē_am	142
mad	126	tē_ar	141
man	148	that	139
mē	124	thē	140
mē_an	145	this	136
mē_at	142	tin	143

Appendix F

Letter Identification (Lessons 41–100)

Letter sound Introduced in	Letter	Letter name Introduced in	Letter name Reviewed on
(k) 144	c	41	43, 44, 45, 46, 50, 54, 55, 60, 61, 73, 74, 81, 86, 90, 98
(101)	a	42	43, 44, 45, 46, 49, 58, 65, 71, 74, 75, 76, 91, 96, 100
101	**a**	91	91, 93, 96, 98, 99
127	f	42	43, 44, 45, 46, 47, 48, 50, 51, 53, 56, 59, 65, 67, 70, 71, 81, 85, 88, 96, 97, 100
(**d**) 123	d	46	47, 48, 49, 51, 52, 56, 59, 69, 70, 76, 77, 79, 84, 87, 92, 93, 98, 100
—	h	47	48, 49, 50, 51, 53, 56, 57, 62, 70, 73, 75, 78, 82, 83, 85, 86, 87, 97, 99
—	j	48	49, 50, 51, 52, 53, 54, 58, 68, 72, 73, 78, 80, 96
104	m	50	51, 52, 53, 54, 55, 57, 58, 59, 62, 63, 64, 66, 67, 69, 73, 76, 77, 82, 83, 84, 92
147	o	52	53, 55, 57, 60, 63, 64, 74, 80, 95
—	p	54	55, 56, 61, 63, 64, 67, 69, 74, 79, 85, 86, 87, 93, 100
109	s	57	58, 60, 62, 66, 69, 71, 78, 80, 82, 93, 96
137	t	59	60, 61, 66, 68, 72, 78, 86, 88, 89, 91, 95, 98, 100
—	w	61	62, 63, 64, 65, 66, 68, 74, 79, 80, 81, 84, 90, 91, 94, 99
—	y	63	64, 65, 67, 74, 75, 77, 79, 81, 89, 94
(ē) 115	e	66	67, 68, 69, 70, 71, 72, 75, 76, 87, 88, 97, 100
119	r	68	69, 70, 71, 73, 75, 77, 78, 83, 84, 86, 90, 97
—	k	70	71, 72, 76, 81, 82, 91, 95
130	i	72	73, 75, 76, 77, 85, 88, 91, 97
—	u	76	77, 79, 80, 81, 83, 84, 89, 90, 93, 94, 99
—	g	78	79, 80, 81, 85, 86, 87, 89, 92, 93, 95, 98
—	z	80	81, 82, 83, 84, 95, 96
140	n	82	83, 84, 85, 89, 96, 99
—	b	85	86, 87, 88, 89, 90, 91, 92, 94, 98
—	l	88	89, 90, 91, 92, 94, 98, 100
—	v	90	91, 92, 93, 94, 99
—	q	92	93, 95, 96
	x	94	95, 97, 99

Appendix G

Letter Writing (Lessons 41–135)

Letter	Introduced on	Steps for Writing		
a	91	a	a	
a	93	c	a	
b	87	b	b	
c	47	c		
d	48	c	d	
e	66	e	e	
f	52	f	f	
g	98	g	g	
h	68	h	h	
i	72	i	i	
j	77	J	j	
k	108	k	k	
l	94	l		
m	63	m	m	
n	82	n	n	
o	55	o		
p	58	p	p	
q	104	c	q	
r	70	r	r	
s	89	s		
t	60	t	t	
u	84	u	u	
v	93	v	v	
w	74	w	w	w
x	102	x		
y	96	y	y	
z	100	z	z	z

Appendix H

Pronunciation Guide (Level K and Level 1 word sounds)

The first 13 sounds are covered in Kindergarten (K)

Symbol	Pronounced	As In	Voiced or Unvoiced*	Introduced in lesson
a	aaa	<u>a</u>nd	v	101
m	mmm	ra<u>m</u>	v	104
s	sss	bu<u>s</u>	uv	109
ē	ēēē	<u>ea</u>t	v	115
r	rrr	ba<u>r</u>	v	119
d	d	ma<u>d</u>	v	123
f	fff	stu<u>ff</u>	uv	127
i	iii	<u>i</u>f	v	130
th	thththth	<u>th</u>is and <u>th</u>e (not thing)	v	134
t	t	ca<u>t</u>	uv	137
n	nnn	pa<u>n</u>	v	140
c	c	ta<u>c</u>k	uv	144
o	ooo	<u>o</u>x	v	147
ā	āāā	<u>a</u>te	v	Level 1
h	h	<u>h</u>at	uv	Level 1
u	uuu	<u>u</u>nder	v	Level 1
g	g	ta<u>g</u>	v	Level 1
l	lll	pa<u>l</u>	v	Level 1
w	www	wo<u>w</u>	v	Level 1
sh	shshsh	wi<u>sh</u>	uv	Level 1

Symbol	Pronounced	As In	Voiced or Unvoiced*	Introduced in lesson
I	(the word I)		v	Level 1
k	k	ta<u>ck</u>	uv	Level 1
ō	ōōō	<u>o</u>ver	v	Level 1
v	vvv	lo<u>v</u>e	v	Level 1
p	p	sa<u>p</u>	uv	Level 1
ch	ch	tou<u>ch</u>	uv	Level 1
e	eee	<u>e</u>nd	v	Level 1
b	b	gra<u>b</u>	v	Level 1
ing	iiing	si<u>ng</u>	v	Level 1
ī	īīī	<u>i</u>ce	v	Level 1
y	yyy	<u>y</u>ard	v	Level 1
er	urr	broth<u>er</u>	v	Level 1
x	ksss	o<u>x</u>	uv	Level 1
oo	oooo	m<u>oo</u>n (not l<u>oo</u>k)	v	Level 1
J	j	<u>j</u>udge	v	Level 1
ȳ	īīī	m<u>y</u>	v	Level 1
wh	www or wh	<u>wh</u>y	v or uv	Level 1
qu	kwww (or koo)	<u>qu</u>ick	v	Level 1
z	zzz	bu<u>zz</u>	v	Level 1
ū	ūūū	<u>u</u>se	v	Level 1

* Voiced sounds are sounds you make by vibrating your vocal cords. You do not use your vocal chords for unvoiced sounds—you use air only. To feel the difference between voiced and unvoiced sounds, hold your throat lightly and say the sound *vv.* You will feel your vocal chords vibrating. Then, without pausing, change the sound to *fff.* The vibrations will stop. The only difference between the sounds is that the vvv is voiced and the fff is not.

Note: Small letters (**a, e, i, k**) are always silent.

Appendix H

Pronunciation Guide (Level K and Level 1 word sounds)

The first 13 sounds are covered in Kindergarten (K)

Symbol	Pronounced	As In	Voiced or Unvoiced*	Introduced in lesson	Symbol	Pronounced	As In	Voiced or Unvoiced*	Introduced in lesson
a	aaa	<u>a</u>nd	v	101	I	(the word I)		v	Level 1
m	mmm	ra<u>m</u>	v	104	k	k	tac<u>k</u>	uv	Level 1
s	sss	bu<u>s</u>	uv	109	ō	ōōō	<u>o</u>ver	v	Level 1
ē	ēēē	<u>ea</u>t	v	115	v	vvv	lo<u>v</u>e	v	Level 1
r	rrr	ba<u>r</u>	v	119	p	p	sa<u>p</u>	uv	Level 1
d	d	ma<u>d</u>	v	123	ch	ch	tou<u>ch</u>	uv	Level 1
f	fff	stu<u>ff</u>	uv	127	e	eee	<u>e</u>nd	v	Level 1
i	iii	<u>i</u>f	v	130	b	b	gra<u>b</u>	v	Level 1
th	thththth	<u>th</u>is and	v	134	ing	iiing	si<u>ng</u>	v	Level 1
		ba<u>th</u>e			I	īīī	<u>i</u>ce	v	Level 1
		(not thing)			y	yyy	<u>y</u>ard	v	Level 1
t	t	<u>c</u>at	uv	137	er	urr	broth<u>er</u>	v	Level 1
n	nnn	pa<u>n</u>	v	140	x	ksss	o<u>x</u>	uv	Level 1
c	c	ta<u>c</u>k	uv	144	oo	oooo	m<u>oo</u>n	v	Level 1
o	ooo	<u>o</u>x	v	147			(not l<u>oo</u>k)		
ā	āāā	<u>a</u>te	v	Level 1	J	j	ju<u>dg</u>e	v	Level 1
h	h	<u>h</u>at	uv	Level 1	ȳ	īīī	m<u>y</u>	v	Level 1
u	uuu	<u>u</u>nder	v	Level 1	wh	www or wh	<u>wh</u>y	v or uv	Level 1
g	g	ta<u>g</u>	v	Level 1	qu	kwww	<u>qu</u>ick	v	Level 1
l	lll	pa<u>l</u>	v	Level 1		(or koo)			
w	www	wo<u>w</u>	v	Level 1	z	zzz	bu<u>zz</u>	v	Level 1
sh	shshsh	wi<u>sh</u>	uv	Level 1	ū	ūūū	<u>u</u>se	v	Level 1

* Voiced sounds are sounds you make by vibrating your vocal cords. You do not use your vocal chords for unvoiced sounds—you use air only. To feel the difference between voiced and unvoiced sounds, hold your throat lightly and say the sound *vvv*. You will feel your vocal chords vibrating. Then, without pausing, change the sound to *fff*. The vibrations will stop. The only difference between the sounds is that the vvv is voiced and the fff is not.

Note: Small letters (**a, e, i, k**) are always silent.